REMARKABLE LEADERS:

Risk Takers Who Dare Us

DORIS LEE MCCOY, PH.D.

American Spirit Foundation Publishing
La Jolla, California

REMARKABLE LEADERS:
Risk Takers Who Dare Us

American Spirit Publishing
5758 Beaumont Avenue
La Jolla, CA 92037-7306

ISBN: 978-0-9773-777-4-9 (Paperback)

This book is printed on acid-free paper

REMARKABLE LEADERS: Risk Takers Who Dare Us
is a trademark owned by the author

The author's web site: http://www.dorisleemccoy.com

Is Dedicated To:

Princess Diana

Joan B. Kroc

Nelson Mandela

Oprah Winfrey

ACKNOWLEDGEMENTS

Obviously this book could never have been written without the help of those who were interviewed. We are all grateful that they shared their deep, important, candid remarks with us.

- **Debra Evans** – who edited with care and excellence
- **Terri Zumstein** – printer extraordinaire
- **Priscilla Wan, Jun Yin, Jullie Chang,** and **Ellen Park** – my amazing assistants
- **Ralph White FN'82** – for helping me through remote and dangerous places throughout the world
- **Elizabeth Morrow, the founder of the New York Press Women's Club** – for her valuable suggestions
- **Gail** – who was a companion traveling throughout the world

I would like to extend my gratitude to **Scandinavian Airlines** for making it possible to attend the United Nations Women's Year Conference in Nairobi, Africa.

Also, much thanks to **Continental Airlines** and **Peggy Mahoney** for allowing me to go to Beijing.

- **Shane, Shannon, Conner, Jeff** *—and all the children of the world who will inherit our earth*

I am grateful for God for putting this goal on my heart, and giving me the energy to follow through this, at times hard, but never boring/incredible opportunity

CONTENTS

- **Nu Skins Enterprises**, Producers of Vitameal
- **Feed the Children**
- **Muhammad Yunus, Ph.D.**, Nobel Peace Prize Winner 2006, Founder of Grameen Bank
- **Steven Pratt**, author of *Super Foods*RX
- **Catherine Bertini, Ph.D.**, Senior Fellow Agricultural Developmental Bill and Melinda Gates Foundation and Professor Maxwell School

Chapter 5...Curing Diseases, Cultivating Hope
- **Bob Wright**, former President CEO of NBC Universal, Co-founder of Autism Speaks
- **Nancy Davis**, Founder MS (Multiple Sclerosis) Foundaiton
- **Tommy Hilfiger**, Assists in MS Foundation, Founder Tommy Hilfiger
- **Karen M. Vanderhoof-Forschner**, Founder of Lyme Disease Foundation
- **Herbert Greenway, MD**, curing skin cancer through Mohs surgery
- **William Magee, MD**, Founder and CEO of Operation Smile
- **Norman McSwain, MD**, Professor, Tulane University, School of Medicine and Trauma Director, Charity Hospital
- **T.Denny Sanford**, Visionary, Philanthropist & Humanitarian

Chapter 6...Environment, Housing, and Pollution
- **Millard Fuller**, Founder of Habitat for Humanity which built over 100,000 houses
- **Dick H. Smith**, Australian Entrepreneur, Businessman, Aviator, Patriot, and Philanthropist
- **Zhengrong Shi, Ph.D.**, Founder, CEO Suntech Power (China's largest Solar Energy company), TIME magazine's 2007 "Heroes of the Environment"
- **Kathleen Duffy**, Manager, New York Marriott Downtown Hotel the Greenest Hotel in America
- **Matt Damon**, Actor, Philanthropist, & Co-founder of Water.org

Chapter 11...The Spirit of Exploration
- **Kenneth Kamler, MD**, Author of *Surviving the Extremes*
- **Sir Edmund Hillary**, New Zealand, first to reach summit of Mt Everest, helped build schools, hospitals, clinics in Nepal
- **Don Walsh, Ph.D.**, Holds underwater diving record
- **Josh Bernstein**, Explorer, Educator & Environment Advocate
- **Angela Fisher & Carol Beckwith**, Photojournalists capturing the culture of Africa

Chapter 12...True Democracy
- **Associate Justice Sandra Day O'Connor (ret)**, First woman Justice in the 191 year Supreme Court of America
- **John Templeton, MD**, President of John Templeton Foundation

Chapter 13...The Joy of Living
- **Barron Hilton**, CEO Hilton Hotels (Ret.)
- **Ernestine Dillard**, Renowned Gospel Singer
- **Les Paul**, father of the Electric Guitar
- **Audrey Geisel**, President and CEO of Dr. Seuss

Chapter 14...Another Kind of Visionary
- **Daw Penjo**, Foreign Secretary, Royal Government of Bhutan
- **His Majesty King Jigme Singye Wangchuck**, Fourth and former King of Bhutan
- **His Majesty King Jigme Khesar Namgyel Wangchuck**, Fifth and current King of Bhutan
- **Dorji Penjore**, Senior Researcher, Gross National Happiness
- **His Royal Highness Prince Jigyel Ugyen Wangchuck**, Prince of Bhutan
- **Her Majesty Queen Dorji Ashi Wangmo Wangchuck**, Queen of the Fourth King of Bhutan, Founder of Tarayana Foundation helping small villages

Chapter 15...Forging a New Future
- **Bob Buford**, TV Executive, philanthropist, author

- **President Bill Clinton, Former Secretary of State Hillary Clinton, Chelsea Clinton, and the Clinton Global Initiative University**
- **Nicholas Kristof**, Author, Journalist with the *New York Times*, Pulitzer Prize winner
- **Author Speaks out about the Future**

Other Non-Profits Making a Difference
About the Author
American Spirit Foundation

FOREWORD

REMARKABLE LEADERS: Risk Takers Who Dare Us, by Dr. Doris Lee McCoy, is a book you just have to pay attention to for what you can learn from it.

I wish I had met Dr. McCoy earlier than when I did in 2009. She is a special lady with an extra ordinary determination to make a difference in the way we look at improving lives. We can do this by devoting ourselves to improving situations using everything within our means and disposal.

I told her during our meeting that she has been divinely touched to bring together the ideas and work of innovative and compassionate individuals who are striving to make the world a more peaceful, secure and happier home for all.

I hope this book will sow the spirit of volunteerism to serve humanity in our own small ways to make a bigger difference to the problems facing the world.

Dorji Wangmo Wangchuck
Queen of the Fourth King of Bhutan
Founder and President Tarayana Foundation

INTRODUCTION

"Give us, O God, the vision which can see thy love in the world in spite of human failure. Give us the faith to trust the goodness in spite of our ignorance and weakness. Give us the knowledge that we may continue to pray with understanding hearts, and show us what each one of us can do a set forth the coming of the day of universal peace. Amen."

> **- Astronaut Frank Borman**, Christmas Day 1968, Prayer sent to Earth from his Apollo 8 mission

While much of our world is fighting over oil and gas, and struggling with political corruption and economic turmoil, a small but very powerful group of people are fighting for the survival and dignity of our human family.

Who are they? And how are they doing their important work?

They are visionaries whom you are about to encounter as you read this book. Some of them you may be familiar with and some will likely be new to you. What they all have in common is that they are people who are actively observing the major problems in the world and are making commitments and taking action.

We live in an extraordinary time in history when we can truly move forward. Many people throughout the world are feeling this overwhelming need, and they are responding with their talents, time, and money.

Nick Clooney and his son George Clooney could be basking in the glory of their past accomplishments, yet they go to Darfur. They do this at the price of putting their own lives at risk.

Nelson Mandela, Sir Richard Branson, and John Paul DeJoria could be taking life easy, but instead they are intent on removing

1

the landmines in Africa that have been left behind from past wars. Princess Diana began this courageous fight to eradicate mines which have left over 50,000 children and adults without arms or legs. This small group is combining their resources and visibility toward a unified goal: to get rid of the bombs with new technology and secure the safety of the African people.

Author, philanthropist, and founder of The Sister Foundation, Helen Hunt, Ph.D. could be vacationing somewhere on a desert island, but she is far too busy helping under-served women in America and throughout the world.

Mimi Silbert, Ph.D. could be making big money in the corporate world. Instead, she chooses to demonstrate how, in the right environment and with the right education, formerly incarcerated criminals, drug addicts, and prostitutes can learn to be productive, contributing members of society. It is my promise that you will be moved by her interview.

You may wonder, "Why do these people do what they do? And why do they make these choices?" I wondered those things as well. So after talking with all but 5 of these individuals in person, and from my interviews with over 3,000 leaders who have shared their stories in the past, my conclusion is that they were moved to take action because it is the right thing to do. They recognize the crossroads we are facing—environmentally, economically, politically, culturally—and yet something has touched them deeply. Something has inspired them to spring into action.

Many of these visionaries are planting seeds of which they may never see the final results. Yet, they believe that their ideas will materialize and develop in the years to come...with or without them. I think you will be excited, as I continue to be, in hearing their stories. I am proud to have talked with them and honored to have them in this book.

Why is this book important to businesses and entrepreneurs?

"A new study of consumer engagement finds that companies that aren't making a difference – to the world and to consumers – aren't going to be around much longer." This quote is from an article by FastCompany on the future of brands.[1]

The article states that companies must build a responsible reputation for delivering products that consistently improve people's lives to cultivate lasting relationships with consumers. Umair Haque, Director of Hayas Media Labs and *Harvard Business Review* blogger studies how businesses can create real value and observes the growing consumer demands for impactful products.

"The Meaningful Brands survey—which spoke to 50,000 consumers in France, Spain, the U.K., Germany, Italy, Mexico, Brazil, Colombia, Chile, Argentina, China, Japan, India, and the U.S.—found that only 20% of the brands they interact with have a positive impact on their lives. And they feel that 70% of brands could disappear entirely without [consumers] noticing."

Haque believes that the trick to make a brand meaningful is to focus on the outcome, not the output. "Did this brand actually impact your life in a tangible, lasting, and positive way?" instead of "Did this company make a slightly better product?"

"More than half (51%) of consumers want to reward responsible companies by shopping there; 53% would pay a 10% premium for products from a responsible company. And they want companies involved: 85% of consumers want companies to be engaged on

---

[1] Morgan Clendaniel, *The Brands That Survive Will Be the Brands that Make Life Better.* FastCo.exist.com; FastCompany, http://www.fastcoexist.com/1678768/the-brands-that-survive-will-be-the-brands-that-make-life-better (Nov. 14, 2011).

global issues, but only 22% think they're getting enough. Haque says that if companies don't start responding to these trends, they will be punished."

The surveys show that people have concerns about their future, and this book will provide some examples of what others have done to further some of these causes.

Why this book is important for everyone

No matter where you are from—which country or continent—this book is for you. You may find yourself intrigued, motivated, laughing, and maybe even shedding a few tears, as you encounter the many ways that people are caring for one another. Good things are taking place right now—even in the midst of economic crises, natural disasters, political uprisings, and profound change.

In truth, dear reader, this book is more about *you* than it is about the people whose great work is discussed here. The courage, creativity, compassion, and curiosity that they demonstrate exist within you too. The capacity to improve the quality of life for yourself and others is hardwired into your heart, mind, and soul.

My hope is that the stories contained here will ignite your imagination and give you new ideas for how to get more deeply involved. Maybe you will decide to become more environmentally active. Maybe you are a teacher and can bring fresh ideas to your students for collectively making a difference. Maybe you are an employer or an employee who takes on the challenge of creating a more positive environment at work. Maybe you have excess food or money that you might share. Maybe you have time on your hands and can volunteer your skills for those in need. There are countless possibilities.

It is my desire that the visionary work of others inspires the Visionary who is alive within you. For this reason, I have included a brief "Visionary Reflection" at the end of each chapter. Each reflection is meant to be like a mini oasis, where you can take a moment to reflect on what you've read—to take a deep breath and make contact with the still, small voice within you. At the heart of the matter, these inner reflections are moments to recognize and acknowledge your own gifts, strengths, skills, and talents. As you connect with your own unique resources, you may see new ways that your life can make a greater difference in the lives of others – whether that's in your own community or on the other side of the globe.

I have talked with people throughout the world, and I can say unequivocally that all of them want to make our planet a better place. They want a world in which their children and grandchildren can grow up, be healthy, and have better lives than they have had.

"Is it possible?" you may ask. Each of the visionaries you will meet here has shown that by putting effort to the challenge, life can be—and should be—better for all people in need.

You will note that my questions, to help the flow of conversation, will always appear bolded and italicized to differentiate between the participant's answers.

> *"This is a pivotal moment in humanity's history, a time when we have the potential to make transformational leaps in our understanding of many of the global challenges we face. I see reason for optimism every day when I walk across the Stanford University campus and talk to today's college students. They are excited — and determined — to make a difference. I am gratified that a graduate of Stanford, Dr. Doris Lee McCoy, has written a book on remarkable leaders that will help point the way."*

> – John L. Hennessy, President of Stanford University

Doris Lee McCoy, Ph.D., La Jolla, California

CHAPTER 1

CLOCKWISE L to R: John Paul DeJoria, Nelson Mandela, and Sir Richard Branson

CHAPTER 1

Eradicating Landmines in Africa

••••••••••••••••••

Photo courtesy of DailyMail.co.uk and Thechrisdsblog.wordpress.com
Princess Diana with sons Prince William and Prince Harry

As our global world becomes smaller, and as we travel more, we are more sensitive to the plight of the under-served. Charity and compassion has led us more into sharing, assisting, and giving back to a world that has provided us such a bounty of gifts. Look around you and you will find many, no matter where you live.

One person who inspired many, who brought a new approach to being a part of the Royal English family, was Diana, Princess of Wales. The late princess not only championed charities in the UK, but with her travels in Africa, she was emotionally affected by the children and adults who had been desperately wounded by landmines left behind by present-day and former wars. As her compassion touched many of us around the world, we listened to her concerns. I recall a moment of shock that spurred me on to get involved. It happened one day when I visited the United Nations building in New York City and saw photographs of how profoundly these bombs, hidden in the ground, can devastate children and adults.

Mozambique is often pointed to as another kind of example of the destructive capabilities of landmines. The country is blessed with naturally rich, fertile soil for growing vegetables, but due to the threat of landmines, much land is not being utilized for planting. Needless to say, the great detriment this has caused to the health, well-being, and prosperity of the people of Mozambique is far-reaching.

Fortunately, many foundations have emerged to address the scourge of landmines. HALO Trust is one of the foundations that Princess Diana brought to the attention of the world. HALO Trust focuses on minefield clearing and works in areas such as Afghanistan, Cambodia, Sri Lanka, Mozambique, Angola, Somaliland, Georgia, Nagorno, Karabakh, Kosovo, and even Columbia in South America.

Strongly connected to HALO Trust and its staff of 7,700 people, Prince Harry appears to be following his mom's great example in his support of the people who work each day in some of the world's most dangerous landmine zones.

Princess Diana traveled to many nations and was an active campaigner for the ban on the manufacture and use of landmines until the year before her death. She truly cared and used her public image to bring awareness to the anti-landmine campaign, which resulted in a Nobel Peace Prize later in the '90s.

Princess Diana undoubtedly educated her two young sons about the ravages of landmines, as well as the need to be involved in other social and human concerns. Prince William became a patron for Centrepoint due to his concern about homelessness in Great Britain, even spending a night on the London streets to gain awareness.

Photo courtesy of People.com

Ten years after Diana's death, Prince Harry and Prince William celebrated her life through a concert marking the 10th anniversary of her death. It was celebrated in London's newly rebuilt Wembley Stadium on July 1, 2007. Prince William said, "We want it to represent exactly what our mother would have wanted–how she was and all that sort of thing. We wanted to have this big concert full of energy, full of the sort of fun and happiness which I know she would have wanted. The main purpose is to celebrate and to have fun and to remember her in a fun way."

The concert's proceeds went to the Diana, Princess of Wales Memorial Fund, which gives grants to communities affected by landmines. Proceeds also benefited Centrepoint and Sentebale. Co-founded by Prince Harry, Sentebale is a fund for the children in Lesotho, Africa.

In addition to the concert, there was a formal church service on August 31st of that year to honor Diana's life. With the young princes overseeing the organization of the events with enthusiasm and care, both were moving tributes. Princess Diana's loving nature and zeal for life is evident in her two boys who continue to keep their mother's legacy alive through their charitable acts and kind hearts.

There are other foundations that have since taken up the charge of eradicating landmines. One shining example is the Mineseeker Foundation, whose members and patrons include Sir Richard Branson, the head of Virgin Group, and my good friend John Paul DeJoria, cofounder of John Paul Mitchell Systems luxury hair care products.

I sat down with John Paul DeJoria to discuss the Mineseeker Foundation's work in eradicating landmines in Africa. We discussed how somebody gets blown up every 15-20 minutes, not counting all the animals. Once they're hit, of course, they're injured for life or they die. We are trying to raise awareness of this and help the foundation raise money for a new technology, which is put on a blimp to detect and record the location of each landmine onto a GPS map, so they are easier to find and remove.

In a turning-point meeting in South Africa, Sir Richard Branson and John Paul DeJoria joined forces with Nelson Mandela, Michael Kendrick, and Alan Oberholzer to discuss how to help solve the landmine problem:

Mineseeker Foundation Global Meeting, hosted by Michael Kendrick:

Michael Kendrick: I want to formally introduce you today to John Paul DeJoria and our new patron. John Paul has been responsible for introducing us to the North African countries in order to obtain the funds we desperately need. All of this started with the gentleman on the left there, Alan Oberholzer. He's actually been instrumental with me helping to establish this great group. John Paul, if you'd like to explain the funding.

John Paul DeJoria: Our goal and our direction is we are going to try not to depend on any country of the world or governments to fund this. So what we have done as a group is decided we are going to try to get the funding. Should anything not happen there, we may have other people standing by that may help fund Mineseeker—our equipment, technology, and getting the first blimp actually floating in the air.

Our goal is to make six or seven of these and have them in various parts of the world. Our overall goal for the funding is to be able to remove every landmine on this planet over the next 10-15 years.

But we are dedicated to getting this done. We may have the financial means to be able to do that without relying on politics to get it done. But we need political help once we are in the country with groups that will help remove them. In the mean time, I am going to Mozambique to help replace some of the limbs of those afflicted.

Michael Kendrick: We are most interested in getting the donation from Libya. Richard and I have visited Libya recently, and they have said they're going to do this. But apart from the money, it's a very good story that Libya has come out and established normal relations and is helping people. That gives Mineseeker a huge awareness around the world so it's on the top of people's mind.

11

Michael Kendrick: There is more concentration in Mozambique, which is very difficult to find, because the water moves the plastic mines. And Angola, we all know is suffering economically because of the mines, so we want to target those two areas first.

Nelson Mandela: That's very good because there are a lot of landmines there. In Mozambique they have done things which no human being ought to do, and one doesn't want to repeat the cruelty which they have committed. And the same thing in Angola. Those countries now are recovering, but it is very difficult because they are recovering from a very difficult background in which there is poverty and lack of education and ignorance. But there are many people that are doing very good work there. And I don't want to mention my wife, she does a lot work, but I hardly mention her because already she is becoming more important than I am. (group laughs)

Michael Kendrick: You are lucky to have her, she is very lovely.

John Paul DeJoria: (Jokingly, John Paul adds) So you really want a job with me?

Nelson Mandela: I do want a job with you because she is very dominating, that is the problem I have. (group laughter again)

Alan Oberholzer: The other thing is in Mozambique, after 30 years of civil war there are weapons that have been hidden all over the country. Mineseekers can go in there and find these weapons very quickly and eradicate them.

Nelson Mandela: That's very good. When are you planning on going there?

Michael Kendrick: We're hoping within 12 months. The British Administration of Defense have given us the technology, and we have to now buy all the equipment and provide the airship and get away, but we're working very hard and very quickly.

Nelson Mandela: Are you going to consult with some people in Mozambique as to where most of these landmines are located?

Michael Kendrick: Your wife has put me in touch with the Prime Minister of Mozambique.

Nelson Mandela: I see.

Michael Kendrick: So, we've already written to him, we're already moving forward on that.

Nelson Mandela: That's good, that's very good. We also have a very good chap in Armando Guebuza who is now president, and he is a very good man, very intelligent.

Michael Kendrick: Oh fine, that will be very nice if we could contact Zelda.

Nelson Mandela: No, no, no, you'll certainly meet him, he's a very good chap, he's very intelligent and very committed to Mozambique.

John Paul DeJoria: We are going to try to make this happen. It's like all of us are paying our rent for being alive on the planet earth. This is one way we are paying our rent.

Nelson Mandela: You're not like me now, because I'm preparing to take my grave because of my old age.

Michael Kendrick: Thank you very much for your time again and welcoming our new patrons. We look forward to a successful future detecting and removing the mines.

Nelson Mandela: I'm very happy to have been with you, thank you, thank you very much. It's always good to see you, Richard.

In order to spread the word further, Nelson Mandela made a video of his appeal for eradicating the land mines in Africa, addressed to world leaders.

"As patrons of the Mineseeker Foundation my wife, Graca Machel, and I, take this opportunity to call upon the world business leaders and space men to support a new technology that can hasten our quest to rid the world of landmines. We believe that with a renewed and stronger effort we can increase our determination to free thousands upon thousands of people that suffer from the devastation of this man-problem. I call upon you to stand hand in hand with us as we move forward to remove landmines from our planet once and for all. I thank you.

On behalf of all of us on Mineseekers and 1,000 angels, please join us."

Doris Lee: That is a wonderful look inside an important conversation. Can you tell us what will be next?

John Paul DeJoria: We agreed that we would carry the word forward for Mineseeker. Our goal is to try to raise the money necessary to be able to get the equipment to do that. Each individual was very excited to be a part of this project. I'll start by buying prosthetic limbs in Mozambique.

We changed the name later to the Soul of Africa and Food 4 Africa, expanding it a little bit further. It's the same organization, we just changed the name. We're not only removing landmines, but also replacing some limbs of those that have been affected by landmine destruction.

It's interesting, because countries like Mozambique, for example, probably have three or four million landmines, Angola probably 10 million, Afghanistan 10 million. It's a very big problem, and we're very excited that the new technology works so well.

The first country to totally get rid of landmines with this technology is Bosnia. We used the United Nations blimp to do it, but Michael Kendrick was able to find some new technology that was put on the blimp that made it more affordable. We're still raising the money to build the first blimps to go to other countries to remove the mines.

How does that work?

These blimps go very slowly, and this technology is on the blimp. It's almost like a laser beam system where it penetrates the ground down seven or eight feet, picking up a signature of every landmine in the ground or any other armament there.

Once picked up, it's transmitted to a satellite, which sends it to a mainframe computer in England, and then it bounces it back to another computer, whatever country we're working in, that prints out the maps.

We haven't gotten the first units up yet, other than the one we did with the United Nations. I went into Mozambique and personally made contributions – on behalf of hairdressers of the world and the Paul Mitchell Systems Company. I'm also personally replacing limbs of landmine victims; we've already replaced dozens of them.

Is it true that there are approximately 50,000 people in Africa that have lost limbs?

I think there are probably more than that, but 50,000 sounds right.

What do you see as the next step?

The next step is to finalize the rest of the money being raised and to get the first hot air balloon up, with the first one probably going into Mozambique. Then we have seven others afterward to be put together to go into the other countries.

What is the cost?

Initially, it is about $30 million, but fortunately, as I mentioned, Michael Kendrick found a less expensive technology that is just as efficient. So after you have the first one up, each one additionally is approximately $10 million. That's for the blimp and the equipment on it and operating expenses as well.

By the way, Richard Branson and I have all picked up our own expenses on this, going to and from Africa. We don't even use donated money. We pay our own way.

All of us get a wonderful warm feeling, a good reward knowing we're doing something for people who, unfortunately, stepped in the wrong place at the wrong time.

Is there anything else that you'd like to mention?

I wish everybody a life of peace, love, and happiness.

You have such a wonderful respect for every human being. How can the public contribute?

They can go online to www.SoulofAfrica.com, or they can go to www.MineSeeker.com and make a donation. All patrons volunteer their time, and our celebrity focus is used to be able to accomplish this.

John Paul DeJoria is now focused on contributing to three states in Appalacia.

Visionary Reflection on...
Compassion

Compassion, in its truest sense, isn't just a mental activity. As the Mineseeker team demonstrates, compassion is a caring that can extend even to people who live in distant lands, people we will likely never meet. Compassion is a depth of empathy that connects us more profoundly to others and to ourselves. Think about a challenge you may be facing right now and ask yourself, "How can I bring more compassion to this situation?"

And now in a very impressive ceremony while millions watched throughout the world, Prince William married Catherine Middleton, who then became the Duchess of Cambridge.

In August 2013, the Royal Couple had a baby now called Prince George Alexander Louis of Cambridge, also known as Georgie to his family.

CLOCKWISE L to R: Rebecca J. Okwaci, Nick Clooney, and Joey Cheek

CHAPTER 2

Stopping Genocide in Darfur

• • • • • • • • • • • • • • • • • •

NICK CLOONEY
American journalist, anchorman, television host, and activist
for Darfur

Nick Clooney has had a richly diverse career; TV personality, a politician, speaker, journalist, and author of three books. Recently, he and his son, actor/producer George Clooney, went to Darfur in Sudan and have alerted the world of the gravity of the situation there.

Doris Lee: Nick, would you comment on the situation in Darfur? One of the specific questions I have is regarding where the Janjaweed soldiers are getting the guns that enable them to go into small villages and kill people and even animals.

Nick Clooney: The background on this is that Sudan, which as many of your readers will know, is geographically the largest country in Africa and has been troubled for many generations. Specifically, immediately following its separation from Great Britain it launched into a civil war, which intensified about 25 years ago between the North and the South. They finally reached a very uneasy truce in 2005. The battle, as always, was over economics. Those in the South thought that those in the North, which is where the capital Khartoum is, were not being represented and not getting a fair share of the resources. That was remedied by a peace effort in 2005. It's an uneasy peace, but it is held now for three years.

At about that same time, the people in the West Sudan region, called Darfur, thought that they also were not receiving a fair share from their government. They started a very small-scale rebellion after having tried other means for about 10 years prior. Unfortunately, a rebellion is exactly what Khartoum wanted, because that gave them the excuse to unleash what many people have called a genocide. The United Nations does not call it that, but President Bush and Colin Powell called it that. It seems to have all the earmarks of genocide, because it appears that the people in the capital of Khartoum, the government of Sudan, want to simply eliminate all of the people of Darfur.

Why would they do that? There are several excuses, one is that they're troublesome and demanding more resources; also, there appears to be much more oil available in the Darfur region than there is in central Sudan now. In addition to that, there's a racial element here. Those in Darfur are African Muslims.; those in Khartoum are Arab Muslims. There has always been some tension, but nothing to match what has happened now in these last few years. What has happened is that 2.5 million people have been driven from their homes, because they're living in camps and the world is feeding them now through non-governmental organizations.

We believe that as many as 300,000 to 400,000 have been slaughtered by, as you suggest, the Janjaweed. Who are the Janjaweed? They are a group of Northern militia nomads actually, themselves having some economic problems because of the encroachment of the Sahara Desert. They are easy prey for the government, which will tell them, "We will feed you, we will pay you, we will arm you, but what we want you to do is drive the Darfurees out of Sudan in whatever way you wish." They have done that very efficiently and effectively, mostly by slaughter, by killing whole families.

As many as 1,000 tiny villages have been burned to the ground by the Sudanese Air Force, by some Sudanese regular forces, and also by these Janjaweed, which translated means "devil riders"—and that's what they are and what they do. They come in on camels and horses, armed to the teeth. They go after these helpless people, slaughtering them and then stealing their cattle and the few possessions they have. This has been going on now for several years.

Some of us have been trying to call attention to that fact. Nicholas Kristof, a great columnist for the *New York Times* and many other reporters have gone over to tell that story, but for one reason or another, it has not caught the attention of our own news outlets. Particularly because of his international fame, my son George and I hoped that going there and reporting what we saw would bring a little more attention to it. It seemed to have done that, but that wasn't nearly enough. We've been flat failures; nothing has really changed and the people are still being killed every day and the dislocation continues.

There are 80 non-governmental organizations, and these wonderful people are some of the great heroes of the Darfur story. Completely unarmed, they're there doling out whatever they can of comfort, food and whatever protection they can give. These are all the people we've known all these years: CARE is there, and Save the Children is there. All of the great humanitarian organizations are there. When George and I saw them, we were shocked at what young people they were; 27-year-olds running large compounds and completely helpless as far as their protection against these militia and Sudanese

21

troops and the Janjaweed. Nonetheless, they stay there and do their best to keep the camps solvent and keep the minimal medical facilities going.

George and I went to several of the camps. We were there only 10 days, but it was a life-changing period of time. Although I haven't been back since that trip, George has been back, not only in Darfur, but also in other parts of central Africa where there is unrest, like the Congo and some of the others. But still, the running sore is Darfur.

We simply believe, as I think most people reading your book would believe, that if we are who we think we are—if Americans are what we have always been—then we have to care about this. This has to matter to us: helpless people being run out of their homes, killed, things stolen from them. This has to matter to us, and we must do what we can to help them.

We've been attempting to do that, we've been trying to get the 26,000 U.N. troops in there to at least keep people alive while a peace process is begun. There have been some steps forward, mostly from the people in the U.S. I've gone out and spoken more than 176 times. George has gone out to speak as well. Many more people are doing this work, and because of that, it is apparent that this problem is not going to be solved top down. Our news people are not going to do anything about it; it's going to come from the bottom up. It's going to come from churches, synagogues, mosques, town meetings, and schools, universities and high schools. There is a grassroots movement from the ground up to help these people, to push our own elected officials into moving this up in priority from priority 50 to priority 30, and maybe to priority 15, to get it on the radar screen again so that we can help these people.

Why is news reporting going so slowly? Are our media people afraid of retaliation of some kind?

I don't think its fear. It is simply that it's a difficult story to report, because it's a closed society. It's hard to get reporters in there, and it's expensive to get reporters in there. There are many news organizations that believe this is not as important a story as others.

As you know, our news organizations have been pulling back from reporting news from around the world, and they've fired or replaced most of their foreign correspondents. We have fewer than 10% of what we used to have even as recently as 20 years ago. That's because we believe Americans don't care about what's going on in the rest of the world; we only care about what's going on within our own borders. We'll care about Iraq, because we're there with our soldiers who are getting killed, and the same is true of Afghanistan.

We found out then that what matters elsewhere does matter here. So what matters in Darfur does matter here. China is deeply engaged in Darfur, in all of the Sudan, and many other nations are as well. It's important for us to at least be aware and understand what's going on, and then if we decide we're not going to do anything about it, that's fine. We should know what is happening elsewhere in the world and particularly where innocent people are dying by the hundreds.

One of the criticisms and questions people have is how much can America police the world?

You're quite right. None of us who have been there would recommend that any American troops be sent there. That would be counterproductive and is not what is required there. What is required is our insistence that an acculturated force be sent there by the United Nations. What I mean by *acculturated* is Muslim soldiers—peacekeepers who are, incidentally, ready to go from Tanzania and Ghana.

The troops are there; they need some equipment, and that's what the United States can provide. They need some pressure at the U.N. and the Security Council. The United States can provide that. Then those 26,000 U.N soldiers can get in there and give the Sudanese themselves the opportunity, the breathing space, to begin a peace process, and to begin dealing with a dictator in the capital of Sudan, Khartoum. His name is Omer Hassan Ahmed Al-Bashir. Recently, it was announced that he was indicted by the International Criminal Court for genocide. The International Criminal Court is the one that indicted Slobodan Milosevic and others for their crimes against humanity.

No, we should not be sending American troops or warplanes there. We don't mean that at all. What we can do, and what appears as proper for us to do, is to apply all the pressure we can. And if there are material things that are needed by that force, to help provide those as well.

The L.A. Times carried an article on the front page concerning the President of Sudan. They declared him as a threat and issued a warrant for him. How do you feel about that?

I've always felt that the best defense is to do the right thing. What's the correct thing to do? What has this man been doing? Is he responsible for killing upwards of 300,000 to 400,000 people and displacing two and a half million others of his own people? If that is true, and if this warrant charges that, then we must serve it—and we must serve the truth by bringing this to the attention of the world. He can

24

ignore the warrant of course, but if he does, all those who have been supporting him—Russia, China, all the others—now must take pause.

This is an arm of the United Nations, as you know, and a National Criminal Court has called him a mass murderer. If they continue to support a mass murderer while attempting to find themselves a place in the sun in the great world organizations, then they're going to have to take a much closer look at the people with whom they're dealing, including a man just indicted as a mass murderer. This certainly will apply more pressure with Russia, China, and with the Arab League itself, which must deal also on the international arena.

This is the right thing to do, which will bring about the best result. If it makes some people uncomfortable or if the shoe begins to pinch for some other organizations, that's a small price to pay.

Then finances are a way in, and we can diplomatically move on that, right?

Yes, and there's something else as well, something that we have not done effectively yet, and that is to apply personal economic sanctions against the individuals in the government of Khartoum. They now have the ability to go to the Riviera, to shop in London at Harrods, or to come to the Cleveland Clinic in the U.S. for their illnesses. If we apply personal sanctions, which we *can* do and other nations can as well, that is a very effective tool.

We have a history of that, because in 1996 the leading citizen of Sudan was Osama Bin Laden. He had been driven from Saudi Arabia by members of his own family because of his radical views. He took up residence in the

25

early '90s in Sudan and became its leading citizen, its richest person, building roads and having large farms. The United States, Britain and France knew that he was a radical, and he had already begun to threaten American and Western interests. They told the individuals in the Sudanese Government, *we are sanctioning you; we're taking away your money. You can't spend your money in our part of the world.* That immediately worked. In 1996 the Sudanese Government pressured their leading citizen, Osama bin Laden, to leave the country, and he indeed did, going to Afghanistan where he continued to foment his plots.

Where can people get more information concerning the situation in Darfur? And what do you think about requesting information for our television stations?

Call your TV or radio station or Congressperson. Don't call just once, because if you call just once, they'll blow you off. If you call a second, third, and fourth time, you'll make a pest of yourself. And each time say, "What's going on with Darfur? I guess it's all solved, because I haven't heard anything from you about it. Tell me what House Bill there is dealing with the situation in Darfur. What is your liaison with the United Nations saying about what's on the agenda now?"

Ask those questions over and over. I know that works, because every time I do that at a speech, I get calls from friends of mine who are in public life, elected officials, and they say to me, "Call them off, Nick. They're bugging me, they're driving me crazy, and I'm doing the best I can!"

Of course, then I tell them, "No, you're not doing the best you can, because those folks aren't home yet. They're not back at their little farms tending their goats and their cattle." That's the goal, get those folks home so they can live in peace. That's all that anybody wants.

Should we also contact our United States Representative to the United Nations?

Absolutely. That's a very good choice, but I'm trying to keep it as inexpensive as possible. You can make local calls and still get your U.S. Representative, Senator, and your news outlet people, city editors and assignment editors.

People can also go to the website: www.SaveDarfur.com. It's a clearinghouse for information for anyone who is online.

I recommend that people do what they've been asked to do so many times before in their lives, but often haven't done. That is to simply contact anybody who has any influence at all, including their elected congressmen.

Good information. Your son George was recently given the honor of being the U.N. Messenger of Peace, is that correct?

Yes absolutely, we're very proud of that, and it's something that George is working on at least a part of every day. It's a great honor for him, and he takes it very seriously, as do all of us. He's been over there again in very difficult circumstances, but he learned a great deal more and came back with what I thought was a marvelous message for the United Nations. He doesn't like me to talk about this, so I won't specifically, but he has other missions for the United Nations coming up very soon.

A lot of people in other countries are trying to attain the freedom and democracy that we have. You have been a scholar of

American History in the past. What really defines America for you?

Our system was set up by a small group of geniuses more than 200 years ago. What they allowed this nation to do, which had not been done before and is very rare today, is to accept, honor and eventually, to assimilate diversity. Our founding fathers said this is what we think the government ought to be, what it ought to look like, and how we ought to treat one another, but if you don't think so, fix it, change it.

Not everything in the Constitution of the United States was sacrosanct, it was not all correct. We decided to elect our Vice Presidents a different way within 10 years of the institution of the Constitution; the body of the Constitution considered African-Americans five-eighths of a person, the body of the Constitution didn't address the issue of women at all. All of those things were changed, and they were changed in an orderly, legal way. It's been painful, we've made terrible mistakes along the line, but we left ourselves open to the possibility of change—and we're still doing that.

Totalitarian nations are inflexible, and they cannot allow change, because change means they might lose power. We don't care about that, because our power changes every two to four years anyway by the election process. It's a brilliant system, and if we don't tinker with it to the point of stultifying it and making it inflexible, we'll continue to grow, because America isn't a place—*it's an idea.*

Looking around the world, is the human condition actually improving? How do you read that?

Those of us who have done news for all of our lives, we make a mistake by not explaining what we're doing for a living. When I was a news director I used to say that if I had the courage of my convictions, I would have a disclaimer at the beginning of every newscast. Say I was in Cincinnati, I would say, *"Today, in our tri-state region, 1,250,000 people woke up and did exactly what they were supposed to do. They took care of each other. They went to work. They went to school. They went to church. They took care of their children. They took care of their elderly, and they did just what they were supposed to be doing. 150,000 people woke up today but didn't do the correct things. Those are the stories you're going to hear today, because news is an aberration."*

News is the chronicle of the abnormal event of the day, spread out all over the world. Consuming news 24 hours a day now, we hear nothing but the aberrants. We don't understand that most people have precisely the same aspirations that we do, want the same things for their families that we do, and most of them are doing the best they can every day of the week. We somehow don't know whether there is general progress being made throughout the world. I think there is. I think all of these things that we're hearing and seeing are very difficult, continuing, growing pains in the world.

Yet at the end of the day, a story of humanity and particularly the story of the United States is a great story...and a continuingly positive story.

Excellent. Tell us about the new job you're moving on to...Will you still be with the American Life TV?

Yes, I'm continuing my work with American Life. They've been just great to me by allowing me to do these special programs, "Moments that Changed Us," which deal with specific people and moments in our history that have actually affected us. I'll also be teaching for the first time in my life as an instructor in Journalism at American University in Washington, D.C., and simultaneously, I'll be working the Scholar-in-Residence Program at the Newseum (museum of news) on Pennsylvania Avenue that just opened in Washington, D.C.

I'm looking forward to those new adventures.

You are a patriot. Your whole family is one that I think others could emulate, because you're out there doing important things that affect a whole lot of people. Bless you for that.

It's good of you to say that. Thank you very much, I wish you well.

- Visionary Spotlight -

GEORGE CLOONEY, son of Nick Clooney, celebrated movie actor, and Darfur activist, passionately speaks out about the ongoing urgency to confronts the atrocities in Africa…

"These crises play to the advantage of [Omar al-Bashir, Sudan's Islamic ruler, and his militants] by pushing Darfur farther from the world's headlines. If we look away and hope it all goes away, an entire generation will disappear."[2]

JOEY CHEEK
Olympic Gold Medalist Speed Skater and the co-founder and president of Team Darfur, an international coalition of athletes committed to bringing an end to the crisis in Darfur, Sudan

After winning the gold medal for the men's 500-meter speed skating event at the 2006 Winter Olympics in Turin, Italy, Joey Cheek gave his $25,000 winnings to the children in refugee camps in Sudan through Right to Play, another athlete-driven humanitarian organization formed by former Olympic champion Johann Olav Koss of Norway. A few months later, he joined Nick and George Clooney on a fact-finding trip to Darfur.

REBECCA JOSHUA OKWACI
Journalist, radio commentator in Sudan, and former freedom fighter

Rebecca Joshua Okwaci is a journalist and the secretary general of Women Action for Development in Sudan. As a peace advocate, Rebecca co-led the Sudanese delegation to the U.N. Fourth World Conference on Women held in Beijing, China in 1995 and facilitated dialogue between women from the south and north.

Doris Lee: Rebecca, you are from Southern Sudan but are now living in Nairobi?

Rebecca Okwaci: Yes, I was part of the revolution for liberation. Now I am in Nairobi and am currently working for Sudan Radio Service. But most of my work is in Sudan. I do news and programs for the radio, but sources are all over the country in Sudan.

What topics do you report on?

Sudan Radio Service is an Education Development Center project—a USAID funded radio. It came at the time when the Sudanese were negotiating the peace agreement signed in 2005, which ended more than two decades of war. The USAID came up with an idea of having radio help in covering the peace process and development.

I contribute to producing a program called *The Road to Peace,* explaining the peace process. I personally covered the signing of the Comprehensive Peace Agreement (CPA) itself, which was a big event in our history. The radio covers and produces programs on good governance, law enforcement issues, democracy and elections processes. We want to have a democratic country.

Later on, I was appointed an executive producer, and now I'm a senior journalist and a manager. I supervise staff and programs that cover the importance of improving health, education and agriculture.

The radio is independent, and very objective. I also initiated and am now producing two important programs for women, *Our* Voices, in English and *Women's Corner,* in Arabic. I focus on all things about women, because I feel women's issues cut across peace, war, agriculture and so on. I talk about the importance of education for women, peace and reconciliation, communication and leadership. We also speak about gender, so that there is no false impression that women are fighting the men and creating opportunities for men and women to work together.

Rebecca, we both attended the UN International Women's Conference in Beijing and heard that one of the directives was the importance of education for girls. How is that going in Sudan?

The conference gave us women an opportunity to share and put forth a plan of action.

I am the Secretary General for Women's Action for Development (WAD)—a civil society organization in Sudan. We focus on education for girls. Our cultures in the past did not see education as important for women and girls. Girls got married at an early age. Now, of course, it has changed.

Tell us about your education.

Education came in through the missionaries who arrived in my area in 1902. Our place, Dolieb Hill, was among the first stations for Christian missionaries in Southern Sudan, so our people learned the Bible and went to school.

My father was among the bright students and was trained as a teacher. He benefited from that opportunity, so education became a part of him. When we were born, he was already educated and my mother understood the benefits of education. My father was an example in his village. He was a Christian and thought that education was not only for boys, but also for girls; therefore, education was embraced in our family of four other daughters. We are happy to be among the educated families that have educated girls. I graduated from the University of Alexandria in Egypt. As well as my sisters Buwar and Sarah. We are not exceptional now in our generation, but still within our communities we are looked at as an example in terms of education.

Ten years before the Beijing Conference, I did a TV special called **Women of the World in Nairobi.** *At that time, an African woman talked about the importance of water and how the people she knew used to walk a half hour for the water. Now it's four hours in and four hours back home. Is water one of the main obstacles that stand in the way of development?*

Yes and no. My country is a country of water and rivers. We have plenty of water. But in some village there is a lack of water. People use water pumps. I personally visited villages where I had to go and pump the water and carry the container on my head, so in some areas women have to walk long distances.

You see that as a part of an engineering problem?

33

It's not only engineering, but also planning and development. I think it's incumbent upon the government to know what kind of services it's giving to communities.

When I was a child in the early '70s, we were living in a mission compound, and water services were much better. Now instead of improving things, they are worse.

Have you found that talking about women's rights in your radio programming makes men angry?

It doesn't make them angry, because you have various levels. If you are talking about the central government, you are oppressed whether you are a man or a woman, so that's one level.

On gender issues, we have our political platform. I do this through our organization, Women Action for Development. So, we're fighting for our rights as *citizens* and as women.

So you stood side-by-side with the rebels?

Yes, I was inside. I was 100% a part of it. I was not trained as a soldier, but I was on the radio. I was a journalist within the revolution, the Sudan People's Liberation Movement/Army, shouting loud for our rights and freedoms. I continued to be a journalist, first for the BBC and now for working for peace and development. But I experienced the war, and I know what it means. If I had not played that role of fighting the oppressors, I couldn't have played this role today.

We were pushed by the oppressive government to fight; that is why we had the revolution. After all the shouting and the fighting, the government is ready to talk about sharing the national cake. Sharing of power and resources has to be negotiated. Today, I am pleased that members of the revolution are in the government of National Unity. The war is over and it is time to talk peace. That's why I'm also very loud about peace-building and reconciliation forums like the Institute for Peace and Justice here in San Diego, California. People are still feeling the bitterness of war.

How did you know about the Institute for Peace and Justice here in San Diego?

Number one, I'm a founding member of the Women Waging Peace Program initiated at Harvard University. Even during the revolution, through my radio programs, I talked about women's development. In 1999, I went to The Hague Appeal for Peace in The Netherlands to talk about peace in our country.

Through the Internet, these organizations found out about me and invited me, and we've now formed a group called the Global Women's Network.

What would you say are the strongest lessons you took back home with you?

I have done a lot of things in life and thought at some point I needed to write my story, which wasn't possible in Africa. Funding is not there for documenting my stories into a book or video documentary.

I'm happy to document my stories, because they will benefit others. If this is shown in a documentary or in a book to other parents, they will know the value of educating women.

Thank you for your courage and conviction, Rebecca.

*In Darfur, women are often portrayed as victims with no ability to influence peace. **These portrayals could not be further from the truth**. Last year, I witnessed Darfurian women coming together to identify common priorities and speak with one voice.*

- *Visionary Spotlight* -

ZEBIBA SHEKHIA
Author and Founder of HealingBridges.org

I met bright, attractive, and very energetic Zebiba at a HUB Conference in Los Angeles. I was astonished with her personal story. Zebiba was born and raised in the eastern part of Sudan. At age 14, she was standing with her parents outside their home when they noticed invaders coming into their village. Her parents immediately realized that these people were there to rob, rape, and kill. Immediately, her father and mother told Zebiba to run. She did.

Zebiba's remarkable story is found in a new book called, ***Healing Bridges***. In her recent newsletter, she shares what she has been doing in her country:

We recently traveled to the Eritrean refugee camps in the eastern part of Sudan, on the border of Eritrea, to assess the situation, provide medical and school supplies and find out what we could do to help.

Not too many NGO's go to these camps, labeled the "Forgotten Refugee Camps," as it's not easy to get to Kassala or get permission to visit the camps.

The situation in the camps is dire. There is over 50% malnutrition in the population and we met many people

36

who had not eaten for several days. Babies are dying from malnutrition and malaria.

Several of the doctors we met were practically in tears of despair as they shared with us how the refugee mothers could not afford prescription medicines for their little ones. The doctors would often pay for them out of their own meager wages.

Our goal is to help provide quality education for the children. Currently education is only provided until 8th grade. The children go to school in run-down buildings with rubble on the floor and have very limited school supplies, if any.

We've been given approval to build a secondary school in Shargarab refugee camp, and with your help, we are moving forward with this.

We're also helping three refugee schools in the town of Kassala. These schools hadn't paid their rent for about a year or paid their teachers salary for six months. With your help, we are helping them pay their rent and pay their teacher's salaries to continue providing education for about 1,000 children.

Our other plans include feeding the children in the schools and providing them with desperately needed supplies and uniforms (a requirement). This will lessen the burden on the parents. Additionally, we plan to build a well at the school to make water more accessible. Children travel for an hour in 120 degree heat to collect unsanitary water. Last year, there were cholera outbreaks due to this situation.

With your help, we can begin to change the lives of the children in the camps. Every donation helps, even $1 to $5 would help us help the refugees.

For more information, please visit www.healingbridges.org

Visionary Reflection on…

Peace

Is there any area of your life where you're having your own personal conflict and strife? Are you at war with a situation, a person, a thought, a feeling, or an old behavior pattern? Today, allow yourself to see one simple thing you could do (or *not* do) that would bring some calm and tranquility to whatever you've been struggling with. Imagine what might support you in having greater peace…not perfection, just peace.

CHAPTER 3

CLOCKWISE L to R: Andrew Young, Ambassador Melanne Verveer, Doris Lee with Xernona Clayton

CHAPTER 3

HUMAN RIGHTS

• • • • • • • • • • • • • • • • •

"Non-violence is the greatest force at the disposal of mankind. It is the supreme law. By it alone can mankind be saved."
-Mahatma Gandhi

ANDREW YOUNG
Former Mayor of Atlanta, Assistant to U.S. President Jimmy Carter and U.S. Ambassador to the United Nations

I began the interview with Andrew Young by asking about my long time friend & the first African American Head of Atlanta's Department of Education, Dr. Benjamin Mayes:

Andrew Young: Dr. Benjamin Mayes was the former President of Morehouse College and Head of a Philosophy of Leadership Development Course that produced Martin Luther King Jr. and a generation of young men at Morehouse College that were committed to making the world a better place.

It was one of the few colleges that was totally intentional about leadership development. They were not just interested in giving degrees. They were interested in creating leaders in nearly every field, like medicine, the law, and education.

Martin Luther King Jr. happened to be the most successful product of that leadership system, but so was Mayor Jackson, who was mayor here in Atlanta as well as Bob

40

Johnson, who was one of the original founders of Jet Magazine with Larone Bennett of Ebony Magazine. In the 60s, more than half of the black lawyers, doctors, and educators came from Morehouse College.

Doris Lee: That's amazing. I've never heard that story before.

There's a book called *Religion and Rhetoric in the Civil Rights Movement* that's produced by Baylor University Press. If you'll read the sermon in there from Benjamin Mayes, you'll find some things that you very seldom hear leaders say to young people.

For instance, my President at Howard University Mordecai Johnson would talk about what was wrong with the United States all the time and he was right.

Is that where you went to school?

Yes, but Dr. King used to say to me often, "If you'd gone to Morehouse, you'd be somebody else." I thought he was just kidding. But Dr. Benjamin Mayes, the President of Morehouse College, went to Gandhi's Independence celebration in 1947 in India, and instead of telling everybody what was wrong with the world, he came back and started saying, "Gentleman, by no fault of our own we're 300 years behind, and my challenge to you is, can you be disciplined, courageous and visionary enough to catch up in the next 25 years?"

The reason that was significant for me was that Martin Luther King Jr. heard that when he was 14 as a freshman at Morehouse College, and he was killed at age 39. This was probably Martin Luther King's first time hearing about non-violence.

Here is where the non-violent movement in America started.

In a profound way, he became a leader not just of America, but of the world. He was a leader that showed that we can make the world a better place by renouncing violence. "You don't overcome hatred with hatred. You overcome hatred with love." At that time, I was at Howard University, and I heard about it and read it also, but didn't believe it.

Because you didn't believe you could change the world?

I didn't believe non-violence was the answer. I was a product of the Second World War and grew up playing commandos—you had to stop the Hitlers of the world. My wife, on the other hand, along with Martin Luther King Jr.'s wife, both came from the little town of Marion, Alabama; both went to schools that emphasized non-violence.

Coretta Scott King went to Antioch College and was a member, as a college student, of the Women's Strike for Peace. Jean, my wife, went to Manchester College, which was a church of the Brethren College. They did not believe in war. It was a pacifist college. Therefore, after we were married, our wives challenged and pushed us to think and commit more seriously to non-violence. When Martin Luther King Jr. died, it was Dr. Benjamin Mayes who was asked to give his Eulogy.

That's the change. You can change the skyline of a city. You can change the quality of test scores in the public education system. But unless we make the world less hate-filled and less violent, toward each other and also toward nature, then we are not making progress.

42

We're now realizing that the abuse of human life and the abuse of nature go hand-in-hand.

Collectively, we have ignored it for a long time?

We still want to ignore it, except that we're running out of water in Atlanta and we have to ask why. I grew up in New Orleans, and we had hurricanes throughout my childhood, but nothing as bad as Katrina.

I became mayor of Atlanta when the metropolitan area was just over one million people, and now we're over five million. Growth and development, in itself, is positive, but the sheer numbers of cars and buildings has put a strain on the environment here. Therefore, we're now in a transition phase. We have been successful in growing an economy, and now we have to make sure that growth doesn't compromise the quality of life. For me, this is a normal process.

I'm optimistic because of the growth and development—and because of the concern about the environment. We're looking at more reasonable ways to generate energy. We're more interested in quality design in the urban environment.

But we also have a health system that's overburdened. I always say, just drinking water and walking a mile a day will improve everybody's health significantly. The earth and the world aren't complicated, but it does require thoughtfulness and sensitivity to each other and to the environment.

This is an important perspective you're providing.

It's very simple. To me, it's a natural consequence of understanding that non-violence includes non-violence towards the earth itself. The reason for Martin Luther King's monument on the mall in Atlanta, as I see it, is not because he was a black leader, it's that he was the only leader on that mall who advocated change without violence.

Where does that leave us in terms of the fact that we're in Afghanistan and Iraq?

It leaves us with an understanding that those were preventable wars. Jimmy Carter dealt with Russia, China, Panama, and Southern African for four years. When I was with the UN, we didn't kill a single person or get a single person killed. We advanced America's geo-political and economic interests without violence.

Through diplomacy and negotiations?

It wasn't just negotiations, because negotiations, implies you're sitting down with opposite points of view. Jimmy Carter was different than any other leader. When he sent me to Africa, he didn't send me with the point of view, with a position to sell. He said, "Ask African leaders what they expect of America."

He asked Israeli leaders what they expected of America, and they told him they were afraid of another war with Egypt. Egyptian leaders told him they were afraid of another war with Israel. So, at their request, he had a basis for getting them together.

The Panamanian leaders told us they were afraid of conflict over the Canal. African leaders told us they needed our help in dealing with Namibia and Rhodesia, but they weren't ready to deal with South Africa yet.

We listened to people. When you listen to people, when you talk with people and not at them, change is possible.

XERNONA CLAYTON
Passionate about African-American Achievements; Founder of the Trumpet Awards Foundation, Inc., Atlanta, Georgia

Xernona Clayton has received many accolades throughout her rich life. Her commitment to the betterment of others began very early. Having accepted a position with the Southern Christian Leadership Conference in 1965, she developed a close friendship with Dr. Martin Luther King, Jr. As the first African-American woman to have her own TV talk show in the South, she has long been a role model for moving beyond obstacles and living to one's full potential. For many years through the scholarship foundation that bears her name, Xernona chooses outstanding minority high school students to spend a year living abroad with the aim of increasing positive international relationships through a global student exchange program. Xernona is an ongoing source of inspiration to me, as she lives a wonderful and exciting life that ignites a sense of purpose and passion in so many others.

Doris Lee: Nineteen years ago, as a Turner Broadcast Vice President, you presented an idea to CNN Founder Ted Turner. The idea was a program devoted to recognizing the untold stories of African-American achievements. You had a dream about this that seemed to evolve. Would you talk about that?

Xernona Clayton: Yes and it's an exciting moment every time I think about it. I guess it's the moment that compels me to tell people to never squelch an idea. You never know where an idea will go. Once you have it and it makes sense,

45

I encourage folks to move forward on it, and that's what I did with this idea.

I wanted so very much to have the image of African-Americans changed; changed from stereotypical views, blurred vision, prejudicial thinking about our people to the reality of our folks. That is making sure that the world knew that African-Americans have been, are doing, and will continue to do great works even when the work is not recognized—and that's what happened to our society.

Bigotry and racism did great harm. I think it gave people the opportunity to disallow the presence and the contributions of African-Americans. In other words, we were denied opportunity, and I use as my prime example Lena Horne who was a great singer. And we could go down the list of great singers, great talents who weren't fully recognized.

Singer and activist Marian Andersen was another real one who had great talent when she went to Washington in 1939 to sing at Constitution Hall. But because of racism, bigotry, and prejudice she was denied the opportunity, and that was the plight of black Americans—denied opportunities.

I wanted to be sure that I used the resources that were available to me to change the story, to change the imagery, to be sure that everybody knew the greater story: Here is a group of people who are reaching great heights, expanding and enriching the lives of people in our society.

I wanted so much to do that. And having the resource of television and the good and great wisdom of my boss Ted Turner, I was able to put that idea into action. I implemented it, and here we are. Going on 19 years later, we have changed negative attitudes. We have proven to the world that our people are not as they were perceived to be. One white caller let me know that she was one among many who was taught that all black Americans were lazy. She had no idea that we've been doing great work, pursuing our goals, and helping people in our society, even though we may have had abusive treatment in our lives.

I feel excited when I tell stories of these wonderful people who have done such marvelous work. And now, for the first time, we're getting some pretty decent recognition; not adequate yet, but decent recognition for the great work we've been doing—not just with black Americans, but courageous people in general who've been changing the world.

You have had 19 Trumpet Award events, and I've been privileged to be invited to them. They have given me the opportunity to meet Stevie Wonder, Gladys Knight, Isaac Hayes, Quincy Jones, Nancy Wilson, gospel singer Ernestine Dillard and many more. Recently you even recognized Clint Eastwood for his long-time love of jazz music. I could hardly believe it when I saw "Dirty Harry" himself playing the piano so well.

You, Doris Lee, have made us happy with your presence. You've witnessed how we strive hard to be an inclusive society. Martin Luther King, Jr. said that we've got to figure out ways to bring people together, regardless of race and gender. Although our program is African-American focused, we include people who are not African-American because that is our mission and our goal. And it's part of my personal zeal to be sure that we do that.

You set a marvelous example for many people to see that we all have something special inside of us, and that all we have to do is take action. You could have kept that dream in your head for

47

years, yet you moved ahead—and in the process brought along so many people with you.

Another Trumpet Awards honoree was Dick Parsons, former Chairman of the Board of Time Warner. His comment to me was that it's important that we choose to be involved in things that will help a large number of people and you certainly have done that.

Yes, and others involved in our program who share that commitment are people such as John Hope Franklin, Maya Angelou, and Muhammad Ali…there are just so many.

One of the joys of my life was to sit next to Rosa Parks and hear her inspirational story—to feel the deep spirituality simply radiating from her.

Yes, General Colin Powell is another one. We have people in our audience who are just as accomplished as the people who we present on the stage. Some of the people who come to the events are people who have the opportunity that perhaps they would never have had had it not been for the Trumpet Awards bringing people together.

The last time I attended your main event, I talked with Nancy Brinker who started the Susan G. Komen Breast Cancer Foundation. It's exciting to see how the little seeds that were planted at the first events have since evolved into major projects. I had a chance to attend the first Susan G. Komen event in Texas, and it's interesting to see the way it has grown over the last 25 years.

Yes, and I'm most pleased with the race relations aspect of all of this. People come together and they meet each other. Different races sit together at a dinner table, and so many deals have been formed as a result of people dining together.

I'm reminded of one story of a woman who had a dream to one day be an entrepreneur. She wanted to go into a franchise operation. That was one of her dreams that she'd kept to herself. As grace would have it, sitting next to her was a man who was the CEO of a major corporation who dealt with franchisees and they just started talking. They did what you would do at any dinner, you just speak to the person next to you. They ended up expressing their dreams and desires. The CEO was a white man who was deeply committed to involving minorities in his company.

There they were, sitting next to each other, and they picked up those napkins at the dining table and signed a legitimate agreement. And the woman did go into business, just as she had dreamed of doing.

It's just been wonderful—the many, many, stories that have come out of the Trumpet Awards and the way people's lives have been enhanced from this one event. That thrills me.

Xernona, you grew up in Oklahoma in a family where your father, a minister, said to you that you're supposed to be nice and respectful to everybody, no matter what creed or race, whether black, red or white. There are many Native American Indians living in Oklahoma, right?

Definitely. I just came back from a wonderful visit with one of the Tribal chiefs in Oklahoma. I shared with him that they have a kinship with us and that their people have not been portrayed adequately, just as our people haven't.

As we continue to recognize and analyze those things that are common to us, rather than the things that are different among us, we'll find that our people can come together with a lot more ease than we've been able to do in the past. There are so many more things that unite us than divide us.

Such a good point. Is there anything in closing you'd like to mention?

One of the joys of doing this work is meeting people like you. You're an accomplished person yourself, seasoned, sensitive, understanding of all the complexities of our society and you're our friend. You see what we're trying to do and you support us so beautifully and so effectively…that's one of my joys.

Thank you so much.

To find out more, visit: www.TrumpetFoundation.org

AMBASSADOR MELANNE VERVEER
Ambassador-at-Large of Global Women's Issues

Ambassador Melanne Verveer most recently served as Chair and Co-CEO of Vital Voices Global Partnership, an international nonprofit that she co-founded that invests in emerging women leaders – pioneers of economic, political, and social progress in their countries. Prior to founding Vital Voices, Ambassador Verveer served as Assistant to the President and Chief of Staff to the First Lady in the Clinton Administration and was chief assistant to then First Lady Hillary Clinton in her international activities. Ambassador Verveer also took the lead in establishing the President's Interagency Council on Women and has served as Executive Vice President of People for the American Way, a civil rights

50

and constitutional liberties organization where she played a key role in the passage of several landmark civil rights bills.

Appointed by President Barack Obama, Ambassador Verveer is the very first member of the State Department to focus primarily on woman's issues on a global scale. I am inspired the depth and breadth of Ambassador Verveer's dedication to raising standards for women throughout the world.

Editor's note: This conversation between Doris Lee McCoy and Ambassador Verveer begins with reflections on the 15ᵗʰ year since the UN Third World Conference on Women which took place in Beijing, China in 1995.

Ambassador Melanne Verveer: We're beginning to ramp up to the anniversary of the Beijing Conference, which spun a movement around the world and chiseled women's rights into human rights. It really created an ambitious blueprint through the platform for action for the kind of things that need to continue if women are going to take their rightful place in the world. It's a particularly good time to look back at what we've achieved and what is the unfinished agenda.

The conference was a blueprint for the kinds of things each and every one of us knows that women need to have: access to education and healthcare. They need to have the opportunity to participate in the economy of their countries and in the political life of their societies.

They need to be free from violence and to have their rights protected, from property rights to everything else. So we can look back and see that in over 15 years, there's been significant progress, but we also have a way to go.

For example, we know that violence against women is a terrible scourge that touches every country. And although so many countries have passed laws to protect women, many of those laws that were passed haven't really been implemented, enforced, or funded, so I think we have to look at the next steps that have to be taken.

Similarly, micro-finance, micro-credits have begun to transform women's lives.

Doris Lee McCoy: Muhammad Yunus discusses this leading-edge topic in this book.

He is still hard at work on this. It's had a transformative impact of enabling literally millions of women around the globe to be able to create a livelihood for themselves and their families and to create economic independence.

Now, we need to keep at that, but we also need to look at ways to really grow small and medium-size enterprises that are women-run, because they will be an engine for economic growth and will enable that many more women and other men to be hired to grow economies of countries.

There's great potential, just as women-run small businesses in the United States have had such a positive impact."

It appears to be a growing sector.

Exactly, and now there's so much more data than we had in Beijing about the fact that women really are the drivers of economic growth. We just need to make sure that they have access to the kinds of skills and capacity development— like micro-finance and credit—that they need to be very successful.

So I think in so many areas we can take satisfaction, as we should, in the progress that's been made. We also need to look at not just what remains to be achieved but also more creative and effective ways for us to do that.

I think what is of great importance is collaboration: the world of public-private partnerships; governments coming together with civil society, businesses, and academia; people working together in a more collaborative way to bring their competencies to bear on the challenges.

We are in a time of innovation and can't even imagine the possibilities of some of the new technology to enable women to grow out of poverty and to move their countries forward.

Your book is coming out at a good time, because we have had a lot of movement thanks to visionaries around the world—people who, decades ago, had a vision of what could be.

Just as the women and men who went to the first Women's Equality Convention in Seneca Falls over 150 years ago, creating a new vision of possibility for women in the United States. They saw what was needed—from the right to vote, to be able to earn a living and keep your pay, to having property rights. Well, the vision now is the difference that women's potential can make if it's tapped into around the globe.

It has not yet been tapped and women still are on the outskirts of opportunity. It is the visionaries, inspirers, and the people who see how things could be that really make all the difference.

Yes. I was at the first Women's Conference in Mexico City and then in Nairobi, Kenya, East Africa, and I could see a little growth at the first one in Mexico City—to see Madame Jehan Sadat, Egyptian President Anwar Sadat's remarkable wife, come without wearing her veil over her face. People were just shocked.

See, you have your stories to tell too.

I had a chance to talk to 8,000 non-governmental organizations (NGOs). I came home and I told my children; they weren't impressed when I told them the talk was translated into five different languages. But I can see the movement taking place. Betty Friedan, Gloria Steinem, Bella Abzug, and Clare Booth Luce were outstanding women who were there. I had a great opportunity to meet and talk with Clare, and we both agree that change was not happening fast enough.

I was just in Bhutan and I was reading in the paper that although the government had given the women the rights to come forward with political viewpoints and even run for office, they weren't picking up the challenge. I think those who have been silent in the past are having trouble coming forward because they may feel they will be seen as being aggressive.

You're talking about Mexico City and Nairobi reminded me that it was the women from Africa who put Violence Against Women on the agenda in Nairobi. And then it was in Beijing that we recognized once and for all that this was a violation of human rights. It wasn't cultural, it wasn't private; it was criminal—and you couldn't do this kind of thing.

What I'm seeing all over the world are women and men coming together to really move women's progress forward, but in different places sometimes it's slower, and other places it's a lot faster.

Here in San Diego we have the Institute for Peace and Justice. The saddest stories that I heard came from a woman attorney in the Congo. She said you would be better to be the enemy of the warring rebels than to be a woman because women were being raped.

Yes.

You know the extent of what happens when a woman is raped, yes?

It's actually a very strategic, systematized, coordinated method of the in-arm conflict. It's to use rape against women as that tactic of war and to go in realizing what it does to dishonor the woman in her own family, how it basically dissolves families and destabilizes communities. And that's what the armed bandits want to achieve.

Don't you think also they're frustrated by not having a wife or a girlfriend in their hometown?

It can't be justified in any way, but I think what we do see is that even in situations where these armed conflicts have ended, or wars have ended, much of this behavior continues. There is an impunity that basically does not prosecute these as crimes. And as long as you don't have to pay the price for this kind of behavior, it is not going to stop.

We have to educate men about respect. Women's station is so low in so many places, they are like property. This is why I think we have to invest in economic possibility and education to raise the level of women's status, but we also have to work with the men.

55

We have to make sure that laws are enforced, because when you have situations of disrespect at the most fundamental level, this kind of stuff becomes a manifestation of a practice that is basically condoned because it's never punished.

You must be traveling all over, because this is a new position, right?

It is. It was something that President Obama created and Secretary Clinton obviously embraced, because it was a recognition that in the United States foreign policy, we cannot achieve what we want to for the world and ourselves in terms of confronting the challenges, whether environmental or governance, economics or security, unless women are fully participating in their societies.

Women are a very big part of enabling our world to address our common challenges, so the place of these issues in foreign policy has been elevated. I must say that in my short time in this position, there's just been tremendous receptivity.

We like to think that we in America can be models. I think the message it has sent to the world about women and the progress of women has been applauded and embraced. Good examples of this are the events that you have personally participated in like the international conferences and at the UN.

In many countries there has been such an outpouring of positive feeling for the United States that we are engaged in these issues.

It may be one of the strongest efforts we have for healing some of the wounds that have occurred in the past—to demonstrate to

*other countries that America does have that kind of concern for
them.*

Yes. Being able to stand up for human rights has been a
great hallmark of this country and certainly a priority in our
foreign policy.

*The fact that you're tying it into the foreign policy now I think is
just outstanding.*

That was really what the leadership intended, and I think
that the way the world is reacting so positively is a message
in and of itself.

*What kind of groups do you find are most receptive to what
you're talking about?*

Obviously, women are tremendously receptive because
they are often on the frontlines of trying to bring about this
change. They are often the people struggling for family law
reform or for an end to the kind of violence we've been
talking about. But also, leaders of countries and leaders in
the business communities that are investing more and more
in women's economic potential are increasingly receptive.

The World Bank has a program called Women's Equality
Equals Smart Economics. Companies like Goldman Sachs
are investing significantly in women's economic capacity
building.

That's the message that has been very gratifying, and it is
so important to say. Yes, these are women's issues—they
deeply say everything about women and women's place in
the world—but they are about creating a better world. They
are about security and economic progress.

Whether the decision-makers sit at high levels of government, in corporations, or universities, we collectively begin to recognize that these are not just "soft" issues, not just women's issues. These really are issues about the heart of whether or not our world is going to be able to deal with some of the great challenges that confront us.

Do you use the fact that, as we know statistically, if a woman has gone to school, this is going to affect the intellectual growth of the whole family?

Absolutely. One of the things we know unquestionably today is that investment in a girl's education is the single best, most-effective development tool that we have. As you said, when you educate a girl, you educate a family, and you change a community.

When she has a family they learn better nutrition. She is more prone to have fewer children. She is more likely to be able to succeed in a job and have her income level be that much greater than it would be otherwise. There are so many benefits that have been reinforced by the data now correlating the investment in an education with these strong positive outcomes.

Do you see the possibility of convening the United Nations meetings again?

You can never say never, obviously. What is planned, for example, with "Beijing plus 15" there is a series of preparatory meetings that are going on. Regionally, they just had one in the Middle East. There will be one for Europe coming up, and there will be a way to sort of take the pulse of what the perceptions are. NGOs are going to be doing this all over the world, as well outside the more official lines.

I think when the Commission on the Status of Women meets in March at the United Nations there will be an effort to really see where we are, to assess ourselves. Also, I know that there are many who are thinking about ways in which younger people can be reached today who did not have the Beijing experience and who want to come together.

There are conversations going on and efforts going on to create different opportunities to come together for women's progress around the globe. I think a lot of that is exciting too, because we talked about creativity and we talked about innovation. The more others are there to embrace all of this I think is good news.

It is in the interest of all of us to insure that women can realize their potential, because our world will benefit from that.

And Doris Lee, you just keep reminding us and inspiring us with your visionaries, because that is what keeps us going.

Visionary Reflection on...

Dignity

What does the word "dignity" evoke for you? Whether it's images of royalty or simply treating people with kindness and regard, today, imagine what would be possible if you treat everyone you encounter with dignity. Even if you don't exchange a word, experiment with holding in your thoughts the significance and nobility of each individual person...including yourself.

CHAPTER 4

CLOCKWISE L to R: Dr. Muhammad Yunus with Doris Lee, Dr. Catherine Bertini, and Steven Pratt, M.D.

CHAPTER 4

Healthy Food and Raising People Out of Poverty

●●●●●●●●●●●●●●●●●●

NU SKIN ENTERPRISES & NOURISH THE CHILDREN
Providing VitaMeal worldwide - An Ideal Food for
Malnourished Children

Since its launch in 2002, Nu Skin's Nourish the Children (NTC) has donated more than 223,000,000 meals to malnourished children around the world. Nu Skin, founded by Blake Roney, Sandie Tillotson, and Steve Lund, teamed up with national nutritional scientist and child nutrition expert, Dr. Ken Brown from the University of California, Davis to create an ideal food for malnourished children (who would die if fed regular food)—VitaMeal.

Nourish the Children provides sobering statistics regarding malnutrition in children and adults around the world. The following is a synopsis provided courtesy of Nu Skin's website that not only outlines the alarming facts but also describes their inspiring and proactive efforts toward eradicating the problem:

SITUATION OF NEED:
• Every six seconds a child dies of malnutrition.
• More than 800 million people in the world, mostly children, are hungry.
• The consequences of malnutrition are severe and include growth stunting, anemia, decreased learning capacity, and a weakened immune system.
MEETING THE NEED:

Pharmanex, the nutritional supplement division of Nu Skin Enterprises™, teamed our own nutritional scientists with child nutrition experts at the University of California, Davis to create VitaMeal, which we believe is an ideal food for malnourished children. Over the past five years, **more than 223 million meals have been distributed throughout the world.**

VITAMEAL PRODUCTION:
• VitaMeal produced for Asia and South America has as the basis rice and lentils
• VitaMeal produced in Malawi, Africa, is a corn-based, porridge-like product to match cultural preferences and local agricultural output.
• VitaMeal plants recently opened in China and Malawi provide economic opportunity in developing areas and reduce distribution costs.
• Each package of VitaMeal provides 30 child-sized meals and retails for $19.95 (U.S.).

VITAMEAL BENEFITS:
• Contains a balance of carbohydrates, protein, fat and fiber
• Provides essential fatty acids required for normal brain development, skin health and immune defense
• Provides electrolytes necessary for maintaining normal fluid balance and muscle function
• Includes 25 essential vitamins and minerals
• Provides vitamin A, which is essential for normal sight and immune functions
• Provides bone nutrients for normal growth and skeletal development
• Allows for easy addition of ingredients to fit every taste and culture
• Is vegetarian and non-dairy
• Each bag contains 30 child meals of nutritious, delicious food

For more information, go to www.nourishthechildren.com. Several recipes that use VitaMeal are available on the website. You can also contact Brent Goddard, Managing Director of Nourish the Children, at: 801.345.2246.

Author's Note: Having tasted VitaMeal, I could not be more excited about its potential. It is so versatile and delicious that I will be planning VitaMeal tasting parties in the future—especially since you can even make a chocolate cake with VitaMeal! Sign up for my mailing list on my website and stay tuned to my blog for more information: www.dorisleemccoy.com

- Visionary Spotlight -

FEED THE CHILDREN

Providing help and hope for a hurting world, Feed the Children is one of the most widely known nonprofit organizations in the world. Founded in 1979, it is one of the 10 largest international charities in the U.S., based on private, non-government support. Feed The Children is an international, nonprofit relief organization with headquarters in Oklahoma City, Oklahoma, that delivers food, medicine, clothing and other necessities to individuals, children and families who lack these essentials due to famine, war, poverty or natural disasters. In 2009, Feed The Children distributed more than 111 million pounds of food and other essentials to children and their families in all 50 U.S. states and internationally.

To learn more about Feed the Children, go to: www.feedthechildren.org

MUHAMMAD YUNUS, Ph.D.
Economist, winner of the 2006 Nobel Peace Prize along with Grameen Bank, Founder of micro-credit for the poor

Dr. Muhammad Yunus received his B.A. and M.A. in Economics at Dhaka University in Bangladesh. He is also a Fulbright scholar and earned a Ph.D. in Economics from Vanderbilt University.

The winner of the 2006 Noble Peace Prize, Dr. Yunus saw a great need and solved it in a way none of the big banks could seem to do. With the creation of Grameen Bank, he changed the face of global finance through establishing micro-credit. His story is uniquely compelling...

In 1974, after the great flooding in Northern India, Dr. Yunus witnessed people seeking refuge in his town, needing only a few handfuls of rice to sustain their life, yet dying in the doorways of those they came to for help. He asked himself, "Why am I teaching Economics when everyone is so poor?" He was deeply stirred and decided to go to the people in a particularly hard-hit village. He asked 47 poverty-stricken villagers how much they needed to be able to survive a month and they said $27.00. He took that money out of his own pocket and gave it to them for the next month, thus beginning the micro-credit movement.

After finding no way for the poor to get through the banking system, this man, who was not a banker at all, founded the Grameen Bank which has grown today to help over 7.5 million women and their families find their way out of poverty. He has always believed that when given the chance, the poor would happily repay borrowed money after using it to lift themselves out of poverty.

In 2006, the Norwegian Nobel Committee awarded the Nobel Peace Prize to Professor Muhammad Yunus and Grameen Bank "for their efforts to create economic and social development from below."

Dr. Yunus said upon receiving the award, "When I lent $27 to 42 people in 1976 in a small village next to the university where I taught, I had no idea that it would be the beginning of a new banking methodology, and it would spread in every country of the world. It feels very strange to realize that, until then, we lived with a banking methodology that kept the doors of the bank closed to two-thirds of the world's population. Grameen freed banking from the limitations of collateral."

Dr. Yunus created the Grameen Bank in order to provide small amounts of working capital to the poor for self-employment based on the concept of capitalism combined with social responsibility. Now, the Grameen Bank has grown. It has loaned out more than $5 billion dollars to its 7.5 million clients in Bangladesh and throughout the world with the incredible and surprising results of a repayment rate of over 98%.

The Nobel Peace Prize Committee said of Dr. Yunus, "Lasting peace cannot be achieved unless large population groups find ways in which to break out of poverty. Micro-credit is one such means. Development from below also serves to advance democracy and human rights."

Muhammad Yunus has shown himself to be a leader who has managed to translate his visions into practical action for the benefit of millions of people, not only in Bangladesh, but also in many other countries," the committee's statement continued. "Loans to poor people without financial security had appeared to be an impossible idea. From the modest beginnings three decades ago, Yunus has, first and foremost through the Grameen Bank, developed micro-credit into an ever more important instrument in the struggle against poverty. The Grameen Bank has been a source of ideas and models for the many institutions in the field of micro-credit that have sprung up around the world."

"Yunus' long-term vision is to eliminate poverty around the world. That vision cannot be realized by means of micro-credit alone. But Muhammad Yunus and Grameen Bank have shown that, in the continuing efforts to achieve it, micro-credit must play a major part," the committee acknowledged.

My first encounter of Dr. Yunus came in 1975 when I attended the first UN International Women's Year Conference in Mexico City as a reporter. I remember thinking at that time what a great idea his system of micro-credit was for the poor of the world. The second time we met was at the second UN Women's Conference in Nairobi, Kenya in East Africa. His micro-credit program was continuing to grow and his audience was very appreciative of the tangible results that were gaining momentum.

Subsequently, I was both delighted and encouraged to see him again—at the UN International Women's Conference in Beijing, China in 1995, and later at University of California, San Diego where he addressed students and faculty of three San Diego-based universities, as well as the general public.

Alex Counts, President of the Grameen Foundation, said about Dr. Yunus's idea, "Professor Yunus is an extraordinary visionary whose unshakeable belief in the power of people to help themselves escape poverty has become a rallying call across the globe. Micro-finance is one of the most powerful solutions to poverty in existence today, and Dr. Yunus is the leader most responsible for developing and implementing it in Bangladesh and globally."

Dr. Yunus also received a letter from Nelson Mandela and his wife Graca Machel upon receiving his Nobel Peace Prize. It read, "As we have come to know, you are a person wholly committed to making a difference in the lives of the poor, and someone who feels deeply about working for peace and justice around the world."

Since 2010, Dr. Yunus has served as a Commissioner for the Broadband Commission for Digital Development, a UN initiative which seeks to use broadband Internet services to accelerate social and economic development. He also serves on the advisory board of the Holcim Foundation for Sustainable Construction, a foundation supporting initiatives that combine sustainable construction solutions with architectural excellence.

Over three decades ago, Dr. Muhammad Yunus simply asked villagers how much money they needed in order to survive for one month. The unprecedented success of the visionary banking system known as micro-credit and micro-finance is a testament to the power of asking the right questions.

- *Visionary Spotlight* -

PAUL COLLIER
Author of *The Bottom Billion: Why the Poorest Countries are Failing and What Can Be Done About It*, Professor of Economics, Oxford University

Professor Collier's book *The Bottom Billion* was the main focus of the Conrad Hilton Foundation's International Humanitarian Symposium in Geneva, Switzerland. The event was attended by people who work in non-profit organizations around the world like World Vision, Operation Smile, and Faith Alive. He spoke very simply and clearly concerning the reasons that the bottom billion of the world's people are failing. He received the 2008 Gelber Prize and the Edgar Graham Prize for his work.

STEVEN PRATT, M.D.
Author of the best-selling book *SuperFoodsRx*

Steven Pratt, M.D. is a world-renowned authority on the role of nutrition and lifestyle in the prevention of disease and optimization of health. He is a senior staff ophthalmologist at

Scripps Memorial Hospital in La Jolla, California. He has been a repeat guest on the Oprah Winfrey Show.

Doris Lee: Dr. Pratt, you are a surgeon, a nutritionist, and an author, which is quite a dossier to have. In addition, you're certainly in great condition!

Steven Pratt: It wouldn't do any good to talk about this stuff if I wasn't.

There's a lot of information out about how compromised our immune systems are these days. How would you suggest people address that?

The only guaranteed way to extend our life span is to restrict calories and be physically fit. Move, burn calories, and the rest is easy. From macular degeneration to cataracts, cancers, heart disease (you name the chronic disease), in almost all cases you can either prevent it or decrease the risk by moving, getting off your butt and burning some calories.

Try to fashion your life like a caveman or woman. If you walked into a modern market, you'd step into the produce section. You wouldn't recognize most of the junk in the stores today, but you would know fruits, whole grains, vegetables, nuts and seeds. You'd recognize some of the meat and fish, but the meat in the store is not what you would eat if you were a caveman. If you look at wild game, it is very lean. It's also full of omega 3, whereas the meat you buy in the store has a lot of omega 6 in it.

So think, *I'm going to live like a caveman or cavewoman as much as I can, but I'm going to enjoy all the advantages of our society. I'm going to be kind to my genes, because my* *genes are back in the Stone Age. They are not 20th century* *genes; they are thousands of years old.*

The genome change is extremely slow, so what did we do 2,000 years ago? How much sleep did we get? Maybe you made love and then you went to sleep, and you probably slept 10-11 hours a night. That's when your immune system replaces and get's ready for the next day. So you want to be kind to your immune system. The key to exercise is "not too much and not too little." There's a middle range where it stimulates your immune system. Lack of sleep is a major issue. With obesity, people say, "Gee, doc, I can't control my weight." And I say, "How much sleep do you get?" If you get less than seven hours sleep a night, you put your body in a metabolic state conducive to obesity.

You have to get seven hours?

Yes, if you want to stay out of the metabolic range or if you are in some sort of inflammatory, pro-diabetic, pro-obesity state. There's an occasional exception to the rule, but the vast majority of people are genetically programmed to require 7-8 hours of sleep a day. Averaging less than seven hours per day puts your body (the only one you will get) into a metabolic state conducive to obesity, high blood pressure, diabetes, inflammation, and perhaps cancer.

So, if you get less than five or less hours of sleep per day, you're 73% more likely to be obese than the same person getting seven hours of sleep. And even with six hours of sleep per night, you're still a little less than 20% more likely to be obese than the same person getting seven hours of sleep.

We now know that inflammation is the cause of most diseases. If you measure inflammatory markers of people who don't get enough sleep, they're all very high. Remember, obesity is an inflammatory disease. I have a section in my *Super Health* book where there's an entire chapter on watching your waistline. As your waistline get's bigger, the risk of cancer, heart disease, diabetes, cataracts, macular degeneration increases. No organ system escapes the adverse effects of a big belly.

What do you think about diets?

No one is able to stay on a restricted diet forever. Everybody can lose calories. If I told you to eat pure lard only, you'd still lose weight if that's all you ate on restricted calories. You wouldn't be very healthy, but you'd lose weight.

I don't see that in the media or the news.

Because everybody wants to make money with their special diet and their own products. I'm saying, you need to stick with whole foods you buy in the market. We have recipes in the *SuperFoodsRx* Kitchen section of our website that are delicious, healthy, and affordable—full of fiber, full of vitamins, nutrients, minerals, and not much sodium.

Remember, when you eat a good meal or get some good exercise, every cell in your body sends an email to your brain that says, "Thank you so much. That was awesome, what you just did."

If you look at centenarians, how do these people live to be over 100? First, you need a little bit of luck. Secondly, they tend to be optimistic.

Optimism, so you're talking about attitude, and that's something people can do something about.

Correct, it's a self-proclaimed prophecy. The more things you do that you know are good for you, the more you're likely to keep doing them. Generally, people will keep doing things if they get positive feedback.

Positive feedback, the way they look at themselves in their clothes, the way their friends say, "You must be losing weight."

Yes, or everybody in the office has the flu and you don't get it, why? Well, because I'm getting more sleep; I'm eating better, taking vitamins, and it all comes together.

With people who live to be 100, optimism is one of the characteristics. Everybody on this planet has speed bumps that come along, like tragedy or the death of a loved one, nobody escapes. Nobody has a life full of pure joy. Again, centenarians in general, move on. They don't dwell on things like, "Ten years ago I had the worst _____." They may never forget about it, but they don't dwell on it.

In fact, in my last book one of my keys is stress reduction, because we don't have time for bad thoughts to go through our brains regarding tragedy. It could be a pet that died. It could be your kids. It could be a hurtful word someone said to you. It could be all sorts of stuff. Everybody's had these things happen, so I learned this from my oldest son Michael. Mike told me, "Dad, if you'll just repeat to yourself 'trust in God' you can drown out any bad thought." There are many techniques like this. If I'm having a bad day, I want to get outside, I want to hear the birds, I want to smell the flowers, and get some exercise. Exercise reduces stress.

In fact, we know that one out of six or seven Americans become depressed in their lifetime. The proven best way to reduce your risk for depression is to move, because you produce endorphins, which are "feel good hormones" that prevent depression. If you have depression and you get on a good exercise program, within three weeks you can do better than you can on an anti-depressant drug. Taking anti-depressant drugs can cause all sorts of stuff to happen and that's enough to depress someone right there. I'm not anti-pharmaceutical by the way, because at some point we all need drugs to keep us alive, but I'm saying there are a lot of natural ways to accomplish the same thing. A pharmaceutical drug may be used to save my life, but maybe the synergy of exercise with my stat drug is better than my stat drug by itself. You may never need a drug, but either way, you've got to lose weight, rest, get proper nutrition and reduce stress. These will augment your immune system as well.

When I talked with Art Linkletter, who was 93 years old at the time, I was amazed at how much laughter there was between us.

You have to laugh because laughter is good medicine. There have been studies that show if you laugh, you help regulate and get more natural cells in your blood that kill off disease.

I'm glad you brought that up. Think about all the old wives tales: Eat your fruits and vegetables; laughter is the best medicine; an apple a day keeps the doctor away. Guess what? All the wives tales work. People figured out that an apple a day does lower your risk for diabetes, obesity, lung cancer, and cardiovascular disease, and that's powerful.

Prevention.

Yes. There will always be people who fall through the cracks who need to be treated, there's no question. But the same thing that prevents diabetes will help you to control your diabetes and maybe even cure it. You won't need any more medication, but you're going to have to burn some calories and eat the right foods.

How can we do that as a country, or even as a world?

I think it's "lead by example"—that's one thing, which is why I try to do the things I talk about. If I weigh 300 pounds and chain smoke, nobody is going to pay attention to what I'm talking about. If I seem like I'm doing pretty well and having fun with my life, then that's a more inspiring story.

If I was the President of the U.S., I'd have my fireside chat once a week with the population, but I'd spend five minutes talking about prevention of disease. If I have a healthier population, we're going to make more money, be more energetic, and spend less on healthcare. We're going to be in a better mood, treat each other better, treat other countries better—and they'll treat us better, which is another self-proclaimed prophecy. The whole human condition is better off if people feel better about themselves.

We should be doing something that unites everybody. Who on the planet wouldn't want better water or better air quality? To get better water, we have to make it so we don't destroy half the industries in the world to get it, because then a lot of people will be unemployed. Then we would be going backward instead of forward.

We need common goals. No one wants to argue that eating fruits and vegetables is bad for you. That's a common unified goal as well. We have to make things taste better, make it more available, because many fruits and veggies you get in the store don't taste like the produce you grow in your backyard, so if it tastes like it does in the backyard you're going to like it better.

You've talked about exercise, rest, fruits and vegetables, attitude, and humor; is there something you want to add to that?

Not all foods are created equal; some are better for you than others. For instance, if you had a million dollar racecar, you wouldn't put low-test gas in that car, because you know that engine needs the best stuff.

Second, we are born to move, so you have to be physically fit. That doesn't mean you have to spend a penny going to the gym. You can walk. You can climb up and down stairs. You can walk with the kids, the dog, with your grandparents, your grandchildren, walk yourself and walk your spouse…

What about weightlifting? How important is that?

Climbing stairs works your quads—that's weight lifting your body every step, up and down stairs. You have resistance exercises you can do, like pull-ups or push-ups. A pull-up bar will cost you $5. Run around outside, garden; you can always do something that includes resistance exercise. So you need aerobic exercises, muscle building, and good food. You have to have good relationships, whether it's a spouse, friends, family—never underestimate the power of close relationships. Get back to nature and treat our environment better.

The future has to be about how to prevent disease. When you look back, Hippocrates, the father of medicine, had it right. He said, "Let food be thy medicine." He also talked about the synergy of food and exercise to prevent disease.

Will you say more about lifestyle choices and the need to reduce stress in our society?

The stress response in humans was initially designed to run away from the bear or to get you through the day when you were starving to find food, not to be turned on 24 hours a day, seven days a week. 10,000 years ago, when we came across a bunch of food, there was no way to store it, so we ate it all. We might not get food for two or four days, so people put the food out in the sun in order to store it.

Historically, people burned about 1100 calories a day moving around. If you wanted to eat, you had to burn calories to find food. You didn't go to the 7-11 or to McDonald's for your chow; you had to physically find it. While men were out hunting for live game, women were out all day long, getting water, hunting and gathering berries, grains, vegetables—whatever they could find. The man was out doing the job that required more muscle power and strength. Hopefully, he found something to eat before it found him to eat…but everybody burned calories.

Now, generally speaking, we burn no calories other than using our hands to put food in our mouths. In addition, we have processed food, which causes disease, whereas whole foods prevent disease. Genetically, we are programmed to use the vitamins, minerals and other nutrients in food to turn on the expression of genes, which create healthier bodies that can handle stress. We now know that food and lifestyle choices help regulate the good genetic enzyme patterns in the body and suppress the bad ones.

75

There's only one proven way to extend life span, which is caloric restriction. But it may be impossible to calorically restrict people in the future, because that's not an easy thing to do. We're programmed to eat food when we find it. We're programmed to eat all we can when we find it. Now the trouble is, we find all we can 24 hours a day, 7 days a week, not once every three or four days or once a week. So we have to find ways to eat slowly, because obesity is obviously a problem, two-thirds of all Americans now are overweight.

Worldwide it's a huge problem, even in China and India. Everybody's getting fat because we're getting all this processed food. You can sit down to eat a whole loaf of white bread and there's no fiber in it. If you try to eat a loaf of whole grain bread, that's five grams of fiber per slice; you're going to get through 2-3 slices, and you're so full you can't eat anymore.

Again, eat slowly, because it takes about 20 minutes to turn on the regulatory pattern between our GI tract and our brains, where brain registers, "I'm getting full, stop eating." If you eat your entire meal in five minutes, you never get the feedback to your brain saying "slow down." We eat tons of food too fast, and 15 minutes later, we feel terrible.

And off Dr. Pratt went to exercise...

CATHERINE BERTINI, Ph.D.
Senior Fellow in Agricultural Development, Bill & Melinda Gate Foundation; Professor of Public Administration at the Maxwell School of Citizenship and Public Affairs at Syracuse University

Doris Lee: Having attended three Women's International Year Conferences, one of the things that concerns me is how women and girls are still being treated as less than full citizens. I know this is one of your concerns too. Would you speak out on what can be done to help women become more equal?

Catherine Bertini: Women and girls do almost all of the work to support families around the world. In developing countries, they bring in the income, they work in the fields. The girls help their mothers take care of the children from dawn until past dusk. The women have to get the firewood, and they have to go a long ways to get it. They have to get water and find food. They take care of the children. They do so much. Women are nowhere near equal to men in terms of the amount of work they do. They do far, far more.

What we have to give to women and girls is the opportunity to get educated, so they can be productive farmers, have healthier children, and find better job opportunities by knowing how to read and write.

This was being discussed 25 years ago in the Women's International Year Conferences. Years later women were asked, "Did you take this information back to your country? What has changed?" They responded, "Nothing different has happened." How do we move to the next stage?

There have been some changes. If you look at the UN Millennium Development Goals that track the progress on girls' education, there have been advancements.

Not enough organizations put their money where their mouth is. As you've said, everybody's been talking about it for decades, but is anyone actually doing something about it? Look at the World Bank, the Food and Agriculture Organization, USAID or other donors, many NGOs and many other UN agencies. Look at what they say, then look in the budget and see what they do for women and girls, or

77

even if they can tell you what they do for women and girls. Many of them can't even tell you that.

It is long past due to invest in this population; real investments, not words—money, support, training, education, action and involvement.

You mentioned USAID and the World Bank. Isn't there a way to hold those companies accountable?

The government agencies, yes. We should be constantly asking what they're doing and writing to the President, our senators, congressman, anybody, and say, "This is important to me. What are you doing about it?"

Internationally, it's true for any country. People should be sure, if they have a representative government, that their representatives know how they feel. In the U.S., it's particularly important. If you think it's important, you need to tell somebody.

At the International UN Women's Conference in Mexico City, I was doing a television show when I met a woman with the Peace Corp in Africa. She told me how the women would get money for their work in the fields, and then the men would come home from the mines, get drunk…and that was the end of the money. So she helped the women field workers set a cooperative for the group to hold their money. That way, when the men came home and asked for money, they could say, "I'm sorry, but the group has the money and I'm not able to get it out right now."

Do you have other suggestions for how women can not only make money but also keep the money they do get?

Some of it has to be based on cultural needs and concerns. Sometimes the men have to be educated about what women are going to do and the money they're going to bring into the household. In many cultures, the woman is in charge of the food and the man is in charge of money. The man does not necessarily spend the money on the family, as many studies have shown. So they have to be educated about priorities for that money.

Somebody had an interesting idea at the conference today. They could work on a debit card. In the U.S., with food stamps for instance, they're now on debit cards. In fact, I'll claim partial credit for that, because remember years ago, there used to be the food coupons. When I was the Assistant Secretary of Agriculture, we pushed this through. We said, "Look this is really important to do, and let's try doing it." The reason why it was important to do is because we knew that these food stamps weren't necessarily cost-effective. If you had a card it would be more cost-effective, and you wouldn't have to print the food stamps and then destroy them later.

It also ended up being better for women, because the coupons used to be mailed and would end up missing. They would say, "Look, I've got to sit at my mailbox waiting for the food stamps to come, because somebody will steal them out of the mailbox." This way you have a debit card with a PIN number. We pushed very hard and asked Congress to make it legal for states to be able to use this electronic benefit transfer system, and they did.

I know you work with the Bill and Melinda Gates Foundation, are you seeing a trend for girls being able to go to school in other countries?

The Foundation isn't involved in that particularly, but it is part of the Millennium Development Goals. When I won the World Food Prize in 2003, it was a $250,000 prize. I asked them to give that check to Friends of the World Food Program for what was called the Catherine Bertini Trust Fund for Girls' Education. We use that for small grants in countries to help put girls in school.

What about the Food Program, is that what the Gates Foundation is working on?

For the agricultural program, they help build sustainable programs that consist of several categories. One is **Science and Technology** to help develop drought-resistant seeds for drought-resistant crops and other technological advances that would help the poor farmers.

One area is **Data Collection**, because there's a dearth of data collected about agriculture, so they're doing a lot of data collection. It's all going to be disaggregated by gender so that there's information both about men and women, because that's also not very well done, so it's hard to track.

There's another area called **Farmer Productivity**, helping farmers be more productive, use better seeds, soils, extension and education.
Then there's one called **Market Access**. Once you grow more than what's needed where you live, where are you going to sell it elsewhere? So there's a whole scheme along that line.

Is it all just a matter of money? Do you have to keep pouring money in? Are there other ways to do this cooperatively?

It has got to be cooperative; no one organization, no one country can fix it, or it would be fixed already. Economic development is really the key and one example that many people will be familiar with is South Korea. In the '50s, after the Korean War, South Korea was very poor. In fact, before the war, regionally it was less well off than North

Korea. Then it split into two countries. But now South Korea is very well off. It's a member of the OECD, the Organization of Economic Cooperation and Development of wealthy countries, and a donor to the United Nations.

In less than 40 years, they grew into an economic powerhouse, so it can be done. There used to be a lot of hungry people in South Korea, but now it's like the U.S. There certainly still are poor populations, but by and large the country is well off.

Do we have enough food for everyone in the world?

We like to say there's enough food on this earth to feed every man, woman and child—and right now there is—but by 2050, we're going to need to produce much more food in order to feed the growing population.

Right now, people in rural and in poor communities have got to produce more food so they can feed themselves locally. It's amazing that in the early '50s it was estimated that just over 800 million people were living on less than one dollar a day. The figure right now is about 920 million people living on less than one dollar a day.

Back to your question, do we produce enough? Right now we do, but the issue is access. Some people are so poor they can't afford to buy the food. Some of them don't have enough income to be able to afford it. Food doesn't get to them because there aren't good farm-to-market roads, or there's a lot of fruit grown and it's very low-cost when it's all ripe, then it rots. There isn't any refrigeration and there are no good storage methods. There are all sorts of reasons why, and the poor spend such a high amount of their income on food.

You said today that we in the U.S. use rice four times as much as in other countries?

Yes, it's quite high, but right now the food prices have started to come down with this economic crisis. Most economists say that they're going to go back up again.

So often, when there's a tsunami or other disaster, the food might even be just 10 miles away, and yet it doesn't always get to where the people are starving. Shouldn't we be able to take care of that?

There are some real problems. If I could brag a minute about the World Food Program (WFP), the agency that I ran for 10 years...One of the reasons I won the World Food Prize is because during the time I was there, I took a good solid agency and made it into a great agency. This is one of the reasons why we have the mechanical, technical, and organizational answers to avoid famine. In 1991, there was the UN Summit on Children. One of the goals was that by 2000 there would be no more famine. Sometimes there are political issues that you can't do anything about, but what we achieved was to create an organization that was the right tool that the international community can use to insure there's no famine. In other words, as long as the politics doesn't get in the way, the World Food Program can get there.

How does that work? If there are no political interventions, you can always get the food there?

If it's a flood, you helicopter food in. If it's in southern Sudan, you fly food in big C-130 airplanes and drop it out of the back of planes because there are no roads. When the U.S. and the U.K. started bombing in Afghanistan after 9-11, the World Food Program was already there and already

82

had food prepositioned. It wasn't enough though, because we had to do it quickly, and we had to open more routes. We negotiated with the Iranians and opened corridors moving American food aid through Iran into western Afghanistan.

In November, after not even two months, President Bush invited Kofi Annan and his senior team, including me, to the White House to thank us for what we were doing. Tony Blair invited me to Number 10 Downing Street to thank me.

In February, when I was in Islamabad I met with President Musharraf of Pakistan, and he said, "I want to thank you, because the World Food Program did what no other agency could do. You were creative, aggressive, and you got food in throughout Afghanistan. I was worried that I was going to have a bigger refugee crisis on my hands, because so many people might leave Afghanistan in search of food."

How about Darfur?

Darfur is a security and a resources problem. At WFP we had to cut rations, because we just don't have enough contributions. It's really expensive because there aren't good roads and the security is bad. WFP has lost over 20 drivers in Darfur. How can you tell the next guy to go and take another load?

Yes, they're losing a lot of NGOs (Non Government Officials) in Darfur.

It's terrible. It becomes a political issue. Why can't politicians solve this issue? Let's get this solved. Humanitarians, in this case, can only keep people alive to the extent that the power structure allows it to be peaceful enough.

Nick Clooney has made 175 speeches to date on this very situation. Guns are coming in from China and are being used by the Janjaweed. China sometimes pays for their oil in Sudan this way. It's such a major problem, and as you said, a lot of NGOs die.

One last question, as a visionary, is there anything you feel very strongly about that you might add?

If we could be sure that every girl has at least a primary school education, we could solve almost every problem that plagues poor people on this earth.

Really? What would it take to do that, more teachers, more schools built?

It depends on the country. Sometimes it's teachers, sometimes it's schools. Sometimes it's school fees, or it's uniforms that the parents can't afford. Sometimes it's a safety or a cultural issue about not wanting your girls to go to school. Sometimes you want them to stay at home and work on the farm.

Sometimes the girls go to school for a while, and then they get to the point in their lives where they need to have some privacy. They leave school because there's no latrine. Sometimes it's that there's no desk, and after they're five or six years old they want at least the modesty of sitting at a desk instead of on the floor.

There are lots of reasons; what we have to do is attack each place. Somebody should work with each government to write a business plan or campaign plan about how we're going to get every girl in Yemen or Afghanistan in school.

Are there organizations you would like to recommend that people reading this information can look at to learn more about what's going on, how they can get involved, or how they can make a donation?

UNICEF does a lot of good work on girls' education. Nike Foundation, it's not something to give to but something to watch, because of their absolute commitment to girls going to school. They have some great information to inspire people about why it's important to help girls (www.nikefoundation.org). They've got some great visuals and lots of interesting activities, so following some of what they're doing would be important. There are a lot of NGOs that are doing small projects here and there. Save the Children, Oxfam, and others are doing girls education projects.

As I mentioned, I have the Catherine Bertini Trust Fund for Girls Education and it's a Friends of the World Food Program, which is www.friendsofwfp.org, and we give small-scale grants. We end up giving $20-$25,000 for furniture for a school or tuition for girls.

Often, even small assistance can make the difference between girls going to school or not?

If everybody does it.

You know the story about the starfish? One time there were thousands of starfish washed up on the beach. There was a little girl going down on the beach, picking up starfish and flinging them back into the ocean. There was an old man walking very slowly down on the beach, contemplating the world, and he saw this girl picking up starfish and throwing each of them back in.

He got to her and said, "Why are you spending your energy on that? There are thousands of them—you can't possibly make a difference."

She looked him in the eye, then she reached down, picked up another starfish, flung it into the ocean, and said, "I made a difference for that one."

That says it all. Thank you so much, Catherine.

Visionary Reflection on...

Resilience

When bare essentials are in short supply, things as critical to life as food and money, people are tested to their core. Time and again, we see the resilience of people who endure the ravages of hunger and poverty. Think of a time when you have demonstrated resilience, drawing on the kind of strength that requires adaptability and the ability to rise up again after adversity.

CLOCKWISE L to R: Doris Lee with Bob Wright, Nancy Davis with Tommy Hilfiger, William Magee Jr., D.D.S., M.D., Hubert Greenway, M.D., and T. Denny Sanford

CHAPTER 5

Curing Diseases, Cultivating Hope

·················

BOB WRIGHT
CEO NBC Universal (ret.) and Vice Chairman General
Electric (ret.), Co-founder with his wife Suzanne Wright of
AutismSpeaks.org

Since its inception, Autism Speaks has committed an unprecedented $128 million in new research funding through 2014 to uncover the causes, prevention, treatments, and cure for autism, making it the nation's top private funder of autism research.

Autism Speaks, in partnership with the Ad Council and the CDC, launched the *Talking to Parents About Autism* educational toolkit. The kit, which includes a training DVD and Early Childhood Milestone Maps, promotes early intervention and encourages educators to speak to a child's parents if they suspect a developmental delay.

Autism Speaks co-founder Bob Wright has a strong history of philanthropy and community service, for which he has received numerous awards and accolades, including the 2005 Humanitarian Award from the Simon Wiesenthal Center. He and his wife, Suzanne, live in Connecticut. They have three children and four grandchildren.

Doris Lee: Bob you were the head of NBC Universal and then recently retired. Now you have taken your talents to another project. You began researching autism and looking for the reasons behind it. Why is this important to you?

Bob Wright: One of the reasons was that my grandson was diagnosed with autism. My wife and I founded the **Autism Speaks Foundation** in February of 2005. Since then, we found out that one in one hundred and fifty children have autism. Boys are much more likely than girls.

Ten years ago, one in every 10,000 people were diagnosed with autism. Today it is one in 110.

Your website www.autismspeaks.org has a wealth of important information.

We found that a lot of people were having trouble getting health insurance. We did the research which can be downloaded from the website. This has made it easier for people to access the information in one place.

Autism Speaks funded $20 million for research in 2006 in four areas: a Pilot Study, Fellowship, Augmentation and Bridge Awards. One new award was presented for early treatment research as autism is now regularly diagnosed at 24 months, and some cases at 18 months. They know now that early detection is crucial for getting the maximum assistance.

The *Autism Tissue Program* has been one of the most important research projects undertaken by Autism Speaks and has made 60+ research projects possible. Dr. David Amaral published a study in the *Journal of Neuroscience* earmarking changes in cell numbers in a part of the autistic brain that may be responsible for behaviors that process emotion and fear.

Autism Speaks findings at Yale University recognized that children with autism failed at focusing on social cues or face recognition. Because parents need to be aware of normal versus autistic child, a video made at the University of Florida shows the contrast.

Don't all of these projects require a large staff?

Yes, we have 200 people working for the Foundation, plus 10,000 volunteers throughout the country.

What is the treatment once autism is diagnosed?

We've made a 100 Day Kit that parents and caregivers can download from the website that has proven to be very helpful; it answers a lot of questions. What we do know is the great value of early diagnosis, by 2-1/2 to 3 years old, because it enables approximately 50% of the children to start developing skills that may enable them to go to regular schools.

How have you alerted people about autism?

Here are some of our best methods of outreach:

- Our website averages 120,000 users each month and that has quadrupled since we began in 2006.
- Autism Speaks produced a documentary called "Autism Every Day" showing the effect on real families.
- Although the National Institutes of Health has a budget of $30 billion, only two and a half percent of it goes to autism. They hope to get donations through the fund-raising walks they have across the U.S., the United Kingdom, and Canada. They already have raised $12 million. Toys-R-Us, Chevrolet Test Drive, as well as celebrities Jerry Seinfeld, Bill Cosby, and Donald Trump made guest appearances at the walks.

Because of your background at NBC, you know the Ad Council has public service announcements for selected causes.

Yes, the Ad Council has already donated media placement of $100 million. At the time of the Beijing Summer Olympics, they sponsored an ad that read:

According to Autism Speaks:
- Odds of a child becoming an Olympic athlete: 1 in 28,000
- Odds of a child being diagnosed with Autism: 1 in 110

Signs to look for:
- No big smiles or other joyful expressions by 6 months
- No babbling by 12 months
- No words by 16 months

Bob, Visionaries salutes your efforts and those of the thousands of people who have helped with all phases of the effort to raise more awareness about this disease.

For more information on Autism Speaks, visit www.autismspeaks.org, or send a letter to: 2 Park Avenue, 11th Floor, New York, NY 10016 or call (212) 252-8584.

NANCY DAVIS
Philanthropist, President of Nancy Davis Foundation for Multiple Sclerosis, and founder of the "Race to Erase MS" annual event

Seventeen years ago when her doctor diagnosed her with Multiple Sclerosis (MS), Nancy Davis was told to go home and go to bed because there was nothing she could do about it. But Nancy is from a family of people who do not quit when faced with illness. Nancy's mother, Barbara Davis, was the founder of the Carousel of

91

Hope, the childhood diabetes foundation. So Nancy decided to get other opinions and also started doing her own research on MS.

Nancy's annual "Race to Erase MS" event usually takes place in May each year. Always a sell-out event, people come from all over the U.S. In the past, bands have performed such as Earth, Wind, and Fire, Frankie Valli & The Four Seasons, and other well-known artists. During my last attendance at the MS event, I even danced a few steps with actor/producer Ray Romano.

Nancy was featured in my last book, *America's New Future*. And, then as now, I experience her great determination to cure this disease. As she holds an annual fundraising event and has her finger on the pulse of the work being done, I was eager to ask her about what is new in the area of MS research.

Doris Lee: Nancy, are there any breakthroughs with new drugs for MS?

Nancy Davis: Yes, we are so pleased to announce that we have three drugs that are already being explored. One is a shot that can be given once a year, another shot given weekly, and one administered daily.

What advice would you give people who are diagnosed with MS?

- Always get a second opinion.
- Make sure that you read all of the material available on the Internet.
- Find out what you really like to do and do it. I have always enjoyed skiing, so I do that as often as possible. I enjoy the rush when going down the slope, feeling the wind and the snow on my face and just love being in that environment.
- Be proactive. Get more involved with projects you really like. I had always wanted to have a jewelry line and have since started my own line.

Knowing our options when faced with an illness is so crucial. Tell us about the book you've written that illuminates many options for those diagnosed with MS.

Lean On Me is a book that I wrote for everyone. Many of us will have to confront a life-altering disease and the book talks about how we can do that with any disease, not just MS. It's a book about options, resources, and hope.

Thank you, Nancy, for your extraordinary work.

For more information about MS, go to www.erasems.org

Special Note: Nancy Davis has created the "My Necessary Medical ID Card"- it lists your name, your closest relative's name and phone number, your doctor's name and phone number, your driver's license, any allergies you may have, and your medical insurance information. They can be purchased by going online to www.verynecessaryid.com or by calling the following numbers:

- *Visionary Spotlight* -

TOMMY HILFIGER
American Fashion Designer & Founder, Tommy Hilfiger Brand

Tommy Hilfiger is the co-chair each year of the "Race to Erase MS" event. Motivated by his love for his sister who has MS, Tommy produces a glamorous and upbeat fashion show that is an integral part of each event.

Fitting in a quick conversation with me, Tommy beautifully summed up his participation: "I have long supported Nancy's efforts; I believe in what and how she is trying to erase MS." I asked him what the noise was in the background, and he said, "I'm walking down 5th Ave. in New York...it's Fashion Week." As busy as he was, I knew of his compassion regarding this disease and appreciated his taking time to share with us his views.

KAREN M. VANDERHOOF-FORSCHNER
Founder of The Lyme Disease Foundation

Doris Lee: Karen, you've been in the forefront of Lyme disease education, but it really hit you directly, right in your own family.

Karen Vanderhoof-Forschner: In 1985, I wound up having a bite that resulted in this enlarging rash on my leg. I happened to have been several months pregnant at the time and nobody in Connecticut, none of the doctors, knew what it was.

My son was born prematurely with multiple handicaps that appeared over the next several months, and one of the things that I vowed is that if I could find out what was causing my son's illness, I would volunteer my efforts to ensure that other people did not suffer the way my son was suffering. At the same time, I was hopeful that we would find solutions to what was causing his illness and save him too.

That led me on this journey that took several years. At the time, nobody knew what Lyme disease was in the State of Connecticut. They were unaware that you could get it while pregnant and pass it on to a child. They were unaware of the devastating consequences. There was no organization that people could call to get information. It was considered a rare disorder, and so there was no tracking of the illness to determine what was happening.

Subsequently, I met many people across the United States who were suffering from mysterious illnesses. I was also contacted by researchers who wanted to study the illness that my son turned out to have, which was later called Lyme disease.

How did you set out to inform people about Lyme disease?

We set up operations in Tolland, Connecticut in 1988. It was in my basement at the time. *20/20*, the television show, came to a meeting we held in Connecticut. They learned about us from some of the scientists who were on our board of directors.

We've created brochures, events, and TV programs. There was a Lifetime television network program that won awards. We also created a PBS kid's special, bilingual and open-captioned for the hearing impaired. We sent out 10,000 copies of the special to schools all across the country. And I wrote a book about Lyme disease so that people could get information and be empowered.

We had no budget—we did this on a wing and a prayer. We wound up attracting a large number of physicians and patients with mysterious illnesses who wanted to know if Lyme disease was something they should be aware of.

What is the next step for the organization?

If you're going to cure a disease, you need a test that can tell who is infected and who is not. We need to get the public back on track in demanding a perfected test. While we're plugging the holes in the education of Lyme disease, raising public awareness, and funding research, we're down to one central issue: we need a test.

What is the message you most want to convey to people right now?

We need to have the mechanisms in place to help facilitate the next emerging disease that happens. Addressing emerging diseases and health care issues comes from the grassroots up. Tackling health care issues comes from the families who can't take it anymore, who speak up and say, "Okay, you've got to do something about my disease." But the government has many issues to address and often can't hear all of the voices needing to be heard. It's going to hear those who use their voices well.

Is there a website that people should visit if they have questions?

Yes. If they have anything that they want to know about Lyme disease they should go to http://www.lyme.org/front.htm.

HUBERT GREENWAY, M.D.
Chairman of Mohs Surgery and Dermatologic Division, La Jolla, CA

Dr. Hubert Greenway is a renowned doctor who has done advanced work in the area of Mohs surgery. Also known as chemosurgery, Mohs surgery was created by Dr. Frederic E. Mohs and is a microscopically controlled surgery used to treat common types of skin cancer.

When I was having my small Mohs surgery, I asked Dr. Greenway when he did his first operation; you often wonder about this as a patient. He responded, "The first operation I did of Mohs surgery was with Dr. Mohs." So I felt assured that I had come to the right place with a man who knew what he was doing.

Doris Lee: Dr. Greenway, I know you are often called the father of Mohs surgery. What would you say to a world that is looking for answers to skin cancer?

Dr. Greenway: There are three areas in cancer.

1. One is prevention, and there is a whole lot of information on that.
2. The second is early diagnosis, and that's why we encourage people to be checked periodically. The skin is the largest organ of the body, so it's one we can see certain areas of ourselves, but there are certain parts that we can't see, such as our back or our inner ear. It's important to get checked as part of your routine physical. Or, if you're at higher risk, you ought to be checked once or twice a year.

3. Then the third is the treatment, and that is where we get into things like the Mohs surgery, which Dr. Fred Mohs at the University of Wisconsin in Madison developed.

You are indicating that the ear can sometimes be cancerous, especially for golfers, is that right?

We know that the ear is an area where the sun actually can touch their skin. This is true particularly of golfers who spend a lot of time out in the sun. Individuals are wise to come to us at the very beginning since early diagnosis is very important. We do screenings here at Scripps Hospital in La Jolla, California.

Although I have a background in family practice, I now dedicate most of my time to Mohs surgery and teaching young doctors how to do the procedure.

Thank you for your outstanding work, Dr. Greenway.

WILLIAM MAGEE JR., D.D.S., M.D.
Co-founder and CEO of Operation Smile, Leading Plastic and Craniofacial Surgeon

Operation Smile is a worldwide children's medical charity providing reconstructive surgery and related health care to children and young adults born with facial deformities. In addition to leading the organization as CEO, Dr. Magee also trains international physicians in craniofacial techniques through Operation Smile's annual Physicians' Training Program.

In 2007, during its 25th anniversary, Operation Smile conducted World Journey of Smiles (WJOS), simultaneous medical missions to 40 sites in 25 countries worldwide. Free physical examinations were provided to 7,414 patients, and 4,086 children born with cleft lips and cleft palates were provided free surgical treatment during WJOS. The initiative mobilized more than 1,900 volunteers from 44 countries and was the largest simultaneous medical mission of its kind.

I had a chance to meet Dr. William Magee at the Conrad Hilton Symposium and Award Dinner in Geneva, Switzerland.

Doris Lee: How did Operation Smile begin?

Dr. Magee: I grew up being one of 12 kids in a family that was filled with chaos and with a dad who was a physician and a great role model. I ended up going through dental school, medical school, then through my general surgery and plastic surgery.

Seventeen years after high school, I finally went into practice with the idea of taking care of children and focusing on that in my plastic surgery career. In 1982, my wife and I were given the opportunity to go to the Philippines to take care of children with cleft lips and cleft palates. As we arrived in an area called Naga City in the Philippines, we were met by over 300 families who—in 100° temperatures and 100% humidity—literally pushed their way into a small room.

Every one of those parents was begging us to take care of their child and every one of those children had a gapping hole in the lip and the roof of their mouth so they couldn't eat or speak an intelligible word. It was probably one of the most overpowering sights I had ever seen in my life. You would think being a surgeon I would have been ready for it, but this was something that I had never in my life dreamed existed. We were only able to take care of about 40 kids that first year and had to watch as over 250 kids were sent away without anything.

I'll never forget, there was a lady that came up with a basket of ripe bananas cradled in her arms, her daughter at her side was about eight years old. She said, "I have very little to give you but these ripe bananas, but I would like to give them to you as a gift for trying to take care of my daughter." Real tears streamed down her cheeks and all we could say was, "Maybe next year." But nobody was planning on going back next year, so my wife and I said, "Why don't we just get a group of our friends, come back here, and take care of these kids?"

That's exactly how Operation Smile began.

I've learned over the years that *reason leads to conclusions, but it is emotion that leads to action.* It was the emotion of that moment that brought us back to the Philippines the next year where we still turned away hundreds of children.

We increased the size of our group the following year and brought back more people. Now, 30 years later, we are in 51 countries, we've operated on over 120,000 children, and we have over 7,000 volunteers who are willing to donate their time to help others.

I think what it speaks to is how there is a human spirit in all of us that wants to give and wants to help, but a lot of people don't know how to take that first step. What we've been able to do is to organize a structure that allows people to take that first step easily, and it gives them the ability to share their talent, time and treasures with other people.

Do you think cleft lips or cleft palates is a genetic trait?

There are definitely genetic and nutritional components to it. We've done studies in the Philippines that show B-6 and folic acid deficiencies. Back in November, we collected

99

one of the largest samples of genetic data on children with cleft lips and cleft palates. We took more than 3,000 samples that we'll be studying to try and find the cause of clefting.

Are you working with a particular hospital?

We're working with many hospitals. We work with universities in the United States like the University of Southern California, Yale, Duke, Harvard, George Washington University, University of Pennsylvania, and the University of Southern Illinois. There are also a lot of hospitals, university programs, and professors who volunteer their time with us.

We also work with the Universities of Rome, England, Ireland, as well as universities in these developing countries. We have a very strong training program that trains thousands of medical professionals every year and they, in turn, volunteer their time to work with us.

It must be a thrill to see a child who hasn't been able to speak well, suddenly talk. Would it be six weeks later after the operation?

Yes, sometimes even immediately after the operation. I remember very distinctly a 20-year-old young man in China who had a bilateral cleft of his lip, meaning that both sides of his lip were open into his nose and the roof of his mouth was completely open, and he had never spoken intelligibly in his life. When he was born, his father said to his five-year-old sister, "Should we keep him?" His five-year-old sister said, "Of course!"

I remember that as he came out of the operating room he groggily woke up, looked over at me, put his thumbs up and said "Thank you" as clearly as you could ever hear a thank you.

What a wonderful gift! What would you say to people who want to help further what you're doing, Dr. Magee?

Every one of us has a gift. We all have strengths and we all have weaknesses. I think that it's so important for each of us to be humble enough to recognize what our weaknesses are and confident enough to be proud of our strengths. We should use our strengths, as best we can, in conjunction with other people's strengths to create change in our world. It depends on where your passion is and where your drive is. The beautiful thing about it is that, as we share our gifts with others, our entire world opens up; we lose nothing.

Sometimes people, especially people who are insecure, are afraid to share what they have for fear that they'll lose something. The reality is, the more openly you share with people, the more you have whether that's physical or emotional.

What countries have the largest groups of untreated cleft lips and palates?

In the greater majority of the developing world, about one in 500 children are born with clefts. For example, in Ethiopia, where there are 85,000,000 people, there are at least 150,000 to 160,000 children with cleft problems. There are only a handful of plastic surgeons in all of Ethiopia, so the chances that a child in Ethiopia with a cleft lip or cleft palate will get taken care of, is miniscule.

In China and India, over 30,000 children a year are born with cleft lips and cleft palates.

China and India. Would those be two of the top of the list?

Yes, because there are over a billion people in those countries. Vietnam also has approximately 85,000,000 people, and that's another 150,000 to 170,000 children with clefts that are in that country.

In as little as 45 minutes you can change a child's life forever?

There aren't too many major problems in our world that can be changed so quickly. It might take years and years to finally find the solution to problems like malnutrition, HIV, and other major health care issues. *However, in as little as 45 minutes you can take a child from hopelessness to possibility.* And by doing so, you can create a metaphor through the face of that child that says: *involvement can create change.* It empowers all of us.

Does the successful future for this falls in more doctors taking on this kind of project as their profession?

It's not just more doctors. Obviously, medical people have to be excited about doing this, and you do have to train more and more people. But it also requires that businesspeople, political leaders, community people, and donors become involved and donate the money so we can accomplish these things.

Success also lies in great educational programs for kids. We bring two high school or college students with us on every trip

How would one get involved?

Go to the website and look at the opportunities that exist. We have student programs in 500 high school student clubs and in 24 other countries right now around the world. Every summer at a different university we have a week of leadership training for high school students.

That's wonderful. Is there anything that you'd like to add?

For each of us—as individuals, as a society, or as a world—we have to make a decision: Are we always going to talk about how horrible things are, or are we going to look and recognize that there is a reality in our world where not everyone has the same opportunities? Are we going to ask ourselves, "What is it that I can do to make one person's life a little bit better tomorrow?"

You also have some celebrities that work closely with your projects?

We have some great people. Billy Bush who hosts *Access Hollywood* has been just wonderful with us. Singer Jessica Simpson has gone with us on a medical mission. Donald Trump Jr. and Vanessa Trump went with us to Nicaragua and are just terrific. Donald, Jr. is actually on our Board of Directors.

Cindy McCain, wife of Senator John McCain, has been on our board since 2005 and she has been volunteering with us since 2001. She's a wonderful lady who asks for nothing special and gets in there just like everyone else does, from dawn to dusk helping out.

We've had the privilege of working with Mark Burnett, producer of *Survivor* and *The Apprentice*, and his wife, the talented actress Roma Downey. They've been very involved in helping us with our direct response TV. In fact,

103

they brought all three of their children with us on a mission to Jordan.

It's important to recognize that this would have never ever happened without my wife, she and I doing this together. We've raised five children, and have 11 grandchildren. Operation Smile was our gift to our children—to help ground them, to have them see life as it really is.

How can people contact you?

Our website is www.operationsmile.org. There is information about Operation Smile and how people can become involved. It also contains how people can donate, volunteer and participate, plus stories of the kids that we take care of.

- Visionary Spotlight -

NORMAN MCSWAIN, JR., M.D., FACS
Professor, Tulane University, School of Medicine
Trauma Director, Charity Hospital

Dr. Norman McSwain has long been a friend since he joined a group of us on a flag-carrying expedition to the Peruvian Rainforest for the Explorers Club. He is an authority on Emergency Room procedures and an author of many books and articles that may be helpful in a serious medical situation:

"The type of, and the cause of trauma, and the medical response systems vary considerably throughout the world. Therefore, understanding the system of the country is critical.

Most of the developed countries have an emergency phone number (911 in the U.S.) for trauma that provides a phone number, which will bring a responder to the emergency site. The training of these responders varies significantly throughout the world, ranging from physicians, to nurses, to emergency medical technicians, and even to untrained personnel who simply know how to drive a car very fast.

To properly move somebody with broken bones, the part of the body that is broken should be immobilized, so that the sharp edges of the bone do not damage other parts of the body.

If responders are expected to arrive quickly, do not move the victim, unless the victim is exposed to hazards that might harm them. If the responders are far away, move the individual to a more comfortable and protected space by completely immobilizing the body. This is most easily done by placing the victim on a long piece of wood or metal to prevent various parts of the body from disparate motion while transfer occurs.

The two emergency situations that will not wait for a responder to arrive are loss of airway/breathing and severe hemorrhage:

Airway
The most common cause of airway loss is a lax tongue falling back against the back of the throat and blocking air. You can either pull the tongue or the mandible forward to open the airway. If the patient is not adequately breathing with an unobstructed airway, assist breathing mouth to mouth.

Hemorrhage
If the patient is bleeding severely, place direct pressure on the bleeding area placed with your hand or a piece of cloth. This will most likely stop the bleeding. Next, cover and

wrap the bleeding area with gauze or some clean cloth to put direct pressure over the wound. Do not remove the dressing even to check if the bleeding has stopped. If the blood is not running, the hemorrhage is most likely controlled by the pressure.

When direct pressure is not effective, a trained operator can use a tourniquet to control hemorrhage from the arms and legs. If emergency transportation is not available, drive the victim to the closest hospital to control bleeding and replace lost blood.

The National Association of EMTs (Emergency Medical Technician) has developed the Pre-Hospital Trauma Life Support Course (PHTLS) with the American College of Surgeons, Committee on Trauma. Information about PHTLS can be found at www.phtls.org. Information about the local EMS system can be obtained from the emergency number in the country involved.

- *Visionary Spotlight* -

T. DENNY SANFORD
Visionary philanthropist and humanitarian

T. Denny Sanford is contributing millions of dollars to move the world forward in health and science, and yet he is one of the most down-to-earth people you could ever hope to meet. Also one of the most likable people, his nickname offers a clue as to his general disposition: WOLT, which stands for the "World's Oldest Living Teenager."

Denny's father instilled in him a great work ethic at the early age of eight, when he took a job working in his father's clothing distribution company. After graduating from the University of Minnesota, where he studied psychology, he went on to work at Armstrong Cork Company as a sales and marketing manager.

Two early achievements of his career were acquiring a chemical company from Sears, Roebuck and Co. in 1971 and purchasing First Premier Bank in 1986. Also forming the credit card company, Premier Bankcard, he grew the bank from 80 employees to over 3,000.

In 1972, Denny took the company Contech, Inc. public at $5/share, and ten years later, he sold it for $35/share. He then started Threshold Ventures, the venture capital company that he remains involved with today.

Denny's philanthropic endeavors are nothing short of amazing. In the last four years alone, he has given away over $700 million, focusing primarily on helping children who are disadvantaged, abused, neglected, or dealing with illness. In 2001, he formed the Denny Sanford Foundation, which has given $18 million for the Sanford Education Project and $15 million to the Mayo Clinic to construct a pediatric center.

Other institutions he has contributed to are the Beacom School of Business, the University of Minnesota, and the Roundup River Ranch in Vail, Colorado (an affiliation of the Paul Newman Hole In The Wall Gang Camps). Denny has also pledged $70 million to the Sanford Science Center in South Dakota.

In 2007, Denny announced a $400 million gift to the Sioux Valley Hospitals and Health System, transforming a pediatric center into a "Castle of Care" in order to appeal to the imagination of the children they help. He also promised $35 million toward the development of the Type 2 Diabetes Project, one of Sanford Health's primary initiatives. In short, Denny has invested much of his time, energy, and money to find solutions and build infrastructures to further the cause of medical research for children.

Devoted to his family, which includes one brother, two sons, and his beloved grandchildren, Denny Sanford is a man who simply loves life. In fact, one of his claims to fame is having coined the term "Aspire to Inspire before you Expire."

For more information, visit: www.sanfordconsortium.org

Visionary Reflection on...

Hope

One of the most powerful healers available to us is hope. As a close friend of faith, hope has the power to give us flight, helping us to rise above seemingly insurmountable situations. What situation in your life right now is asking for you to have hope? Where could you use a dose of optimism? Whether it pertains to you personally or someone else, take a moment to remember that there is always hope...

CLOCKWISE L to R: Linda Fuller, Dick H. Smith, Dr. Zhengrong Shi, and Matt Damon

CHAPTER 6

Environment, Housing and Pollution

• • • • • • • • • • • • • • • • • •

MILLARD & LINDA FULLER
Founders of Habitat for Humanity and Fuller Center for
Housing

Habitat for Humanity is known by most of us as the organization that builds houses. Some executives lead from the offices but others, like Millard Fuller and his wife, Linda, lead with a more hands-on approach. I met Millard at the Social Responsibility meeting Win New York City where he was being honored.

Doris Lee: On the front cover of the book, The House That Love Built, written by Dr. Bettie Youngs, about Millard and his wife, President Bill Clinton is quoted as saying, "Millard and Linda Fuller have changed philanthropy, and instead of just asking for money, they ask people to swing a hammer." You are the founders of Habitat for Humanity, and it sounds like you move people into action.

Millard Fuller: Absolutely. There's a fundamental basic principle of fundraising: money follows involvement. The way you capture the heart is to get people involved, and that's what we did in Habitat for Humanity. We are now also doing it in my new organization, The Fuller Center for Housing. We don't just ask people, as former President Clinton says, for money, we ask for their involvement.

The volunteers get to know the homeowners, they renovate a house in five days, and at the end of the process, we have a house dedication service where we give the keys to the

110

new homeowner. Because this is a project that is openly and unashamedly a Christian program, we give a Bible to remind the people that the work being done is out of a motivation of God's love. Many tears are shed, a lot of hugs given, and the volunteers who participated are deeply moved, as the homeowners are. It captures the hearts of people, causes them to want to do it again, and that's why over the years we've been able to build up a huge army of volunteers. They go all over the world building these houses. The volunteers contribute, get their churches, companies, and friends to contribute, and that's how it grows, and has been growing dramatically over the last 30 years.

None of us can dismiss the fact that living in a decent home provides us with the basics for a decent life. How do people register a request to get a house?

Every local group of Habitat for Humanity and The Fuller Center for Housing has a Family Selection Committee, and by various means, this committee learns about people who are in dire circumstances. In the case of a man in West Virginia, obviously the bus was not well-insulated, miserable conditions by anybody's definition. That situation came to our attention and the family was chosen.

That's how it happens with both organizations—people from the Family Selection Committee will go out and interview the prospective family. They explain to them that their involvement will be necessary, that they will need to put in so many hours of sweat equity to help build the house.

What does sweat equity mean?

There are various ways in which people can help, from driving nails and sawing boards, to providing meals for volunteers—whatever is needed to get the job done.

We are primarily renovating houses for senior citizens, thousands of whom still own their own homes. They live on fixed incomes, maybe a social security check is all they have each month and the front porch is falling off or the roof leaks and three windows are broken. We go in with The Fuller Center for Housing, and with volunteers we fix whatever needs to be fixed.

What about the new loans that are involved directly in going to the bank? How does the credit work out that way, Millard?

When you build a new house there is a mortgage. It's a typical mortgage as would be on any house purchased, the only difference is no profit is added and no interest is charged. The Bible teaches if you lend money to the poor, do not charge interest, so we follow that ancient Biblical principle.

Good idea, because some people just couldn't even think of the possibility of building a house unless that was part of the agreement, right?

That's right. A typical house built in the United States is financed through the bank, and there's an interest-bearing note. Currently in this country, thousands and thousands of people are losing their homes, because they can't make the payments on the houses and they're being foreclosed on.

After the house is completed, the money is paid back on what we call The Bible Finance Plan, at no profit and no interest. We give them a little wooden box called a Greater Blessings Box, because the Bible says, "While it's blessed to receive, it is more blessed to give." The people who are the recipients of this renovation work have the opportunity to pay the money back, but it's not a legal obligation. And as they are able, they give the money back. The money then can be recycled and reused to help more families.

In the case of Fuller Center for Housing, we charge no interest and add no profit on the house, so when a family gets one house, they pay for one house. Whereas in a typical situation financed through the bank, they get one house, they live in one house, but with the mortgage interest rates, they may pay for three houses at the end. If you've got a good income, you can pay for three houses. But if you are a waitress, the person who picks up the garbage, or has some other minimum wage type of job, you cannot afford to pay for three houses.

How long does it take most people to pay you back?

In the United States, a typical payback period is 20 years. Outside the U.S., in places like Mexico, Nigeria, Sri Lanka, or the Philippines, the payment period typically is less, somewhere in the range of ten years. As it is paid back, the money is used to build another house.

You've actually put into the system something for continuing the program for other people, and it just doesn't end with that one house?

Absolutely. In every community that we work in, the idea is ultimately to end poverty housing there. The idea is to continue building so that *everybody* in that town or in that community will eventually have a decent place to live, and that is based on the theological principle that God's love extends to everyone. That's why from a theological standpoint the goal that we had for Habitat for Humanity,

113

and now The Fuller Center for Housing, is to provide a house for everybody.

Similar programs have been launched in other places such as my home area where I was raised, a place called the Chattahoochee Valley in east central Alabama. We have embarked this past year on a campaign to build 500 houses there to make sure that every single family in that area has a decent place to live on terms they can afford to pay. That will involve building hundreds of new houses, plus renovating many other houses, but at the end of the process.

A wonderful program, Millard. You've done some things in Louisiana, what about New Orleans?

After Katrina hit in 2005, we started a program called "Building on Higher Ground," because thousands of people fled from the coast to higher ground and 20,000 people went to Shreveport, Louisiana.

Tell me how you got started doing this?

A former business partner and I went into business when we were still in law school at the University of Alabama. We made a fortune in business. What happened in my situation was that I became addicted to making money. I was just a moneymaking machine, and I neglected everything else in my life, including my wife. She ended up leaving me and going to New York City. We were almost divorced, and it was out of that personal crisis that a decision was made to drastically change the way we were living our lives—from chasing money to seeking God's kingdom first.

The Bible says get your priorities right and all of the other things will be added. My wife and I just went on a spiritual pilgrimage. We asked God to guide us into a life of Christian service and that led us to Koinonia Farm, a small Christian community near Americus, Georgia. That is where Habitat for Humanity was born.

Our new project, The Fuller Center for Housing, began in 2005. The new ministry is now taking off like a rocket, building houses in a number of locations all across the United States and in other countries. We're a strong Christian ministry. We reach out to people of other faiths and build houses for people regardless of race or religion, but the core motivation remains strongly centered on Jesus, His life, teachings, and examples.

While Habitat for Humanity hasn't totally abandoned their Christian witness, I would say The Fuller Center for Housing is more overt or more open about the proclamation of the Christian motivation behind what we do. We are a more grassroots effort that runs a bare bones operation in order to build more houses for more families.

In reading Dr. Bettie Youngs' book The House That Love Built, it seems like you jump into a project without any guarantee of repayment. For a lot of us that would be scary, but it seems like you have a sense of hope and goodwill.

Yes, it's what we call building on faith. If you're going to build houses and you don't have the money in the bank, then you have to build on faith. Millions of people around the world live in a crisis situation where they need somebody to step out in faith and say, "You need some helping hands, and here we are."

I'm sure you have some data to back that up, or you would not continue to follow that ideal, is that correct?

Absolutely. For example, when we started building houses in Shreveport, we launched a 10-house blitz—to build ten houses in a week—and that was going to require in excess of $600,000. We didn't have $600,000, but we ended up building the ten houses. All of the money came in, we paid all of the bills, the families moved in, and the project was a big success.

What actually happened for you to get that money? Were there people involved that helped you do that?

Absolutely. First you have to ask. The Bible says that if you want to receive you have to ask. We're constantly asking people to contribute, letting them know what we're doing and that we need support. Not everybody can help, but a large number of people responded. The money has a way of coming in, but the only reason it comes in is because we keep asking. And if you keep asking, you keep receiving.

Who would you go to? Would it be churches or Kiwanis Clubs in those smaller communities? How would those people go about finding that additional money that you need?

The primary partner for our work with The Fuller Center for Housing is the church; we go to different churches. We also do direct mail. We mail thousands of letters out to people who we think are likely to be supportive. When they contribute they go on our mailing list, and some of them become Abundant Life Donors and they give to us monthly.

How can people contact you?

Our website is www.FullerCenter.org. We're in Americus, Georgia, and people can phone us at 229-924-2900, or write us at The Fuller Center for Housing, PO Box 523, Americus, Georgia 31709.

Special Message: Millard went on to build more houses until his death in February of 2009. His work continues today with his wife, Linda Fuller, and their strongly committed Board Members and volunteers.

- *Visionary Spotlight* -

DICK H. SMITH
Australian Entrepreneur, Businessman, Aviator, Philanthropist

Doris Lee: Dick Smith, what a variety of talents you have. How did all of this get started?

Dick Smith: It was amazing, because until the age of eight, I couldn't even say the letter "s." At school, I used to say my name was Dick Mith or Dick Fish. One day I was called up in front of the class. The teacher didn't understand. All the kids laughed when I had to say my name, and I said Dick Fish...then I said Dick Mith.

Finally, she sent me to the head principal of the school thinking I was being smart or rude. Luckily, the principal rang my mother, and my mother said, "He can't pronounce the letter 's'."

In the early days, I hated school. I always thought I'd be a failure, but I had two interests: the outdoors and making crystal radio sets. I finally quit school at 15 to work in a factory. But found that I hated that even more than school, so I went back to school for two years and got what we call my learning certificate.

Then, I went back and worked in a factory again. One day, when I was about 22 years of age, I was working for a company that was fixing two-way radios for taxicabs, and they decided they weren't going to fix the radios anymore. I said to my fiancé at the time, who's now my wife, "Let's start a business." It was 1968. She was only 19, and I was 24. I had $600 and she had $10, so we put the $610 together and started a business called Dick Smith Electronics.

Our ambition was to have three or four people working for us. We saw a business called Howard Car Radio in a Sydney suburb, and we thought "wouldn't it be great to be like that." Twelve years later, I sold the business for $25 million. We did incredibly well. I have a very simple formula, which is: ask for advice, surround yourself with capable people, and then work very hard.

Here I was, at 39 years of age, with over $20 million. I gave $3 or $4 million to charity, because I felt a bit guilty and thought I should. I then started on a life of philanthropy and adventure.

When I was a young boy, it was beyond my comprehension that I'd ever be able to learn to fly, but I learned. One day, when I was running Dick Smith Electronics, fixing mainly cab radios, I found that for $24 per hour you could go out to Banks Town Airport, near Sydney, and learn to fly. I used to go out at 5:00 am each morning and finally got my fixed-wing license. I never enjoyed flying fixed wing, because if you could actually see anything on the ground, which was interesting, you could never land there because there wasn't an airstrip nearby.

A number of years later, in 1977, I was stranded with my fixed-wing plane in New South Wales in bad weather—and a helicopter arrived. It was a Bell Jet Ranger. I walked out to the pilot and asked, "Is this an instrument-rated helicopter?" He said, "No, with a helicopter you just fly beneath the cloud, and if the cloud gets too low you stop and have a cup of tea with somebody."

I thought, wow that's my type of machine! So I bought a helicopter and started to fly it around Australia. Then I came up with the idea of doing the first flight around the world by helicopter, and this was my first adventure. In 1982, I ended up buying a new Bell Jet Ranger at the Bell Factory, and I flew it across the Atlantic solo.

The first fixed-wing solo flight across the Atlantic was by Charles Lindbergh. Well, the first rotary-wing solo flight across the Atlantic was by Dick Smith. No one had ever thought a helicopter could go that far, but I went out via Greenland and Iceland, then I continued around the world.

It takes a lot of courage to move forward on something that nobody has done before.

As a family, we used our helicopter as the ultimate off-road vehicle. I called it a magic carpet. We traveled around Australia on heli-camping trips, we called them. We'd go up the Canyon Stock Route, a very famous stock route where they drove cattle across the desert. We'd go right across the Nullarbor Plain, down to Tasmania. That was the way I learned what a helicopter could do. Most people think helicopters are only suitable for flying short distances over cities with television crews. I realized I could put a big tank in the back, so I did some experimenting and flew 600 nautical miles with one tank of fuel. So then I figured I could get around the world.

I could have gotten right around the world if Russia had let me land. Wiley Post, my hero, had flow around the world, which was the first solo fixed-wing flight around the world...but he had flown right through Russia. The highlight of my flight was that it was in the middle of the Cold War, and I was not permitted to land in Russia—and maybe that's why no one had ever flown around the world in a helicopter.

What I ended up doing was getting four barrels of jet fuel and putting it on a ship that was going between Yokohama, Japan and Seattle. When it was halfway across the Pacific Ocean, I took off and landed on the ship halfway between Japan and Alaska and then refueled. From there, I flew to Alaska, and that's what got me right around the world.

My helicopter had no floats and only one engine. If I put floats on I couldn't get the range because they were too heavy, so it was quite a risky flight. The whole flight around the world was 10,000 nautical miles over oceans, but I managed to succeed—and lived—so that was the main thing. I didn't die.

You had a wife and children at home. How did they feel about you taking those risks?

I wouldn't have let my wife take that type of risk, but she let me. She tells me now that she thought that was going to be my one-and-only risky adventure. She didn't realize, it was just the beginning. She was very good and put up with it.

I've now done five flights around the world, and we have just completed a drive around the world of two and a half years and 40,000 kilometers. We've driven across the USA, Russia, Kazakhstan, Mongolia, and then across Australia. So that was our last great adventure.

I love adventure, because it is unpredictable. I consider myself a good risk-manager. The whole key to managing risk—and the most important thing in an adventure—is looking at what can go wrong, asking advice, and copying the success of others. But of course, when no one's ever done it before, it's a bit hard to copy that success.

I've done two balloon flights, one across Australia and one from New Zealand to Australia, and that's an interesting flight. Balloons always fly in the westerly winds, so they fly from west to east. A prominent businessman in Australia bet me that I couldn't fly from New Zealand to Australia, which is against the wind. I said that's impossible, you can't fly against the wind. Anyway, he said look, you can do anything. He said, "I bet you $100,000 that you can't do it."

You were betting against yourself?

I managed to talk to the Met Bureau, and they said if you were to have a high pressure system sitting on the Tasmanian Sea and you fly very low, just skimming the waves, you might just be able to do it. After about two years of waiting for the correct weather we managed to fly, with my co-pilot John Wellington, from New Zealand to Australia. It was very exciting; we actually surfed the balloon gondola in on the waves onto the beach. So I've had some very lucky adventures.

I consider my philanthropy as a duty. It's quite interesting in America you have a history of philanthropy; if people do well they tend to believe they have an obligation to put money back into society, and I really like that. That's not so apparent in Australia, so I'm considered to be a bit unusual there. I've managed over the years to give over $20 million away, and I sometimes feel guilty that I don't give more.

I'm not religious, but I believe in karma. If you do the right thing, the right things will come back to you. I think there's a very good reason for that; it gives you the self-esteem and confidence to be able to succeed.

I recall a conversation with you years ago where you talked about the year you took off after selling your electronics company. You spent part of that year helping young people to understand how the media was conditioning them to think that smoking was a cool thing rather than something that was harming them. You said 13% less children smoked in Australia after that year.

Absolutely. What happened was that I was a supporter of an organization called Life Education Australia. Life Education brought young school children, normally between the age of five and ten, into a building called the Life Education Center. We'd built a number of them around Sydney, and we had portable ones on caravans. These electronically showed outlines of the human body and how fantastic it is. They also showed the effect of drugs. They didn't preach. They didn't say do not take drugs. They just said, "Look, this is how your body works and this is how the blood system works through the brain. If you take drugs everything slows down, everything is affected."

I was funding that for a number of years and was very proud of that, but then I found that the smoking levels for young girls had risen to about 30%. I'm a marketing person, and the reason I've been good in business is I know how to write good advertising. I was seeing these advertisements in Australia clearly directed to children smoking. One of the most popular ones was Peter Jackson

Cigarettes, an American company. The ads had a young girl sitting on a park bench with her boyfriend with their legs entwined. There was a law that said no one under the age of 26 could appear in a cigarette advertisement, but they'd picked this particular girl who looked 15. The impression was that this gorgeous girl would get this handsome bloke if she had a Peter Jackson cigarette. I got so angry with this, so I spent about half a million dollars on some very effective advertising attacking the cigarette companies.

I ran a constant campaign in the media about directing cigarette advertising to children. Within about a year, it was completely stopped, and they just weren't allowed to run their ads. Now it is illegal in Australia. There's hardly any advertising at all of cigarettes, but to have any cigarette advertisement geared toward young woman is against the law. It was 30% of young girls smoking. Now it's down to less than 15%, so it's dropping all the time.

You did another advertising stunt in Sydney Harbor. Will you tell us about that?

Everybody was complaining about a shortage of water, so I announced to the media that I was going to tow an iceberg into Sydney Harbor and cut it up into ice cubes. I said the ice is very different than normal ice, and I'm going to sell them for ten cents each and call them Dicksicles, for people's drinks.

The media was a bit suspicious. Anyway, it was getting near April Fool's Day, so I arranged to get a huge barge, 80 feet long, 20 feet wide. We covered it with white plastic and then put firefighting foam and shaving cream on it. We towed it out at midnight through the Sydney Heads. I had about 400 staff working for me at the time, and I gave them a list of all the radio and TV stations. I said, "At 5:00 am in the morning you've got to call up this list of stations and tell them to look at what's coming in through Sydney Heads. It looks like an iceberg." Every switchboard was jammed, so the media thought that thousands of people were phoning. Sure enough, here was the Dick Smith iceberg being towed. It got publicity around the world, even on the front page of the Chicago Tribune. It cost me $1,200, which is basically free publicity.

At the same time, I've always made sure my business was close to my family. I've always been a very strong family man.

How did you do that?

Since I haven't worked for anyone since the age of 24, I've made sure that my business and my home are close together. When I got into helicopters in 1979, I used to fly to work every day. I built a house with a helipad. I have my Bell Jet Ranger helicopter under the bedroom, and I have a separate hanger for my twin-engine Augusta Helicopter, so I keep both helicopters at home. At the local airport, which is 12 minutes away by helicopter, I have my other aircraft.

I've been incredibly fortunate. I was born in Australia in the 1940s. I just missed out on going to Vietnam; I was a bit old, which was fortunate for me. I won this lottery of life. I've always been very thankful, which is why I thought I had an obligation to give something back.

I've been the chairman of the Civil Aviation Safety Authority twice in Australia, equivalent to America's FAA. The first time I made a number of changes; second time the bureaucrats worked out how to stop me from making any changes, which is a great pity. I still have hope that one day we'll be able to complete reforms, which will get more people flying.

You also attribute part of your inquisitiveness to having been a Boy Scout.

Yes, it's interesting. Like Chicago businessman Steve Fossett, I came right up through the scouting movement. Steve was a good friend of mine, and I was his main support for his balloon flights in Australia. He would come down for scouting functions in Australia, and we'd fly together in his beautiful Citation 10.

I started off as an 8-year-old Cub Scout. I went right through to 23 years of age. I got my Baden-Powell Award, which is the only certification I have. When people ask if I have a university degree, I say, "No, but I have a Baden-Powell Award, and I'm very proud of it."

Scouting allowed me to be an individual; it allowed me to take risks, which I called responsible risk-taking. In starting a business and starting Dick Smith Electronics, the financial risk was not great, because I only had $610. But to me, that was a very important responsible risk-taking adventure.
When I was a Boy Scout, we'd all climb in the back of a scoutmaster's truck and go to a scout camp. These days, you have to have a seatbelt on; there are all these new rules and regulations to protect people from themselves. I've been very vocal. I'm giving a major donation to scouting this year of $1 million, and it's to be directed at encouraging responsible risk-taking in Boy Scouts.

When I was 20 in 1964, I sailed from Sydney to a rock spire in the Tasman Ocean, which is to the east of Sydney, 300 miles out to sea. I jumped off a yacht, swam in, grabbed hold of a ledge, and then started climbing on this 1,800-foot spire of rock rising up out of the ocean. I failed to get to the top then, but I went back in 1980 and actually got to the top.

I like to complete adventures I've started. That was my first real risk-taking adventure and it taught me responsible risk-taking. With my five flights around the world now, I have never ever been late, called search and rescue, damaged an aircraft or anything, and that's by very good organization.

You went into a grocery store, as I understand, looking for jam. You found English and American jams, but not Australian jams. So you went out and started your own company.

That's right. When I sold Dick Smith Electronics for $25 million, I thought, *I'll never have to work again. I'll now just do worthwhile things.* One of the worthwhile things was to start a magazine called *Australian Geographic.* I loved the outdoors, so I started *Australian Geographic* in order to give money to help the environment. The magazine and the shops were very successful, and I ended up selling those for over $40 million. Over the years, we donated about $10 million for adventure, scientific research, and exploration.

One day, after selling *Australian Geographic*, I was in a shop in Australia and found that just about everything was foreign-owned and made. I said, "Why can't we own something ourselves?" So I started Dick Smith Foods, and it has now done about $200 million in turnover. It has breakfast cereals, jams, peanut butter and other products. But it will gradually fade out, because now the big supermarkets will only buy from big companies. It's globalization, which is quite sad, but that's the way it goes. We've given $4 million away, so far. It's run a bit like Paul

Newman, where the money is given away to environmental and social causes.

My wife and I have investments in industrial buildings, and that's how we get our income. And then I work on aviation reform. And I'm still doing a bit of adventure.

What do you see in your future?

In the future, I'd like to continue doing philanthropic work. If possible, I'd like to finish my aviation reform. I'm building a "solar dog" at the moment, which is a solar-powered vehicle designed to go to the South Pole. It's got six wheels, low-pressure tires, and a big solar panel. In the summertime in Antarctica, there is actually about 60% more solar power there because of the 24-hour sunlight. And it's cold, so the solar cell works well.

It's an incredible story...and it's one in which you're still enjoying the journey!

ZHENGRONG SHI, Ph.D.
Founder and CEO of Suntech Power based in China, the world's largest producer of crystalline silicon photovoltaic modules

Dr. Shi is a man of extraordinary accomplishment. He was Research Director of Pacific Solar Pty. Company in Australia; leader of Thin-Film Solar Cells Research; holds eleven patents in PV (photovoltaic); was named China's Green Person of the Year 2007; and was one of *TIME Magazine's* 2007 "Heroes of the Environment." He was recognized with the PV-SEC Prize at the International Photovoltaic Science and Engineering Conference.

Doris Lee: What would you say are the most crucial environmental issues that we face in the world today?

Dr. Zhengrong Shi: I think what we are facing first is climate change, because this requires the strongest effort and longest time to combat. For example, if we say a lake is polluted, maybe we can fix it within a year or two. But climate change is on a macro-scale, so it requires everybody on our earth to act upon it. I think that's why it is a very tough job. If only you and I do something about it, it's not enough.

Some people are still questioning whether global warming is true or not, but I think the majority of individuals are realizing it's crucial. The way that you've chosen to deal with this is through photovoltaics. Is it true that only a small percentage of people in China are aware of this?

Yes, I think so. We have done a lot of lobbying work in China at different levels. I think the problem here in China is unlike the United States; in China there are still a lot of people who live in poverty. The Chinese government has too many agendas, and I think the priority on the agenda is still trying to address the poverty issue.

Now there is the environmental issue, because in the last 30 years the Chinese economy has grown so much and caused a lot of our pollution problems. I think the government now is on top of this pollution issue, which is good. Of course, they also realize the importance of addressing the climate change issue, but I think that requires much more effort, especially in educating people. You can imagine that a farmer who is starving doesn't know there is a climate change issue. I think that's why education in China is so important.

From our point of view, when I address the industry, I also say we have to make solar happen. That means we have to reduce the costs dramatically. We need temporary support from all government subsidies, because if we don't have the market, no matter how hard we work we will not make it happen. With temporary government support, it will give us a chance to reduce our costs dramatically. Maybe in three to five years we won't need any further subsidy. Then we will become a real market.

Let me add a little more. The major reason China's government cannot promote this technology or its products is because it is too expensive. So we lobby the governments and try to tell them that in three to five years with the electricity generated from our products, the price will be similar to the price we are now paying. If that's the case, I think they will not think the cost is the issue.

I've read about the outstanding research you have done. It seems like one of your strengths is doing the necessary research, yet you are also the CEO. That's another facet you have to handle— what a great challenge.

The majority of my effort, actually, has been diverted to the role of a CEO. Understanding the industry and all the technologies is especially important in this time. Many people say it's a boom period and they all jump in. Because we understand the situation, we know what is real and what is not. On the other hand, the financial crisis is impacting every industry, including solar. I try to raise confidence, assuring everyone that it's just temporary.

Your background is amazing. You were raised on a farm, went to college in China, then later went to Australia, and that's where you worked with Martin Green and learned about the new solar energy industry. Then some of your Chinese friends encouraged you to go back to China. You said that if you had missed those conversations, you might not have gone back like you did.

Yes, it happened all of a sudden because I always planned my career to be academic, a scientist, and I never imagined I would come back to China. All of a sudden people were telling me that so much had changed in China. They said, "You have the technology and skill we need."

I found that my skills and knowledge were really needed there, because there's a big lack of understanding of updated technology. That was the initial motivation for me to come back to China and to establish Suntech. After a while, my own thinking was also lifted. From a simple motivation, it was a transforming experience—we can now really make it happen and solar can provide solutions to combat this problem we are facing.

What would you attribute that shift in your thinking to?

I'm not an inborn businessman, and pursuing profit or fortune is not my only interest. In the last couple of years, because I travel and fly a lot, I can be alone with my thoughts and think. The analogy I use is sometimes you need to leave the earth to really see it—to look at the country, the industry, and your company. Looking at it from an entirely different angle, you can see things much more clearly.

It's an education, traveling and seeing new things, isn't it?

Yes. For a company to survive, to exist for a hundred years, we need to consider what service we can provide to society. What solutions can we provide, not just how much money can we make, do you know what I mean?

Yes. Your value is contributing to the needs of the world rather than just collecting more possessions.

Exactly. Thinking like that, you can actually see the future. You can say, "Okay, in that case, here is what our company should do in three or five years time in order to provide a solution or a service. It helps you to streamline your strategy very well, and when you have a good strategy and good execution, you will never struggle making money.

You also say that it is important to focus and work hard.

Yes, I'm a very hard worker.

It wasn't easy to do what you did; you made amazing gains and you have a vision. Did you have your vision all along, or did it grow as you went along?

Yes, it continues to grow, and I see more possibilities. You keep lifting yourself up, and that makes you believe more and more in your vision.

In addition to solar energy, are you working with wind power or turbines?

I think wind power is already one step ahead of solar, because it's relatively cheap. People use wind power more than solar at this moment. But we need to basically change our lifestyle. We can still enjoy what we ought to enjoy but in ways that don't harm the environment. For example, in China people's life standards have improved, but not necessarily in the most environmentally friendly ways. Back in the 1970s and '80s, people had a habit of drinking tea from their own cup, but now it seems that people are getting lazy. They use paper cups, then just throw them away when finished...like bottled water. Of course, when you travel it's not convenient and we have to use bottled water. But when you are at home or in your office, you can use your own cup.

Also, people get used to switching on lights, even during the day when you can open your curtains and let the natural light come in. Another thing I have noticed is with public bathrooms. When we wash our hands, we have gotten used to using paper towels instead of cloth towels or electric fans. Of course it makes you feel more comfortable, but if you think twice about it, where does this paper come from?

It comes from the trees. I've done research in 17 rainforests, so I know the price that we've paid for wanting more paper. For one thing, it robs us of oxygen we need to breathe with in the rest of the world.

Exactly. My point is, we just need to be a little careful to review how we lived before and how we live today. The habits I just mentioned show that it would not have any negative impact on our lifestyle at all.

No, it's just being a little more thoughtful.

Yes. In our company, we have a rule: For any office that has windows and natural light, in the daytime we're not allowed to switch on lights. Every evening in every office, we have a person in charge of making sure all power is off. Also, we don't drink bottled water; we all use our own cups and want our staff to do the same—and to influence their families and friends to do the same.

You and your wife are philanthropists. Is it true that you will be teaching environmental awareness and methods for living a green lifestyle?

Yes. My wife and I have two farms in Beijing; one is her family farm. We continue to educate people and to protect the environment, and that is the biggest charity because that's our biggest belief. The houses we live in use a geothermal heat pump in the house, so we don't feel guilty.

We use solar and other renewable technologies to build automobiles and design houses, so we've already grown this competition in China in the last three years. We find these young people really fascinating, students who are very creative in looking for ways to use this technology.

Also, our foundation sponsored the Himalaya competition in the Olympic Games last year. Because there's no electricity there, we used our solar products to sponsor all the mountain climbers and the local schools and so on in Tibet.

What does the future look like then? You're still working on solar and you see that becoming more valuable in meeting the world's needs, is that correct, Dr. Shi?

Yes, more valuable and more practical. I will keep working on this. I think it will become my mission for the rest of my life.

You kept making breakthroughs when you were in Australia. Is that something that you're still able to do with your busy new life?

Sure. I'm a very critical thinker, so I also can stay focused. I'm a very solution-oriented thinker. Usually, I don't easily accept what seems to be the fact; it is not easy for me to do that. We always try to find solutions.

You're still a scientist at heart, aren't you? How do you see us getting back to the simple days?

I think this comes from human nature. I read many books about the Chinese philosophers of 2,000 to 3,000 years ago, like Kung Fu Chi, and I found that we have a lot of similarities with the philosophy these men proposed thousands of years ago. It all comes back to how we should live our lives. There is greediness in human nature. But I think there should be a balance. It really comes down to fundamentals. I think education is the answer. I don't think government alone can do that, because the government's performance somehow is driven by greediness. The whole financial crisis is caused by greediness.

We can always talk about reducing pollution and changing our lifestyles, but I think in order for this to happen, we need to have an internal change of fundamental thinking. If a person does not change their fundamental beliefs or thinking, then *how* we should live is probably half of the issue. People are sort of forced to be different, and yet are not really willing to be different. That's why in China there are a lot of education programs.

We should have a balanced and harmonic relationship with nature and our life; that's what our ancestors thought and promoted a long time ago. So maybe we should come back to this level and get back to basics.

Nowadays, we have iPhones and all these fancy technologies, but we don't have as many musicians, thinkers, novelists, or writers as before. There's a reason for that. In the past, people lived a simple life. People tended to think, and that's why they could write. Now people are in a hurry, most to make more money.

Instead of having that wonderful cup of tea that you and I talked about. When one goes to China, as I had the opportunity to do, the unhurried pleasure of tea becomes very important.

Dr. Shi, I'm so pleased to have you as a part of this visionary conversation. Is there something else that you might like to add?

All people living on the earth should be aware of the crisis we're facing. I feel especially sorry for African people, for those who are living in the poor regions, because it is not their fault. They did not create this climate change. It is the people of the developed countries—USA, Europe, and now China—that have caused this problem. I think those of us who polluted and caused this problem should show the leadership and address the issues.

- Visionary Spotlight -

MARRIOTT HOTELS & MARRIOTT INTERNATIONL
Making a difference from New York City to the Amazon Rainforest

In my research, I found that Marriott Hotels are making great advancements and leading the way for hotels that are "going green." A press release by Kathleen Duffy, Director of Public Relations in New York City, includes the following details of their efforts to reduce carbon emissions and more:

Marriott Downtown is the First Hotel in New York City to Install Energy-Efficient Tri-generation Plant:

In a major initiative to reduce energy and carbon emissions significantly, the New York Marriott Downtown, a 500-room full-service Marriott hotel managed by Marriott

135

International, Inc. and owned by Host Hotels & Resorts, Inc., celebrated the inauguration of its new "microturbine farm" with a ribbon cutting on June 3, 2008 in Lower Manhattan.

The installation of two hotel owner-funded PureComfort® systems built by UTC Power, a United Technologies Corp. company, makes the hotel the first in New York City to use this ultra clean technology to provide its own electricity, cooling, and heating on-site. Waste heat generated by the system's 11 microturbines is used for space heating, hot water and air conditioning.

On an annual basis, two typical PureComfort systems will reduce carbon dioxide emissions by about 1,700 tons (the equivalent of 360 acres of forest) and nitrogen oxides emissions equivalent of the 530 car emissions. The system will offset about 5800 megawatt hours of electricity, enough to power 700 homes each year.

The press release concludes with a clear commitment to the future:

Marriott is also trying to reduce the company's water waste and energy use by greening their supply chain and building greener hotels in the future. "We are all guests on this planet and that's why an integrative green strategy is a business imperative," says Kathleen Matthews, Executive Vice President of Global Communications and Public Affairs and co-chair of Marriott's Green Council.

A spotlight on Marriott International...

Marriott International has pledged $2 million and invited its customers, suppliers and other stakeholders to contribute to a fund that is administered by the newly created Amazonas Sustainable

Foundation, which, together with the State of Amazonas in Brazil, monitors and enforces the protection of 1.4 million acres of endangered rainforest in the Juma Sustainable Development Reserve.

As an adventurer and member of the Explorers Club, I am very aware of the results of clearcutting in the 17 seventeen rainforests worldwide that I have visited and researched. According to Nature Conservancy leaders, the reason for clearcutting in other countries is often for construction purposes. Some individuals have even been killed for protesting this kind of clearcutting. It's essential to understand that approximately 25% of the oxygen that we breathe every day comes from the rainforests, primarily from the Amazon region.

Marriott's team should be applauded for their efforts to protect this magnificent rain forest. According to Marriott's bulletins:

- *The Amazonas program goes beyond rainforest protection and looks toward long-term sustainability by empowering Juma's 500 residents through a variety of means including:*

- *Expanding the community's one-room primary school to include the new J.W. Marriott, Jr. School for middle and high school students.*

- *Distributing one "Bolsa Floresta" stored value card to each of the local families. The cards are credited with 50 Reais (about 25 US dollars) per month.*

- *Providing speedy new emergency boats, including an "ambulance" for transport to the Novo Aripuana Hospital.*

- *Purchasing mosquito netting for houses and other buildings to cover windows and other openings. Malaria is spread by mosquitoes, which often bite after dark when people are asleep.*

- *Making a new microscope available to the community to help detect malaria.*

- *Installing rainwater cisterns that are used on the small, basic family house structures.*

- *Chlorine is added to the water to avoid spreading of disease. Residents previously drink river water, often causing diarrhoea.*

To learn more about Marriott's Amazonas Sustainable Foundation, visit www.Marriott.com/environment.

- Visionary Spotlight -

MATT DAMON
Actor and Philanthropist, Co-Founder, Water.org

Matt Damon is a one of the finest actors of his generation. With a career in the film industry that continues to flourish, he sees acting as his job. His life, on the other hand, is his family. Perhaps it is a desire to ensure a bright future for his children that spurs on his passionate interest to help developing countries and address environmental issues.

The seeds of his activism were sown early in his life. As a teen, Matt's mother, a professor of early childhood education, would take him to spend part of his summers living with local families in Guatemala and Mexico. Seeing poverty at an early age produced in him a caring heart for the disadvantaged.

Today, Matt is tackling the world's number one health problem—unsafe and inadequate water supplies. On a trip to Africa in 2006, he got a taste of the realities of living in an area without clean water, which opened his eyes to the essential need to have a communal well in such a community. One of the people who had a strong impact on Matt was a 14-year-old Zambian girl who regularly carried a 5-gallon water jug back to her home for her family. Understanding that people with clean water live longer than those without it, he saw that having access to clean water could be the key to this young girl having a chance to move forward in life and achieve her dreams. In addition to the body's basic need for water, having a community well would also serve other important needs. Not only would it help to prevent the spread of contaminated water, but it would also mean that the children who were responsible for gathering the water would have a great deal of time freed up, enabling them to spend more time in school.

In 2009, Matt joined forces with Gary White to create Water.org, an organization dedicated to addressing the issue of the one billion people who lack access to clean water and three billion without proper sanitation. Since its inception, Water.org has already helped hundreds of communities in Africa, South Asia, and Central America to gain access to safe water and sanitation.

Matt also founded WaterCredit, a micro-finance initiative aimed at connecting impoverished villages to local bankers who lend the money to build toilets and systems for tapping the water wells. This project is evidence of the far-reaching view that Matt has of the crises at hand. In a recent *Fast Company* article, he spoke about the importance of connecting with the local people in the communities in which we are working.

The risks involved in micro-credit have already proven worthwhile, as their model is now being successfully adopted by other organizations. In 2009, Gary White won the Skoll Award for Social Entrepreneurship. For more information, visit Water.org.

Visionary Reflection on...

Gratitude

We live in a stunningly beautiful world, one that is counting on us to take care of the food, air, and water that sustains us. Today, think of something you love in nature, whether it's the grass outside your door or the smell of spring rain, and allow yourself to be uplifted by gratitude for that which you love.

CLOCKWISE L to R: Roxanne Spillett, Dr. Mimi Silbert with Doris Lee

CHAPTER 7

Saving At Risk Kids
&
Turning Prisoners and Drug Addicts
Into Productive Citizens

• • • • • • • • • • • • • • • • • •

ROXANNE SPILLETT
President Boys and Girls Club of America

Roxanne Spillett is head of the Boys & Girls Club, which is known as the largest group of healthy children that are less likely to be on drugs, girls less likely to get pregnant and boys less likely to go to jail. In addition, it is a safe and productive place to go after school.

Roxanne, what is the core purpose or mission of the Boys & Girls Club?

Our mission is to serve all young people with a special emphasis on those who need us most. We have 4,000 clubs located in urban, suburban, and rural areas, including Native American and Native Alaskan lands.

We have many clubs in public schools and about 450 clubs in public housing. We also have clubs on U.S. military bases around the world. The clubs are staffed by about 50,000 full and part-time professionals, supplemented by hundreds and thousands of volunteers. Last year alone, we served 4.8 million young people.

Let me just put this into perspective for you. In 1998, we celebrated our 2,000[th] Boys & Girls Club. It was the Andre Agassi Boys & Girls Club in Las Vegas. Colin Powell, who was on the board in 1998, was there for the dedication where he challenged us to open 3,000 clubs.

In 2001, we opened our 3,000[th] Boys & Girls Club in Camden, New Jersey. And in 2006, we opened our 4,000[th] club in Houston, Texas.

And yet, there is still a great need in this country. Life as we used to know it has changed dramatically. When kids come home from school, they're not coming home to a mother and father who are at home. With two parents working and a large number of single-parent families, there needs to be a support system for children. Our intent is to assure all kids in need that we'll be there for them. That's what fueled our growth: the will and the need to do it. Boys & Girls Clubs are physical places that come in many different sizes, shapes and venues.

We do an alumni survey every three or four years. It's very clear when you compare our Boys & Girls Club alumni to the general population that something magical is going on. We learned that 28% of our alumni said that if not for the Boys & Girls Club, they would not have graduated from high school. Our clubs are helping kids stay in school and lead productive lives. The responses on the surveys reflected three important lessons taught by the club: what's right and wrong; how to obey the law; and how to succeed in school. 57% said that the Boys & Girls Club literally saved their lives.

One story that strikes me most is from an alumnus who grew up in a circle of 19 friends. Almost all of them died prematurely from drugs and violence. What was interesting was that of the three surviving friends, they were the only members of the Boys & Girls Clubs.

What is the difference between what the members in your club do as opposed to what kids do in school? Is it less structured or more structured?

When you walk into a club, it's like walking into a candy store. There are many fun choices that you can make. You can go into the game room and play table tennis, air hockey, or football. While playing games, they learn lessons that teach them the importance of waiting your turn, respecting others, and solving differences and problems. Therefore, even in the course of fun, important life lessons are taught.

What is the most dangerous time for these kids?

The greatest dangers lie in transition years, especially in the change from elementary school to junior high school. They're distancing themselves from their parents, relying more on peer groups, and going from a lot of teachers in elementary school to fewer teachers in middle school. It's a tumultuous time. We are able to deduce 75% of kids who are going to drop out of school by the time they complete middle school. I would say that most kids who drop out of school don't drop out because they have poor cognitive abilities. They drop out of school because they don't feel safe or they're bored. Most of the time, kids who drop out of school think nobody cares. Often, nobody reaches out and tries to bring them back, which is an important role our clubs can play.

I also think the most dangerous time during the day for kids is right after school, from 3:00 PM to 6:00 PM, which is when most of the violence takes place. It's our responsibility to make sure that there are productive, safe places for kids to go after school.

Colin Powell gave a heartfelt speech at the Andre Agassi Boys & Girls Club. He walked up to the podium and he didn't say anything. He just kept looking around. Everybody was waiting for him to say something and finally he spoke. He said, "I'm looking at all these cinderblocks. I'm looking at all these ducts. I'm looking at all this material, and you know what I'm thinking? I'm thinking that it takes this much stuff to build a jail." He went on to say, "We need to build more Boys & Girls Clubs and fewer prisons."

At an earlier event, in 1995, Mr. Powell had a turning-point experience. He gathered one afternoon with a group of kids and shared about how he had grown up with a supportive family and how much they meant to him. One of the kids raised their hand asked, "If I don't have a mother or father like you describe can I ever hope to grow up to be like you?" It was then that he decided to join the board. His answer was, "Do you see these people here? These people love you, they care about you, and like my mother and father, they will not let you fail."

You also have other well-known people on your board, like Denzel Washington.

He was a member of a club in Mt. Vernon. He often says, "If not for the Boys & Girls Club, I wouldn't be where I am today or who I am." His mother said, "The Club has taught my son to be a man."

What do you see as your next step? Is this Keystone Program something you do every year?

We have a Steering Committee made up of teenagers that actually run the Keystone conference. It's a great growth experience; it's an experience that helps kids understand that they are masters of their own destiny and that they have so much talent. We are very serious about making deeper partnerships with schools so that we can identify the kids who are at risk of dropping out of school. If there are 75 kids at risk of dropping out, that club needs to be on top of that right away. We need to recruit them to the club and give them the love, support, help, and tutoring they need to develop stronger belief in themselves.

Often times, I find people struggling because they don't see all the options for themselves. Is there something that would help kids figure that out?

You've just put together something important. If you don't aspire to do something, it is hard to reach your goal in life. We have kids growing up in public housing where there are very high unemployment rates that lead to limited thoughts about what their career options might be. At the Club, we help promote the exposure of career opportunities with our Career Exploration Program where people from the community come in. We help build a support system by bringing successful alumni back to the club. Alumni can include police chiefs, principals, state assemblymen, and successful family members. We're developing a new ad campaign that's going to feature the life and times of our alumni, so you might see Denzel Washington talking about growing up in our next series of public service announcements.

On a related note, we have a program called "Youth of the Year." We identify young people who have distinguished themselves academically, given back to their club,

146

community and family and have overcome some very serious obstacles.

In 1997, we elected Eddie Armstrong to become our National Youth of the Year. He was one of the first minorities to lead the Community Affairs Department at Tyson Foods Meat Company. They went on to found their own 501(c)(3) to develop a scholarship program for minority students who are from single households and who wish to attend the University of Arkansas.

If somebody wants to sign up, how do they do that?

Our philosophy is to keep our fees affordable. If a young person cannot afford our fees, they're given a project to do to earn them. The idea is that we don't turn kids away. We keep our dues extremely low and we're primarily located in neighborhoods where there are families that have few discretionary dollars. It could be $10 or $15 a year. One man stood up at a Congressional breakfast, reached in his pocket, and took out a five-dollar bill. He said, "You see this five-dollar-bill, do you know what this bought me? This bought me two gyms, this bought me homework help, this bought me the people who loved and cared about me, and this bought me my success–five dollars a year."

Your major focus is through the transition years you spoke of?

The most vulnerable age group is 6 to 18. Our vision is to assure that success is within the reach of every child and that we inspire young people. What's important to us is not only that kids succeed in school, get good jobs, make money, and have a house. It's important that they are good and gracious human beings and citizens—not just of their community or of this country, but of the world.

Do you see your organization being duplicated in other countries?

We're starting a program in Mexico now with counterparts in Canada, U.K, and South America. We provide everything we can to launch this program. We invite them here to take tours of clubs and we go there to help them. We have already expanded to 5,000 clubs.

How can people find you on the Internet?

Visit BGCA.org and you can find a location near you. If they don't have immediate access to the Internet, they can call 1-800-854-CLUB and be directed to the club closest to them.

MIMI SILBERT, Ph.D.
Founder, President and CEO of Delancey Street Foundation, a residential self-help education center for ex-convicts, ex-addicts and ex-prostitutes

Dr. Mimi Silbert, I have followed your career for many years, and you are one of those featured in my book **America's New Future: 100 New Answers.** *What would you say is the secret behind helping people with major challenges to create a productive and happy life?*

Before I even answer, I just have to say you're fantastic, and your constant commitment to moving life forward for all of us is great.

To me, one of the most important things behind what we do is that, unlike most nonprofits, we don't have a staff and we're not funded. Instead, we rely on the people who have the problems to become their own solution. And we do that

148

by something we call, "Each one teach one, and each one help one."

Our average resident is now a third generation gang member. They've gone in and out of prison, basically, their whole lives. They even have grandmothers in gangs.

Grandmothers in gangs too?

Grandmothers in gangs—which speaks to a level of despair, because when it spans three generations you don't even have role models to look to. Violence just becomes what life is to you, and you're mostly at the receiving end of life. You are the underclass of society, which either receives help, donations, or punishment. But you are never called upon to give.

Society is always worried about what we can do for them to get them to stand up, be stronger and healthier, but at The Delancey Street we need them. When you have no staff and you have no funding, you need the people in your extended family. We've run it like an extended family, you need them to rise up the best of themselves and give to each other.

It's in that process of acting as if you are already a better person—a responsible person who can be counted on—that you actually become one. Our residents have to teach what they've just learned to the newer person; that's what they spend more time thinking about. It's in the teaching that they learn themselves. For example, if you read at the 10th grade level, you're tutoring someone who reads at the 8th grade level, and that person is tutoring someone who reads at the 6th grade level.

If you have started to understand why it's important to never lie about the little things, then you begin to teach other people. It's not just the big things that matter, it's the slow development of character and the fact that your word means something; the fact that you stand for principles. What matters is that you believe in things that are bigger than you and come to know that you can affect those things. It's in the doing that we actually change. I like to say change is a verb. It's something we must do. We can't talk about it, we can't just hear about it, we can't feel it. We have to jump up and do it.

They're forced to do that at Delancey Street, because there's no other way to do it for them. And it's phenomenal what they then rise up to.

Is there a system that they have to follow?

We laugh and call them the 999 basic rules. It starts with everything. You know, many of our people have lived on the streets. They have to learn how to take a shower, how to make a bed; we're down to the very basics. We're still bouncing quarters off of the beds to make sure that the bed is made correctly. You learn your most basic habits. You learn how to speak and how to develop your vocabulary so that everyone speaks the best form of our language.

People are tutored to get their high school degree equivalency. We also teach art appreciation where everyone goes to museums; and music appreciation where we go from blues concerts to jazz concerts to the opera and the symphony.

We teach people through our business training school. We have a restaurant, a moving company and numerous products that we make and sell. They all learn three marketable skills. Although they learn academics, and they learn how to dress, how to communicate well, how to interact productively, most importantly they learn the values and attitudes that give rise to integrity. That's our primary focus.

What do you mean by integrity?

Integrity, decency, and helping others. Our entire place is run by volunteers, including me. I live here, and I don't take a salary. All of our job positions at every level of the organization are to be positive role models. We are also extraordinarily structured, very strict. We need to be, because as I said the majority of our people have been in gangs. These gangs are sworn to kill one another by race or by where they live. They've had a lot of violence and they need to balance out their past by giving and helping and making the world better. We teach them to believe this is our society and it's up to us to now make it better—especially those of us who have caused society a little more pain. So they volunteer with kids in schools, and they help the elderly.

We have no violence. It's just phenomenal that people who are sworn to kill one another are living together in integrated dorms. We teach each other to read, spell, and learn the values that eventually make people proud of themselves instead of guilt-ridden and angry.

I saved a letter your group sent out after 9/11. It was a touching Valentine's Day greeting about the need to learn how to get along with people different from ourselves in order to end terrorism.

Exactly. You might disagree totally on the fact that my God is blue and your God is green; my beliefs are purple, your beliefs are orange. But it's the joy of life to put them all together to make a rainbow. The idea is not to wipe out some of the colors of the world...the purples, the greens, and the oranges. It's horrible to live with hate inside you, believing that revenge will solve the issue. It never has; it never will. You can't live with hate dominating your life.

Mimi, could you take us through how somebody new would come into your facility, maybe angry at another gang member who is right on their same floor? How does that start to change people?

First of all, you have to write us. For example, no judge, no president, and no mommy can say "Please help this person." Whether you mean it or not, you would have to write from jail or wherever you are and ask for yourself: "Please help me." If you're on the streets, we have a bench that is right at the front when you come through the gate in our front office. You can just sit yourself on it 24 hours a day. It means, "Please come interview me. I need help."

We don't take sex offenders, because I believe they need professional help and we do not do professional counseling. But otherwise, our interview process isn't based heavily on the past. We base everything on the fact that you can start all over again. You can learn; you can learn to be decent, you can learn to be kind, and you can learn love, which is really the center of it.

The interviews, which are done by residents, are primarily about listening to the tone with which you tell your story. When the focus is on a person you hate or you're blaming, we will stop the interview and ask, "Then why am I interviewing you? If it's another gang that's caused all your problems or it's a particular person you hate then I should interview that person, because obviously that person controls your life. You don't control your own life, because all you're telling me is about someone else." They have to stop and say, "No, I control my life. This is what they did to me."

Then we again say, "No, we can only help change *you*. You have to understand that this is what *you* do to you. No matter what someone else does to you, you have to live the right, decent, correct and good life, or you will hate yourself, and you will just keep doing stupid things."

It all starts in the interview and our refusal to focus on the times in their lives when things have been horrible.

The message is that it doesn't matter what anybody else does—this is *your* life; you control it and what matters is what you do with it. We each get to choose how we respond to life, and upon arriving at our front door, people find out that choosing hate and anger doesn't work here.

We put everyone in integrated dorms. We have learned that we can't change our lives by ourselves, so here we are. We're one big "we." I tell our people, "You're all the 'we', and I'm a 'we' too, because I live here." No matter how many tattoos—in many cases, hatred is made visible through tattoos—we are here together, sleeping next to one another. A person with swastikas, lighting bolts, and pro-Nazi comments, sleeping next to a Mexican mafia gang person covered with entirely different tattoos, or a black person covered with the symbols and statements of his gang.

These people thought they hated, then hate becomes just too mean. I sometimes tease them when they can't sleep and tell them, "Okay, so the person you want revenge on is sleeping soundly in their bed, and you are staying up all night like a lunatic, pacing and angry. You can't let them win that way. Get rid of your hate and sleep."

I'm like a mother figure. I love them. They love me. And we're climbing a mountain together. I tell them, "I might be closer to the top of the mountain, and you might feel closer to the bottom. But the truth is the people at the bottom hold the power. If you pull in a negative direction, we'll all fall

153

down the mountain—and Delancey Street will be over. If you pull each other up, we'll all make it up. And the pie is big enough for all of us, so here we go."

Initially, they don't feel it, but out of respect for a place that took them in when no one else wanted them—that believes in them when they don't believe in themselves—out of just that simple basic loyalty, they don't act on their hatred. Slowly as time goes by, they see themselves doing better.

When you take your model and look at the world, how can this be used? Can this be used in India and Africa?

We've started a training institute where we're teaching people from 20 different countries. Singapore sent people here. We have people come here who are working with Aborigines in New Zealand and Australia. It's interesting, because in all countries, including our own, it's easier to start with the people who have hit bottom, because everyone recognizes that change has to happen there.

The wonderful thing is when people graduate from a place like ours and they can teach it to their own children. They can also teach the system to their families, their friends, and the people they work with. It penetrates and bubbles up into society.

This system is slowly making its way around the world and the country. We now have about eight locations. They can't call themselves The Delancey Street, but they can call themselves a replication of The Delancey Street, and on their own they're taking the model forward.

We can't force change, that's why prisons just don't work that well, because the people themselves haven't chosen to change.

You're talking about power. It would be good if you told readers how tall you are.

With a little poof on my hair, I am five feet even.

Many of our residents are gigantic, muscular. Some of them have spent a total of 25 years in prison, and that's 25 years spent pumping iron. They are huge!

They say that the gentle giants treat you in a very gentle way, because they respect you.

Yes, and in all honesty, I love them. It's like they are my children, and my family. And it helps them to understand love a little better and to understand the power of love, which is extraordinary. Together, we discover that caring, giving, and doing provides an extraordinary sense of power. With that power, people start to really listen to you.

Looking at our people struggling against all that negativity, and trying so hard to help someone else, I feel like it saves my life every day. It's a difficult time in the world right now, and it is all too easy to get cynical. Truthfully, you come to a place like The Delancey Street, and it brings back every childlike belief in hope and goodness.

It's refreshing and renewing?

Exactly, refreshing and renewing, and sometimes you forget that incredible things are possible. If you only looked at the lives of our 500 people in San Francisco on paper—what they have been through and how much hatred dominated their lives—it would be easy to just say the world is spiraling downward.

Then you listen to them tell each other how they were once one to kill and now they say, "Here, let me show you. I can make this easier for you. We can do it together." It makes you believe in the system.

You're saying 500 people are now in your facility?

Yes, in San Francisco alone. We've got several hundred in Los Angeles and a couple hundred in New Mexico. The facilities are of different sizes. For example, our North Carolina facility is very small, 35 people, because there are some who actually need a very small family. They're so pulled inward and so hopeless, and 500 people are just too many for them to feel connected to.

Each facility looks different, but it's the same process. You have to make your bed the same way. We teach everyone to "act as if": act as if you are decent, act as if you care, act as if you're a professional, act as if you're an executive at one of Bill Gates' companies so that you walk with your head held high.

I must say, we differ from many modern companies, because we teach our people to wear coats and ties. It's a joke I make when we go to certain big events and some of our people come with me. I say, "You can tell who the ex-convicts are in the room amongst the doctors, lawyers and professionals: We're the people in the suits."

Mimi, what happened when you were honored by the University of California and you brought some of the Delancey people in tuxes with you?

To be Alumni of the Year at UC Berkeley, everyone else is a Nobel Prize Winner…and then there's me. I gave my little speech. I talked some about my experiences, they

156

showed a nice video, and then I said, "This beautiful thing you've given me belongs to the residents of Delancey Street, and there is one person at each of your tables. Yes, they are former gang members, armed robbers, prostitutes, etc. These people have carried on intelligent conversations with you. Would our people please stand."

Our people stood, and within seconds everyone in the room stood up for them. It's extraordinary how much people are moved by someone's ability to change, because if people with that level of anger and hatred can change, then the world can change. That is what changing the world is. It's getting at the root of the hatred that underlies the poverty and the horrors.

In most cases, your people don't end up back in jail. Do you have any statistics?

Right now in California, 70% of the people who get out of prison go back to prison. I can claim that, at the minimum, 70% of what are now over 15,000 graduates of Delancey Street don't go back to prison or jail or do drugs.

For our 30th anniversary (we're now in our 38th year), we spent a lot of time tracking graduates and inviting them all to a *prom*. You have to remember, most of our people have never gone to high school, so we had a homecoming weekend and a prom. We tracked 14,000 graduates, and talked with many of them on the phone. Most were doing something in addition to raising healthy families and working hard—they were volunteering at something, doing pancake suppers at church, bringing food to people with AIDS, working with kids in need, and some were volunteering in other countries.

When one of our 15,000 people goes back to prison, that one person has probably positively changed the lives of ten people. I like to say, "It's not just that we've stopped them from doing negative acts—yes, that statistic is good—but there's a statistic that no one can measure: how many lives a positive life can change. That's a great statistic."

Is there something that you see different now than you did when you started 38 years ago?

Yes, when we started people were first generation drug addicts and criminals, and now, on the average, our residents are third generation.

When we started people had positive role models—they just weren't following any of them. Now our residents honestly don't know what we're talking about at the start of our program. Having positive role models is not a world they know.

We so desperately need to reverse that. Hatred and revenge are getting embedded. When you look at poverty and the horrible struggles happening to people, you say, "I can understand how they feel angry and vengeful." I understand it too, but we just have to stop it.

Understanding it isn't enough.

The divided way we're living today, it will never solve anything. We all best jump in the one lifeboat—that is our world—because no one is going to win if we keep this up.

There are so many ways to help; teach a little class, send some books, or send a letter that I could read to everybody. George Schultz, former U.S. Secretary of State, is a dear friend. He regularly stops by, and he simply tells our people, "I admire you. I admire everything you're doing, and thank you for making the world better." Sometimes just your words of belief make all the difference in the world.

Wonderful. And people can buy your Christmas trees each holiday season.

Exactly, buy our Christmas trees. We sell them at every facility around the country. Call us if you have a big building! We win awards for decorating buildings.

We also have a national moving company and have received the BBB "No Complaint Award" for many years. We've been voted by several magazines as the best moving company, because our people are earnest and want to help.

Any final words?

*Thank you...*because spreading hope is what you do phenomenally well. Honestly, what the world needs now are people who keep spreading the word that impossible things are possible. It just takes the willingness to take some risks and fail, and then pick yourself up and take more risks, and then succeed! You're doing that, you're spreading that word, so my final words are "thank you."

I appreciate that. How can people who are interested in helping The Delancey Street Project do that?

People are welcome to call us, our headquarter number is 415-512-5190.

If you know people who have totally hit bottom, then call 415-512-5104, and that way we can help them.

People can donate money, or when they're moving, they could use our moving company. If they're hungry, they can hire us for catering in New Mexico, New York, North Carolina, or Los Angeles. Or they can eat at our restaurant in San Francisco.

Dr. Mimi Silbert has shared with us her years of experience, her years of struggle and joy. She's such a gift to this whole world. Thanks so much, Mimi.

Visionary Reflection on...

Meaning

As too many of us know, going through years of chronic stress, turmoil, abuse, or addiction leaves us feeling disconnected from our own inherent value, significance, and contribution. Very often, regaining a sense meaning comes from stepping beyond our limitations in order to benefit others in some small or large way. Today, simply take inventory of the things that connect you with meaning...and give thanks for them.

CHAPTER 8

CLOCKWISE L to R: Doris Lee with Jhang Hemming, Ph.D., Vanessa Bezuidenhout, and one happy panda

CHAPTER 8

Saving Endangered Species

• • • • • • • • • • • • • • • • • •

A JOURNEY FROM CHENGDU TO WOLONG, CHINA TO TALK WITH THE GIANT PANDAS

A brief story of JHANG HEMMING, Ph.D
Director of the China Conservation and Research Research
Center for the Giant Panda, Wolong, China

When I was in Chengdu, China—the area which was later struck by an earthquake in 2008—one of my students, his driver, and I drove three and a half hours to a small mountain village called Wolong. Wolong is the home of China's largest research center for pandas. Pandas are the pride of China and often thought of as the main symbol of the country. It was a trip well worth taking.

The road up was very steep and was being repaired because of all the huge tourist buses that often use this route. Personally, I would never try to drive up these steep roads. It was my student and friend, Vanni, who had arranged for his driver to take us to this mountain area. Stepping outside my comfort zone to travel there made it possible for me to interview the director of the largest panda center in the world.

Upon arrival, we were served a very tasty meal. My lunch companion, a young staff woman working with the pandas, told me the mushrooms in the soup had been growing wild up on the side of the mountains just an hour prior. Some of the older women in China make a small living picking the mushrooms. If not used soon, they will be dried and sent to the city. One restaurant that we later visited listed over 360 different kinds of mushrooms.

Dr. Jhang Hemming, the director, had obtained his doctorate in animal husbandry in Utah. He had taken on the challenging goal of discovering how to keep the baby pandas, born in captivity, alive after birth. Before Dr. Hemming began this work, most of the babies only survived a month or two.

He and his team of scientists were up for the task. Along with his colleagues, and with additional research support from the San Diego Zoo in California, they were able to create new food supplements in the form of small biscuits. A specially formulated biscuit gave these magnificent animals the nutrients they needed in addition to their favorite food, bamboo leaves. With Dr. Hemming's permission, we visited the Panda Bakery.

Dr. Hemming was proud to show me pictures of the 30 baby pandas born that year. It was seven months later, and they were all alive.

One good-humored observer who knows about my passion for interviewing said that it looks like I'm interviewing the panda in this photo. I'll never tell...

According to the Chinese news reports, these pandas were not harmed by the earthquake, but over 80% of the buildings of the center were partially destroyed. And since the earthquake, the pandas seem to show more stress, so the handlers are touching them more and connecting with them more. There are 200 pandas in captivity at the Wolong Research Center. The estimated 1,600 pandas in the wild have not been evaluated. They may have lost their habitat, food, or some may have been killed by the earthquake itself.

The San Diego Zoo gets their pandas on loan from the Chengdu Research Center, and so the staff in San Diego was greatly concerned after the earthquake. Because of their close connection with their Chinese counterparts, some of them even traveled to China soon after to help rebuild the compound.

It was interesting to learn that the mother of my student host helped identify the original pandas found in this valley when local farmers thought they had discovered a new breed of raccoons because of their similar eye features.

The icing on the cake: I was given the opportunity to hold a six-month old giant panda. I must say, he was soft and cuddly.

To learn more about the in-depth work of the Wolong Center, visit: www.ahfan.com/wolong. And to learn about the Chengdu Research Center, visit: www.panda.org.cn

Visionary Spotlight -

GREG CARR
Entrepreneur and Philanthropist

Since childhood, Greg Carr has been an environmentalist at heart, with a lifelong love for biology. While studying history in college, he also developed a passion for human rights. In time, he would discover a way to bring all of his greatest interests together.

After attaining his Master's degree, he saw the telecommunications field as a promising career path and co-founded Boston Technology, which became the nation's number one voice-mail provider to telephone companies. After serving as chairman to Boston Technology and Prodigy, Greg resigned in 1998 to pursue his true passion—human rights. In 1999, he established the Gregory C. Carr Foundation, a nonprofit dedicated to the environment, the arts, and human rights. Eventually, this work led him to Africa.

Though Mozambique is considered the "jewel" of Africa, it is also one of the poorest nations on earth. Sixteen years of civil war have wreaked havoc not only on the people but also on the land and its animals. When Greg visited Mozambique's treasured Gorongosa National Park in 2004, it was still largely in ruins, with buffalo herds that had decreased from 14,000 to 50 in number. The park had been closed in 1983 without any hope of revival.

Through the Carr Foundation, Greg is now pioneering one of the largest animal reintroduction efforts in Africa. Not limited to Africa, his endeavors are a response to the waning global biodiversity. One of the primary aspirations of the foundation is to spur development without harming the environment. In 2005, Greg pledged up to $40 million over 30 years for a restoration project centered on ecological restoration and economic development.

Greg visits Gorongosa National Park once a month, overseeing its communications, business and scientific activities, and its community relations. Just one year after the project began, the park's staff increased from 100 to over 500, and their visitors increased from under 1,000 to over 5,000. Greg also aims to build an eco-tourism industry in the region, which he believes will provide jobs to the locals and have a snowball effect, improving education, health, and the overall standard of living.

For more information, visit: www.carrfoundation.org

Visionary Reflection on...

Interdependence

St. Francis of Assisi said, "If you have men who will exclude any of God's creatures from the shelter of compassion and pity, you will have men who will deal likewise with their fellow men." In the fullness of our lives, it's so easy to forget about our interdependence with all life, including the exquisite animals, birds, and sea creatures that populate our earth. Today, allow yourself to contemplate your innate connection with all living beings.

CHAPTER 9

CLOCKWISE L to R: Joanne Wolf with Doris Lee,
Former President of Mozambique Chissano with Doris Lee, Marilyn Tam,
Rebecca Di Domenico, Conrad Prebys, Helen Hunt, Ph.D.

CHAPTER 9

The Power of Non-Profits
People at the Leading Edge of Philanthropy

· · · · · · · · · · · · · · · · · ·

HELEN LAKELLY HUNT, Ph.D.
Founder of The Sister Fund

Helen LaKelly Hunt has been very active in the women's movement for over 25 years. She is the founder of The Sister Fund, which is a private women's fund dedicated to the social, political, economic and spiritual empowerment of girls and women. She has also helped to fund many other groups, including The Dallas Women's Foundation, The New York Women's Foundation, and The Women's Funding Network—national and international organizations that work in partnership with women, empowering them to find respect and dignity in their daily lives. She is recognized for her leadership in building The Women's Funding Network and was inducted into The National Women's Hall of Fame.

Doris Lee: Helen, tell us about some of the exciting projects that you're involved in right now.

Helen LaKelly Hunt: I think I would like to start by noting that we are on the cusp of a historical time for women. Around the world, women are political and business leaders; the world is beginning to be more open to listening to what women have to say. For centuries women have been asking for a place at the table. They've wanted to have a voice around policy-setting tables. They've wanted to have a say about how their communities are run, yet in the past, most of the world has turned a deaf ear to what women have had to say. But now, people are listening.

You mean men are listening as well as women, Helen?

Yes, men too. Men are curious and want to know: If you're a leader, how would you lead differently? What would you have to say? People are listening, which is why I also think it's very important that women take the time to form their thoughts and their views in circles of women, so we can put well-formed ideas out there.

You're supporting women to tell their stories, is that correct?

Yes. I think it's important for women to come together and share their experiences with each other. Women often work well collaboratively when developing policies and procedures for running a community, an organization, or a culture. Working in collaboration, these organizations are developed out of experience and community.

Women can bring a myriad of life experiences to the table that are relevant; from the experience of what it's like to raise a family, to what it's like to live in areas where some people have most of the resources and others have few. Handling the disparity and discrepancy in the amount of resources and voice in society one has—this is an experience many women can speak to. How do we redistribute wealth so everyone has a chance for a decent education and everybody has a chance for a stable base from which to start your life?

How do you encourage countries where women, particularly girls, are not sent to school? It's been on the agenda of the United Nations Women's International Conference for 30 years, but it hasn't taken hold throughout the world. Do you see a change?

I think solutions can, and will, emerge if women stay in touch with each other across the cultures. Women need to find, or actually found, organizations that do that kind of mentorship—women helping women.

I think there are affluent women who have financial resources and want to help women and girls go to school and succeed in life, but they don't know *how* to help. This is the reason I feel like there's a real onus on the organizations that do this kind of networking, to get their messages out and get the messages out loudly, smartly, and broadly.

An excellent point. Is there information on your website that would be helpful to others who might want to start a group?

I'll share with you the philosophy of the organizations that I have worked with, which are women's foundations. When I got involved with women's foundations over 20 years ago, there were only 14 women's funds in the world. When we were starting up The Dallas Women's Foundation, there were only 13 other women's funds in the world. The first fund was the Ms. Foundation for Women. The Ms. Foundation broke the ground for women's funds, and the idea began to proliferate. Today there are nearly 130 women's funds around the globe.

Women's funds are simply women coming together to pool their resources and leverage one another's dollars. They pool their money into endowments to support women and girls in their communities. Women's funds often support areas where there have been the fewest resources for women and girls in their communities—including

170

education, medical assistance, violence-related support, and economic justice.

These funds pose the question: Do women have work opportunities so that they can bring home the paychecks to stabilize their families? Do women have the financial opportunities that will allow their children to be nutritionally fed, well educated, and well prepared to emerge into adulthood?

Is there one organization where people can get information about what is being done in specific cities, such as Dallas, New York City or other places?

Yes. There is an organization called The Women's Funding Network and their website is www.wfnet.org. The Women's Funding Network (WFN) is the overarching organization that works to coordinate with approximately 130 women's funds worldwide. Currently, there are over 90 women's funds in the U.S., one in Canada, one in Mexico, one in Central America, and one in South Africa. There are also women's funds in Bulgaria, India, and Nepal. One of the early women's funds is in Amsterdam, and we're all jealous of its name, it's called "Mama Cash."

These funds work to pool women's energies, ideas and resources so they can respond to the needs of women in their communities. Over the last 20 years, they have raised $450 million in assets and endowments. They have also raised $400 million that has gone directly back into the communities, in grants to others. All in all, women's funds have raised a total of $850 million to help empower women and girls.

There is a group of us that are also currently working to raise the last $150 million to send women's funds crashing through the billion-dollar mark. Just think what changes a billion dollars for women and girls' empowerment might be able to create.

This initiative is called Women Moving Millions, and isn't there a website of the same name where people can find information?

Yes, and the Women Moving Millions initiative is a part of The Women's Funding Network, and we are working to raise that last $150 million from million dollar donors. The other monies have been raised from women's fund supporters from across cultural, social, and economic lines—million dollar donors and $10 donors. Every donation to women's funds is valuable.

Recently however, some of us have been talking about how high net-worth women have been sitting out of some of the most important work that is being done for women. This initiative is an opportunity for women of high net-worth to step up and begin to prioritize funding women.

Are women members of that organization once they've made their donation?

That's a great question. Although it is a funding initiative and not an organization, it does have its own separate website: www.WomenMovingMillions.org.

WomenMovingMillions.org is in partnership with The Women's Funding Network. We're going out and telling women that it's time to write the million-dollar check.

I am working with the WFN around this initiative after taking a little time out from my activism work to get a doctorate on the origin of American feminism.

Yes, I hoped you'd talk about that.

In studying early feminism, I learned that the leaders of the suffrage movement were exasperated by the lack of funding for the women's work. I found a letter that one of the women wrote to her friend, basically saying: *"My Dear Elizabeth, I am so frustrated today. I've opened the paper and there's yet another article on another woman who has funded another museum. Why won't women fund suffrage?"*

That's when I began to wonder, *did* women fund the suffrage movement? I gathered beside me a couple of 19th Century scholars, and we went back and read every set of minutes from every suffrage organization meeting. The truth is, men were the main financial contributors to the suffrage movement. That is one of the reasons suffrage took so long. The high net-worth women were funding museums, their husband's alma maters, and houses of worship, but they weren't funding women's voices and status in society.

We're inviting high net-worth women to the table. Women's funds offer, for the first time in history, the perfect vehicle for funding. Women Moving Millions is working to create a contagion of this energy.

Before we began this initiative, we uncovered about 30 million-dollar donors who had helped fund and support women's funds over the last 15 years. And since we began the Women Moving Millions initiative a year ago, we've raised over $93 million for these women's funds.

Wonderful. Are you seeing any trends as to how people are getting involved?

Yes, we're learning what women want; what they want to see in terms of impact studies. And we're also learning that these women want to meet each other and work together. Women do philanthropy and activism work differently than men. Women do it *relationally*. Women love to work together. They love to get together for meetings—to strategize together and dream of what's possible if we unite.

Good information. The doctorate you mentioned was related to faith and feminism. I know you have a book out by that title. Would you comment on that?

I wrote the book as a Christian, because that's my tradition and that's the tradition I know best, but the dynamic of the book is true for all religions. Women who are part of faith-based institutions are struggling with one of the most entrenched patriarchal energies in the world. The women's movement needs to recognize the women in religious institutions who are struggling to lift up women's voices there as well.

I encourage women in faith-based institutions, as well as women operating and organizing outside of religious institutions or who may call themselves secular feminists, to begin to link together. There is so much we have in common. I'm encouraging women to think of the potential we can create by *working together*.

Where I came to this thesis was another avenue. It was after meeting with women who wanted to lift up women's voices and see the potential of women being the fulcrum for social change in the culture. If you talk with these women, many of them are faith-based women, but they don't feel free to talk about their faith within the women's movement and its organizations. They don't bring the voice of faith to the table because there has been a sense that women who stay in faith-based institutions have sold out to a patriarchy, but I don't think that's a fair assumption.

Many of these women are insisting that their faith tradition is important, and they're not going to give up their faith simply because men have dominated its leadership. They're excited about working with anyone who will dignify women's roles in religious institutions. After all, women have shouldered most of the daily work within these houses of worship. It's because of the attendance and work of women that most of these houses of worship remain open, so women should not have a subordinate role within them.

The work we do as faith-based feminists is about a vision, ontology and the sacred order of life. It's the way life is meant to be—where everyone is treated with dignity and respect, and that is what women want in their houses of worship.

Recently, the sermon at the Rock Church in San Diego was that Jesus came to destroy the barriers between male and female, Jews and Greeks, saints and sinners. It's like there's something there, but we haven't claimed it.

That's right, Galatians 3:28 hits the nail on the head: "There is neither Jew nor Greek, slave nor free, male nor female, for you are all one in Christ Jesus."

Regardless of what countries or communities we live in, how would you encourage women everywhere to make equality possible?

I think every woman has a responsibility to be a part of a women's organization, whatever organization in your community seems most vital and alive. Women need to stay networked with other women, because we are the majority. If we unite and work together, we will make progress toward the values that we hold so near and dear.

Great ideas, phenomenal work. Thank you for taking the time, Helen.

MARILYN TAM
Founder and Executive Director of US Foundation and Visioneer HealthWalk

Marilyn Tam is a consultant, speaker, and author. She has had an extraordinary and diverse life, from her beginnings in a traditional Chinese family in Hong Kong to her rise through the executive ranks of the international business world. As the former CEO of Aveda, President of Reebok Apparel & Retail Group, and Vice President of Nike, she became an influential corporate leader and has become a respected humanitarian throughout the world.

Doris Lee: Marilyn, how did the US Foundation start and what are some of the projects you're involved with?

Marilyn Tam: Us Foundation really is an accumulation of my many, many, years of working in the non-profit sector, as well as the for-profit world. Having been in the corporate world, but coming from a developing nation, I've seen both sides of the equation.

I've always had the dream that one day I would be able to devote more of my energies to giving back, so an opportunity came in 1996.

I started the US Foundation because there is really no "them." It is only "us" here, and that is why it is the name of the foundation. We work on creating more harmony and understanding between people and the planet. Our mission and purpose is in line with unifying and creating more collaboration and communication among all aspects of life and how we are integrally impacting each other, no matter where we are.

You've held many leadership positions in corporate America, including Miller's Outpost, May Company Department Stores, and Britannia Sports Wear. How did that work translate for you into putting the US Foundation together?

When I was doing all those corporate-type jobs, I also integrated the giving back and humanitarian aspects of life into the work. Whatever we did, I always considered what kind of impact we were having on the community at large. Not only in terms of which products or services we were providing, but also how we were purchasing our goods. So it was all connected.

When it came time for me to shift my emphasis between for-profit and non-profit, it was an easy shift because I had been working on the same things all along.

The US Foundation is still working in New Orleans. Could you say something about that?

Well, Hurricane Katrina and the storms in New Orleans, Louisiana and Mississippi have really impacted the people there. After the large charities came in and did their work, everybody went home and forgot that people there still have no homes.

Also, they still need jobs, support, and how to redevelop their businesses. Basic things like how to get water back into an area. US Foundation, and some other organizations we were connected with, adopted two towns across the river on each side of the two states. We said, "We are going to be staying with you, working with you, until you get back on your feet again."

It's not the glamorous work that you read about in the paper. It's more just the day-to-day things that need to happen to move forward. You need to find transport to get to work, or you need childcare so that you can get out of the house—fundamental things.

You're working on a project in Santa Barbara, too. Could you speak about that?

It goes back to helping people help themselves. We have a beautiful community here in Santa Barbara, California. Compared to many parts of the United States, it is a safe and healthy environment. Yet we still have youth gangs, young people who feel like they don't belong in the upward mobility or educational system because of unhappy or dysfunctional home lives. They get very attracted to belonging to a community of *any* kind, and that's where gangs come in. They attract our young people into a role that is not a healthy long-term one for them.

After one unfortunate incident with gang violence, several members of the community decided, myself included, to do something. The Us Foundation was a spearhead in this, to create opportunities for young people when they transition from sixth grade into seventh grade. It is an important time when the first break in education comes because children transfer schools and their community from sixth grade is disrupted. They have to go to another school and create a new community, and if the children are not focused or interested in school, they are very vulnerable to joining gangs. What we do is take those students that have that tendency to stray and give them focus and opportunity to do something else.

We are working with the district educational people, the superintendent of schools, the police chief, and the mayor to create a new system for an apprenticeship program.

In a new school program, for the first half day certain children will attend classes, and then the next half day, we will work with the teachers to help identify areas of interest that these children may have beyond school. There are those who aren't doing well academically, and also being disruptive in class. We will find out where they have interests and then help them to become an apprentice to a business for a half day.

They will be paid a small amount of money that will be given to them at the end of their high school years, so they are given an incentive to stay through graduation. That money can go either into vocational training when they get done with high school, or it can go into a college or junior college fund, depending on how their interests develop.

What we see is that children get very excited to have somebody actually focus attention on them. They're showing a sense of responsibility and the ability to know that they have talent and a way of making a difference in the world. I'm really quite thrilled about this program.

It sounds like a great idea. I would hope that what you are doing can get circulated throughout the country.

You're reading my mind. That's exactly what we hope to do once we get this program established, but this is not really a new program. If we look back into Europe, and even parts of Asia, there has always been the tradition of apprentice-type or vocational education for children that may not be on the academic track.

In all my studies and interviews, I have found that if young people find their potential, they are home free. They are not dreading going off to work just to pay bills. There is more enthusiasm about the job.

In my corporate life, I work with a lot of Fortune 500 leaders, and that really is the same thing for them. They have to have a passion and love for what they're doing or else it will be—no matter how much money they're making—a job that they feel like they have to do rather than one they enjoy.

Let's look at some of the things that you've done internationally. Last fall-summer you worked with 25,000 Indian children and helped them to attain a healthier way of life. I was overwhelmed when you said you could organize a group this large. How did you do that?

We know we aren't the only people on the planet doing this work, so what we do is identify other groups who have interests in the same area as we do, and we collaborate with each group to have them do what they're best at. Together we can make a bigger difference.

About an hour out of Bangalore is this area called Nandi Hills, which is a desperately poor area—under a dollar a week. The children there have a high danger of becoming malnourished. When children do not get enough vitamins between birth and age ten, there's a very high tendency for nutritional deficiency-caused blindness, as well as all the other ailments that can damage a child, often times permanently.

180

Working with an organization in India, we collaborated with two more organizations—Vitamin Angels Alliance is an organization that gets donations of vitamins and anti-parasitic medicine from different pharmaceuticals. The Airline Ambassadors is another organization that carries the goods and products that we want to bring to India. There is great enthusiasm about the program and many people are donating their time, resources, and energy to make this happen. Between the four groups, we organized this ongoing health and education program for 25,000 Indian children.

We flew over there carrying bags and bags of vitamins and anti-parasitics. And we organized a health and education training with graphic posters, so that they can understand, because literacy is low in this area. The graphic posters were written in their own language.

Working with teachers, local communities, and families, we actually dispense anti-parasitics, because there is no clean water and almost all the children have worms and other parasites. Giving them the anti-parasitic medicine first, before the vitamins, is necessary or else the vitamins will just support the parasites. It's an ongoing program. Every six weeks we have another team going over to follow up to make sure that the program is continuing, but educating them on how to eat and on personal hygiene. We show them how to obtain clean water, boil it, and wash their hands before they eat.

All the basic things that we take for granted are not available for people who are on such marginal, subsistence-type living. We will be starting another one later this year in another part of India. Our goal is to help 100,000 children.

Are there other projects that you've worked on with the Us Foundation that you're excited about?

We have so many exciting, rewarding, projects; I'm so grateful. One that may be very interesting to your readers is that we have an exchange program, more like a pen pal program, between a school in San Francisco and a school in Bhutan. Bhutan is a country between India and Tibet in the Himalayas. We have an exchange program of letters—pen pal information, email—between sixth graders there and a school in San Francisco.

It's been very wonderful for both sides to get an opportunity to understand another culture, and also being able to articulate and appreciate their own in this exchange. We've had American volunteers go over and take pictures, to share pictures of the students between countries.

The appreciation and understanding of each other's culture is growing. I think that's the first step to a more harmonious way of appreciating and dealing with other cultures.

Are there any final thoughts that you would like to share?

I would like to urge your readers, wherever they are, to make an effort to get involved in their community, in their passion of giving back. It is so rewarding, not only for the community but also for you too.

If they want to get more information, just go to www.UsFoundation.org.

Great. Thanks very much Marilyn Tam, a woman who is making a difference in this world.

Special Note: Marilyn has also written a book called *How to Use What You've Got to Get What You Want*, a fascinating read. You can learn how to succeed in your life's purpose using what you have right now.

A new *book Living the Life of Your Dreams* where she reveals the principles and strategies she and other experts learned and used to achieve a balanced, healthy and joyful life.

- *Visionary Spotlight* -

STEVEN M. HILTON
President and CEO of Conrad N. Hilton Foundation

I was invited to attend the Conrad N. Hilton Foundation annual conference, entitled *"Reaching the Bottom Billion: Is There a Tipping Point?"* I was so overwhelmed with the prospect that this one-day event could provide answers to this huge question. And after a day fully packed with outstanding presenters from all over the world, it was clear that some of these major issues could indeed be addressed.

Steven Hilton shared this vision for where the Hilton Foundation is headed:

The Foundation's future starts NOW– by cultivating an organization with competent people who exercise wise stewardship of the assets entrusted to our care and share a passion in carrying out Conrad and Barron Hilton's philanthropic vision of humanitarianism on a global scale. Following the directive in Conrad Hilton's Last Will, we will continue to alleviate human suffering with an emphasis on children and the work of Catholic Sisters in serving those most in need. And encourage staff to infuse their efforts with the same entrepreneurial spirit that inspired Conrad and Barron Hilton in making Hilton Hotels a world-class hotel company. At the end of the day, we as a dedicated group of individuals can, hopefully, look back and say that our collective

183

efforts "added value" by translating a visionary legacy into practical and effective programs benefiting those most in need.

Addressing the conference in his welcome, Steve said:

The prize ceremony will be a fitting ending to today's symposium which is dedicated to finding new ways to help the bottom billion escape from their seemingly endless poverty trap.

It is also appropriate that we are meeting just three days after the World Poverty Day as we struggle with the dilemma that certain countries continue to fail despite years of increased financial assistance and new attempts at interventions. Just two months ago, the World Bank adjusted the international poverty line from $1.08 to $1.25 a day, immediately increasing our bottom billion to 1.4 billion.

The consensus was that all major donor countries have endorsed the Millennium Development Goals, but unless new strategies are embraced, it's not likely there will be much impact on the 58 countries that continually experience no growth and have the unlucky distinction of being members of the bottom billion.

This is the 13th year the Hilton Prize has been awarded and the tenth Hilton symposium on humanitarian issues. We all remain committed to overcoming the poverty that causes so much suffering in the world, but the problems remain often stubbornly entrenched at the bottom where they afflict the most vulnerable. While statistics mount that point to global triumphs over human suffering, and millions of people continue to realize a better life for themselves and their children, others remain behind, virtually untouched by human progress, falling farther behind and cut off from the mainstream. The very fact that there has been so much progress casts a glaring light on those left behind.

To contact Hilton Foundation, go to www.hiltonfoundation.org.

- *Visionary Spotlight* -

PRESIDENT CHISSANO
Former President of Mozambique

Joaquim Chissano served as the president of Mozambique for 19 years, from 1986 until 2005. In 2006, the United Nations Secretary-General Kofi Annan appointed President Chissano the Special Envoy to Northern Uganda and Southern Sudan to resolve conflict there. He worked with the United Nations Office for the Coordination of Humanitarian Affairs and with the International Criminal Court.

President Chissano spoke in Geneva, Switzerland at the Conrad Hilton Foundation event on the topic of *Reaching The Bottom Billion*. While there, I had an opportunity to ask him about the landmines that still need to be removed his country so that the people can begin to utilize their very fertile ground for raising food crops. I was interested in this topic since a group of patrons made eradicating landmines in Africa one of their major projects: Sir Richard Branson, John Paul DeJoria, Nelson Mandela and his wife, all featured in an earlier chapter. President Chissano confirmed that they continue to work on this crucial issue.

- *Visionary Spotlight* -

KENNETH KAUNDA, Ph.D.
First President of Zambia

Dr. Kenneth Kaunda was the president of Zambia from 1964 to 1991, in its first years as an independent state. I met Dr. Kaunda at a Project Concern International event in San Diego, California. He was being honored by Project Concern as an outstanding leader. Having faced great struggles and overcome many obstacles as the

185

first president of Zambia, he is a man of grace, wisdom, and good humor. It's worth noting that Dr. Kaunda is still very positive about the future.

- *Visionary Spotlight* -

JOANNE WOLF, Ph.D.
Former clinical psychologist, founding member of Kids Korps USA, and one of the authors of the book *Teaching Kids to Care*

In 1995, a visionary group of women came together to show their children how to care about the world. Born into relative privilege, they wanted to give their kids the opportunity to contribute to the well being of others and the welfare of their communities. Inspired by the Peace Corps model, they founded Kids Korps USA.

One of the founding members is Joanne Wolf. I have been fortunate to know Joanne for a few years now. Although her own children are now grown up, Joanne graciously goes about her continued support of the organization. She recently co-wrote a wonderful book called, *Teaching Kids to Care: Nurturing Character and Compassion.* The title says it all.

Kids Korps USA is a 501(c)(3) nonprofit youth volunteer organization that engages young people, ages 5-18, in community service. Each year, thousands of youth freely give their time to engage in community service efforts to make the world a kinder, better, safer place—activities such as: feeding the hungry, building or restoring shelter for the homeless; removing graffiti from public buildings; visiting seniors; and participating in environmental conservation projects.

When California experienced major wildfires not long ago, the kids were there to contribute water and food for the firemen and later honored the workers with a celebration of gratitude. For special American holidays like Thanksgiving and Christmas, they help to feed communities and distribute toys and clothes to other children,

The children of Kids Korps USA are making a tremendous difference through their practical acts of kindness.

For more information, please visit www.kidskorps.org

REBECCA DI DOMENICO
President of the Compton Foundation

Dorothy and Randolph Compton, founders of the Compton Foundation, had been friends and colleagues of mine for over 40 years. Dorothy was the daughter of another visionary, William H. Danforth, Founder, CEO and President of the Ralston Purina Company. Like her father, I would see them annually at Camp Minnewanka, a leadership training conference on Stony Lake, Michigan. Dorothy was known for her enthusiastic early morning swims in the very frigid Lake Michigan.

The Compton Foundation's history began with the vision of Dorothy and Randolph, which they later passed on to their children and now their grandchildren. Shortly after the United States entered World War II, all four of the Compton children served their country. After the untimely death of young John Parker Compton, Dorothy and Randolph established a charitable trust in 1946. The mission was to build a foundation for peace and help prevent another world war.

They believed that world peace would only be possible if the conditions that brought about war could be eliminated. As a result they focused their funding on three key areas: (1) rapid growth of the human population, (2) the destruction of natural resources because of population growth, and (3) increasing consumption levels.

The Trust was converted to a Foundation in 1973, and in 1987 expanded its international focus. Through the leadership of Rebecca Di Domenico, President, Dorothy and Randolph's vision is still alive today and very much a part of the Foundation's legacy. I had an opportunity to talk with Rebecca about the important issues the foundation is addressing. Their mission statement reads,

> "The Compton Foundation focuses most of its grant-making in the areas of **Peace & Security, Environment & Sustainability**, and **Population & Reproductive Health**, with a special emphasis on projects that explore the interconnections between these categories."

Doris Lee: Peace and security is such a big topic, how can you make a difference?

The Compton Foundation funded a Security Manual that will help countries after a war has been concluded, helping them to move forward.

Another important project that the foundation has done is fund the convening of NGOs (non-government organizations) and the military to see how they can work together toward change in the future. One example is the Naval Post in San Francisco in which one of their grantees took on this assignment to evaluate its long-term effectiveness.

Regarding the environment and sustainability, what has the Foundation been able to do in that area?

We continue to follow the information on climate change and some of our awardees are making that their major projects.

Another area is the importance of water and its use, particularly in large city areas. For example, the Klamath Oregon River Project has been supported by a couple of grants that enables them to use this as a pilot project, to try to change the culture and see how business is actually transacted in these areas.

Another project is to bring ranchers together to see if they can restore the usage of some of their unused land. They are brought together to ask the question whether this is a project that will be helpful, not only to the environment but also to them as ranchers.

I visited one of your funded offices out of Tijuana, Mexico. How have those small offices helped educate people on reproduction?

The Foundation is trying to increase reproductive information on an international level. One organization that we co-partner with is Advocates for Youth in which young people from developing countries and their families look at how these decisions in reproduction affect their young people. They take videos and share those with the youth in the United States. These observations enable parents to view reproduction from the standpoint of young people. This project is being carried out in Jamaica, Ethiopia and Nigeria.

The Foundation seeks to foster positive and sustainable models of change in each of our three program areas. We encourage creative collaboration between institutions and/or foundations, and projects that advance human knowledge by connecting theory with practice.

Thank you for your far-reaching, integrative work and for carrying on the vision.

For more information, please visit comptonfoundation.org.

Special Note: The Compton Foundation is committed to arts and culture through their programs, and Rebecca has creatively furthered the Foundation's focus on water, environment and sustainability, peace and security, and population and reproductive health through her imaginative art. She has had numerous exhibits of her artwork throughout the country, including the Denver Art Museum.

RICHARD ENRIGHT
Established nonprofit entities and foundations for individuals and corporations

Richard Enright is a tax attorney with an additional gift—he helps individuals find their talents and start foundations based on those talents. Many years ago I met Dick at the Explorers Club, and I told him I was interested in setting up a foundation—which ended up being called "The American Spirit Foundation." Dick was so helpful in those early stages.

Doris Lee: Dick, why do people want to start non-profit foundations?

Aside from just a charitable motivation, focusing on the tax-side of it, folks will be able to set up a foundation and avoid estate tax. That's the principle reason I've seen for the set-up.

They also have a deep-seated concern about a cause or a need, isn't that the case too?

I have a little different approach. When I start working with people, I generally approach it from the idea of the enlightened self-interest of the charity. Most people I deal with do not have families that they're planning to pass on wealth to, so they're ending up at the end of their life with a large estate or a corporation that they own. When they die, their heirs will be facing a very heavy estate tax, as high as 55%. So I work out a program for them where they would avoid that estate tax.

As I start talking to people who have formed these corporations, we discover what motivated them to start their corporations in the first place. We find out that they didn't start the corporations just to make money. When you dig deep enough and listen long enough, you can find a genuine charitable purpose that motivates all people.

Is it hard to get a non-profit foundation?

No, it only costs a few hundred dollars to file the application with the IRS; application Form 1023. One can get publication #577 from the government for free, which describes it all.

But it's a different story running a charity. If an individual sets up a charity, it's called a Private Foundation. It has severe rules on how it can be run, what the individual can take out of it, and it's full of pitfalls. The preferable way is to establish a "private charitable interest" within a larger charity.

For example, a person could say that they want to set up a program to do some form of evangelism in California. A better way is to set up a new charity. I'd tell them to set up a program first as an endowment, like a program under the American Spirit Foundation for example. They could run that, and if they start getting into large amounts of money, then you can split it off.

But you need a management team, and you need tax advice. That's what big community organizations do, like the New York Community Trust. They allow you to have a bank account within their organization, and you work under their tax ruling.

It's like having an umbrella. As a matter of fact, my American Spirit Foundation was first founded under another foundation. I have felt much more secure knowing that I can pick up the phone, call you, and you can give me advice as an attorney, which is extremely helpful. Is there anything else that you'd like to add, Dick?

I certainly want to encourage people to look at this as a way of dealing with their estate. And again, find somebody who can understand what you're trying to accomplish, someone who can explain the joy of giving and the satisfaction that comes in the latter part of life.

Mr. Brewster Kopp, who was Assistant Secretary of the Army, started the Stewardship Foundation in Boston. They provide free management services and allow the use of their organization without charge for what we call component funds.

You've done a great deal with your American Spirit Foundation, and I wish it all the success too.

When you and I talked with a man who had made several millions of dollars on the stock market, he told us he felt that his foundation was giving him more satisfaction than anything he had done in his life.

That's true for my brother also. My brother was one of the founders of Rockwell. He's 93 years old, and he says he's getting more joy out of founding organizations and helping with charitable groups.

How can people get in touch with you?

On a private basis, people can email me at dseree@bellsouth.net.

Good to talk with you Dick. Thank you.

Entrepreneurs in Collaboration with Non-Profits

BRENDON BURCHARD
International speaker and author of *Life's Golden Ticket;* combines partnerships of corporate and non-profits

I have continued my personal education by attending conferences that are productive for learning how to get the stories of these people I have interviewed out into the world. One of the best training programs I have found is led by Brendon Burchard. In this interview, he shares some of his newly discovered wisdom.

Doris Lee: What's amazing, Brendon, is that you're a young man who wrote a book after you had a near-death experience. That seems to have pushed you to search for the meaning of life earlier than most people.

Motivated by what you've learned, you have forged a new approach for promoting transformational books and services. You take corporations and co-partner with non-profit foundations. How is this different from any other approach that you've seen?

Brendon Burchard: What's different is the ability to reach millions of people more quickly with their message, brand, product, or business. Many people struggle for years to get their message out. What I've discovered with what I call the *"partnership model"* is that it allows us to not have to

193

do everything on our own. You ask most entrepreneurs, "Why aren't you succeeding?" They all say the same thing: "I'm not doing as well as I could in my business because either, a) I'm trying to do it all by myself, or b) I can't reach enough people to get enough customers."

I was in the same boat. I was trying to do everything myself. I couldn't reach anybody, and here I was launching a new part of my business based on my book *Life's Golden Ticket*. I thought, there must be a way to get my message out in a quicker, more effective way to make a greater difference in the world.

Most people start by trying to do it on their own, building from scratch. I said, that's a crazy model that will take decades. What I figured out with the partnership model was that I could partner with major non-profits and Fortune 500 companies who where already doing things that were similar to me and already trying to reach a demographic, an audience, that I was also trying to reach. So, if I could just partner with them in a way where everybody wins, then I win. That would be something magical.

What's different about it is this isn't some "get rich quick" strategy or marketing ploy. This is a whole different model of working in the world, in which I teach you to partner with other organizations so you can accomplish your goals.

You have three non-profits that you consistently work with: Kiwanis, Junior Achievement, and the YMCA. When you go to other companies, how do you pitch your idea? And what companies can you pitch to these days when the market is so tight?

I figure out a product, a program, or a promotion; those are the three things. I say, who's interested in what I'm doing

194

or trying to reach the demographic I'm trying to reach? I look for corporations, for example, who can become corporate sponsors. If I'm going to launch a book, I'll find a corporation who will help sponsor my book tour or a non-profit that will allow me to speak on all their fundraising stages.

Do partnerships and sponsorships still work in a down economy? The answer is absolutely, and here's why: Sponsorship in the corporate world is a phenomenon that happens in their marketing departments. Do their marketing departments get cut in down times? Yes, sometimes, but they've realized that what keeps the business going is marketing. The worst thing you could do as a business is stop marketing when the economy goes down because then there are no new clients coming into the business. They know that sponsorship is one of the most effective ways of doing that.

It's not so much that they're tighter on money; it's that they're smarter with money. Every corporation that is going to sponsor or partner with you is essentially asking two questions:

1. Does this product, program, or promotion align with our strategic priorities? In other words, does it align with **what** we've decided are the big things we have to do this year in the marketplace?

2. Does it align with our marketing initiatives? Does it align with **how** we're going about pulling in new clients, gaining greater awareness or getting more sales?

If you can come up with a project, program, or promotion that aligns with a company's strategic priorities and marketing initiatives—and they could see the alignment—

they could say there's a return on investment and doing this is going to get new business or generate more awareness. It becomes an easy yes for them.

Yes, in a down economy it's more challenging, but the only reason is because people are more fearful to let that money go. Because they're more fearful, they're just watching opportunities more closely, so you have to be really aligned with them. It has to be very clear what the return on investment is. It has to have what I call the *manageability factor*. Whatever you're doing with a partner has to be very manageable. It has to be easy for them to understand and do because they want to win, not take risks.

You're saying make it simple, but how do you do that?

It's the old answer of doing your homework. It's the most important thing in all partnerships. If I'm going to partner with a non-profit or a Fortune 500 company, I need to know a lot of information about them.

I need to know, how do they already serve their clients, and is my idea going to make it more difficult or easy for them to do that? There are basically ten questions we ask in this partnership model about whether or not it's going to be something they're really attracted to or interested in.

The problem with the partnership model for most people when they start is they think they have to go into these relationships knowing all the answers. You have to do your homework on these companies, but then when you get on the phone, it's a collaborative endeavor, because you don't know what's going on inside the halls of that corporation or that non-profit.

You can do as much research as you can, but once you get somebody on the phone you might find out there's lots of politics or no politics, there's lot of money or no money, or that they're interested in working with other people or not. What's important is that it's not about having all the right answers. It's about going in with a collaborative mindset that says, "I understand that the number one rule in business, in partnerships, is that people always support what they create." You're not coming with the answer but with the idea—and then fleshing it out *with* them. Now they're part of the process, now they're excited about it. **People always support what they create.**

How do you make a good pitch? You might have a lot of good ideas, but you have to get to it quickly and succinctly.

Yes. Make it compelling. A pitch is always the same in the partnership model. When you're going to approach a partner, whether a non-profit promotional partner, a Fortune 500 company, or a corporate sponsor that's actually giving you cash, the outline of that pitch is essentially the same. It starts with:

1. "Here's what I'm doing and here's why it aligns with you."

You start with yourself, saying what you're doing rather than what you've read about them?

Yes. You start off with a very quick summary of what you're up to in literally two to three sentences.

2. Flesh out the project a little bit more, "Here's *why* I'm contacting you. Here are the *benefits* you would get by becoming involved in this."

You would know the benefits upfront?

Absolutely. You think, okay, this is going to help them create a greater affinity with this audience, create better customer loyalty, spread their message, reach a new demographic, or help them get this type of awareness in the media.

If you think about it as a partner, here's what they want to see. They want a letter that says, *I'm doing this, it totally fits with me, and I'm going to get tons of benefits by being involved.* The next section is, *here's what we would need and what we're requesting. What we request is for you to be the sponsor of this project, tour, or promotion, and that would require a phone conversation between you and me to figure out how to make it work.*

The whole pitch these days is incredibly short. It's one page covering these points. The key today, because of the down economy is, you're not selling the sponsorship or the partnership in the pitch letter or the pitch call. *You're selling the live meeting.* When you have a live meeting, then it's about really fleshing things out. The live meeting is so important, because in a down economy, trust is so important. They need to look you in the eye and believe in you and your project. Salespeople know that a live meeting is a hundred times better than over the phone, as long as you're not ugly and have smelly breath.

You don't really make the pitch through a letter?

If it's a letter, it's one page. If it's a pitch call, it's a short call to get the meeting and get them excited. In some cases, they may say, "This sounds great, send me something." You can send them a summary of the call and more points or a full proposal, depending on how complete you are in terms of knowing what you want to do with them.

I still recommend today, though, in the down economy to get the meeting with somebody. Flesh out some ideas with them, already have your proposal 70% done in your mind, but then go back after the meeting and incorporate everything they said. Put that into the proposal and send that off to them for approval.

Partnerships have been around, but you're doing it in a different way. You've brought non-profits and for-profits together. Do you have to have the non-profits? Is this part of your personal philosophy, or does this make good business?

Great question. I think it's both, Doris. It's definitely part of my personal philosophy. All of my life I volunteered, and I have a big heart for giving back. Something that's always driven me is how can I make a greater difference in the world.

I thought, as I grow my business, I don't want to be one of those people who decide to give some money away at the end of my life to some foundation. I want to see the difference in the world now, and I think my generation really speaks to that. Let's not just throw our money into something that we can't see when we're dead. I think that really drove me.

The reality is, can you get corporate sponsorships for your projects, dreams, and promotions without non-profit partners involved? Absolutely, you can. Is it easier with a non-profit involved, and does it make a greater difference? Absolutely.

If a corporation is going to sponsor your small business, event, product launch, or promotion, they get excited if it really aligns with them, and that's all great. But if that audience is a large non-profit with the demographic they're trying to reach anyway, then the sponsor is like, "Oh, this is perfect." It basically gives you more of a base, more of a platform to work from.

Sure. It's like if you go to SC Johnson, which has a strong interest in wildlife. If you then go to Conservation International, for example, which is a non-profit, then you are helping sponsor a project that they were involved in. They already have a toe in the door anyhow because they feel those same things are important. Is that correct?

Yes. Every major corporation, Fortune 500 company, wants to make a positive impact or at the very least want to be perceived as someone who's making a positive impact. Basically, I help partner them with non-profits and projects to help them raise funds and awareness. It also helps that corporation get their message, products, and services out. By tying them together, it's a win-win-win situation.

I basically show a triangle at some of my partnership seminars where I say, "Here's you, here's the non-profit, and here's a Fortune 500 company. All you have to do is figure out a way to triangulate a project where everybody wins. Suddenly that sponsor and that non-profit are going to help you reach millions of people, and everybody is going to win."

The last time you did a teleseminar, Brendon, I noticed that you had an international number to call. Now we're dealing with an international clientele.

People are responding to the partnership model worldwide. They're saying there is a different way of doing business, and that different way is by doing things together and doing well together.

200

What do you see as your next challenge?

My next challenge is a program I call the Global Partnership Summit. It's bringing together the senior leaders of Fortune 500 companies, the top 250 non-profit organizations, the top 250 foundations in the world, and putting them all in a room with 500 social entrepreneurs and asking them explicitly: How can we partner together to address some of the greater challenges our world is facing?

My greatest challenge right now is getting more people to partner together to handle the challenges of the world. You have hundreds of non-profits who are doing the same exact thing, but they don't even know about each other and have never really combined efforts. Everyone wants to start their own foundation and to make a difference, and that's wonderful. The challenge is seeing that sometimes the best way to make a difference is to support a cause that is already there and has an infrastructure.

How can we leverage each other's resources, assets, infrastructure, clientele, consumers, and staff members to address these issues of poverty, homelessness, water, and sustainability?

It's a question I will always ask, for the rest of my life. When I see a problem, I ask, "How can we get a whole lot of people, different partners, involved in solving that problem?" The world is an interesting place right now. There is a lot of fear and worry, but there is also a lot of need. In times of great need, crisis, and fear, it's even more important to get groups to ask the simple question of what can we do together to address this.

Right now I think the real influences of our society, whether they know it or not, are following the partnership model. The partnership model is so powerful because it's saying to entrepreneurs, people like myself and like you who aren't huge companies, we *can* partner with these huge companies. We're not huge non-profits, but we can partner with them in ways that get great messages out into the world. Obviously, we can do it in a way that grows our business and generates revenue, but at the end of the day it's about what message we are all perpetuating.

I would just encourage anybody who happens to read this just to think about this one question: *How can I address the number one problem in my business, community, or the world that I'm passionate about by bringing in more partners, a non-profit, or a Fortune 500 company to assist with this?* When you triangulate that kind of firepower, you will light the world.

How can people contact you, Brendon?

People can go to PartnershipSeminar.com or to my general website BrendonBurchard.com and find out more information about our events, causes, or what we're trying to fight for.

Thank you, Doris. I appreciate you interviewing so many influential people and helping them share their message. Thank you for the opportunity.

TOM PETERS
World Wide Leadership Management Consultant

I have known Tom Peters for many years as an exceptionally wise person, so I was looking forward to his views on today's financial situation. As this book is being compiled and written, we're in the midst of a financial crisis. Most companies are saying they just don't have the money to do what they've done in the past. Non-profit foundations are saying that fundraising is very difficult, and they too can't do what they've done in other years. And social entrepreneurs are left using their own money exclusively. It is the perfect time for the perspective of a visionary.

Doris Lee: Tom, you've been a master, along with Peter Drucker, of speaking out on leadership. Could you provide some insight that would help people to have some hope for the future of their organizations and companies? Are there some clear guidelines?

Tom Peters: First, I would offer a few guidelines...

Guideline #1: Transparency and straightforwardness.

For example, if you are running a non-profit, it is true that the money is not going to come in at the level that it's come in the past, and there is a good chance that it might not come in at that level for two to five years.

Self-delusion is not a good thing, and I don't mean being over-pessimistic, but I do mean understanding the pickle we're in and sharing that information in particular with your staff.

Guideline #2: Have decency in all you do.

There are any number of companies, non-profits, governmental organizations, and so on that are in a budgetary situation where they have to let people go, cut back their hours, or cut back their salaries in general. There is utterly no reason why that can't be done with decency. I have written something that I have called "The Decent Organization and The Thoughtful Organization." It's about people who move a little bit more gently in the world.

Guideline #3: Experiment with new programs and new ideas.

I remember years ago when there was a huge change in the tax policy in California and the community college budgets were hit very badly. After the screaming and the shouting were over, the smartest of the community college presidents reshaped the curricula so that the community colleges were far more responsive to the local community than they had been in the past.

I don't want to put on rose-colored glasses, but I do believe that there is significant opportunity for reshaping programs and missions. It's not about getting more bang for the buck. It's about absolutely reforming what you do have—creating new projects and looking at the entire mission of the institution in a new way. That would probably be at the top of my list. There's a chance that, four years from now, the organization could look very different than it does today and be exceptionally effective.

The classic case-in-point that you have addressed are the social entrepreneurs. A lot of them do amazing things with astonishingly small budgets. They do it because they depend on their users, their customers…and they depend on imagination. Big budgets are, more often than not, disadvantageous rather than advantageous.

Okay, some may have a little trouble understanding that right now.

There's a guy I used to work with at Digital Equipment, and I remember him once saying, "I've never seen a project being done by 500 people that couldn't be done better by 50 people." And I absolutely believe that.

One last point is this…

Guideline #4: Fully utilize the new tools of the Internet.

As was evidenced by Mr. Obama's presidential campaign, the ability to build community, build support, and get feedback is matchless—MyBarackObama.com was just an extraordinary happening.

Why do you think your co-worker at Digital Equipment suggested the view that it was easier to work with the 50 than the 500?

The advantage is less bureaucracy, more focus, and aiming at the stuff that's important.

Could you mention some of the smaller organizations that are good examples?

Organizations in my little town of 3,000 people, like the daycare salaries. It's scholarships for kids who don't have the money to buy equipment to use at the local hockey rink. Those are the kinds of things I'm talking about.

As I go around the country, I see outstanding projects that are having trouble connecting with the people that could fund them. For example, there's a group in Oklahoma that is working on alternative energy methods, but they can't get through to the people for fundraising.

I'd say a couple things, first is you can't believe in the tooth fairy. The reality is that when the price of gas is $1.70, there's a lot less money available—even if we were in good times—than there will be when the price of gas is $4.50.

Even though we all complain about it when the price of gas goes up higher, right?

Exactly. When the price of gas goes up to $4.50 that means the venture capitalists have money to support one of these programs. When it goes back down to $1.70, the money dries up overnight.

On the other hand, the sorts of things that are entirely possible are working with a local utility or a community to raise money so that people can insulate their pipes. In cold climates, like where I live in Vermont, you can raise money and awareness relative to putting weather stripping around the door. Everybody laughed at Obama when he said keep your tire pressures at what they're supposed to be. The truth of the matter is there are dozens, if not hundreds, of things that are either free or cost a relatively small amount of money. You can be the first on your block to change your bulbs instead of the last one on your block.

How do you get to people like President Obama, who are obviously overwhelmed with the challenges?

That doesn't interest me in the least. There are people who do it, good for them. But I'm interested in smaller units where you can make a *specific* difference. I worked like hell for Obama, my wife did too, and that's a terrific thing. However, I am not interested in large-scale stuff. I will leave that to my betters.

During the election I kept giving $10 every week to the Obama campaign. I was part of the process, but I would rather work on insulating pipes in Brooklyn.

Because you can do something about insulating pipes.

206

Absolutely. Over the long haul, it is the people who insulate their pipes and meet in associations with other people who insulate their pipes that fundamentally create the groundswell that makes the change happen.

I believe that it's more likely to happen under Mr. Obama than Mr. Bush, but the reality is, until "the people" are in favor of it, no president can do a lot about it. Presidents don't make changes fundamentally unless the nation is ready for it.

Again, I would stick with engagement in the local community. You can be with your friends and you can make a difference that's measurable. And if you want to go on and be the head of a state chapter or something like that, I will applaud you until the proverbial cows come home.

Remember that Mr. Obama started as a community organizer in a fairly small sphere of influence. I remember before the election I happened to be giving a speech in Atlanta, and on the way out of town I stopped by Ebenezer Baptist Church. Every time I do, I shake my head. Martin Luther King Jr. started out in one of the smallest churches known to human kind.

I stand by the Margaret Mead quote that says, "Never doubt that a small group of thoughtful, committed citizens can change the world. Indeed, it is the only thing that ever has." It's true. Who would have thought that little Ebenezer Baptist Church, 50 years later, would lead to an African-American President?

I'm grateful to you for your time, Tom. I look forward to meeting you somewhere along the trail.

207

CONRAD PREBYS
Successful Businessman and Philanthropist

Military: ROTC; Army service: 1956-57

Career: Industrial relations manager; pizzeria owner. Prebys arrived in San Diego in 1965 from a blue-collar Indiana steel mill town with $500 and the shirt on his back. He is now founder of Progress Construction and Management Company in San Diego and now has "between 6,000 and 7,000" rental units countywide. Prebys has grown to be one of our county's largest landlords.

Prebys, in 2007, donated $10.1 million to revamp the polar bear plunge and elephant care center. Later, he gave $15 million to the **San Diego Zoo** to renovate its big cat and koala exhibits.

In addition, Mr. Prebys has donated to UCSD's new Music Center and Concert Hall, Sanford-Burnham Medical Research Institute's Center for Chemical Genomics, The Old Globe's theater center, the Scripps Mercy Hospital trauma center, an endowed chair at Salk and on numerous checks to other local charities.

Conrad Prebys recently donated $45 million to San Diego-based **Scripps Health** to support construction of a $456 million cardiology center at Scripps Memorial Hospital in La Jolla. This is the largest gift in Scripps' history. "This gift is huge," said Scripps CEO Chris Van Gorder. "It will allow us to build...the largest and strongest cardiovascular program in the West." Conrad explains his approach to philanthropy in an article from Scripps Memorial Hospital News website:

"I've embraced Andrew Carnegie's philosophy that excess wealth is a sacred trust that one should

contribute for the good of the community during one's lifetime. I liken myself to Scrooge who wakes up on Christmas morning and discovers it's not too late to acquire the joy of giving. San Diego is where I enjoyed my prosperity, and this is where I plan to give to the community that enabled me to do so well."

He attributes any success he's had to his mom, who believed in and instilled confidence in him since he was young.

"If you are interested in contributing, just put your foot in the water and experience the joy of giving. You don't know what you've been missing. If you don't have funds, give of your time."

One leader said:

"I've found that the more generous I am, the more I get in return, and the more I get in return, the more generous I am."

T. Boone Pickens,
American Oil and Natural Gas Magnate

"The most important and beautiful gift one human being can give to another is, in some way, to make life a little better to live."

– **Ellen Browning Scripps**, Founder Scripps Memorial Hospital/Scripps Metabolic Clinic, 1924

Visionary Reflection on...

Purpose

Having a strong sense of purpose—feeling connected to our higher reason for being—is an incredibly fulfilling and motivating experience. On the other hand, losing touch with our purpose can be very painful. Experiencing life as meaningful and purposeful often involves being of service in the world in some way. Today, write down on a piece of paper what your purpose is at this stage of your life. What connects you to your reason for being? And if you're feeling out of touch with your purpose, let your imagination soar...imagine what *could* ignite the flame of purpose for you if you put some attention there.

CHAPTER 10

Top to Bottom:
Doris Lee with Larry King

CHAPTER 10

The Media
Past, Present & Future

• • • • • • • • • • • • • • • • •

LARRY KING
Host of *Larry King Live*, Emmy Award-winning interviewer of
40,000 people over more than 50 years on television

Larry King was born in Brooklyn, New York and is known all over the world as the host of *Larry King Live*, which aired its final show on December 16, 2010.

Larry's awards and honors are many. He has been inducted into the Broadcasters' Hall of Fame, won two Peabody Awards, ten Cable ACE Awards, and an Emmy Award. He is also a recipient of the prestigious Alan H. Neuharth Award for Excellence in Journalism. In addition to interviewing thousands of the most influential people in the world, Larry has made cameo appearances in scores of TV shows and movies, including *Shrek 2* (which I'm sure his kids loved). He has also authored multiple books, including the recent book, *My Remarkable Journey*.

Larry's generosity is far-reaching and includes founding the Larry King Cardiac Foundation, which has raised millions for lifesaving procedures for needy children and adults. He also established the Million Dollar Journalism Scholarship for students from disadvantaged backgrounds.

Larry is married to singer-actress Shawn Southwick King and is the father of five children and one stepchild.

The following interview was done shortly before *Larry King Live* aired its final show.

Doris Lee: Larry, you are incredible. How did you get started doing all this?

Larry King: It's all I ever wanted to do. When I was a little kid, my earliest memory of being five or six years old was listening to the radio and wanting to do what the announcer did. I don't know why. I thought for a while I'd be a comedian, because I liked to tell funny things and would imitate radio people and go watch radio shows.

My father died when I was nine, so I graduated from high school but didn't go to college because I had to help my mother. One day I had an opportunity to go down to Miami so I went around, knocked on doors, and got into a small radio station. I thought I'd be a sportscaster, and that was May 1957.

I got into interviewing a couple of years later when a restaurant wanted a show to come out every day at the restaurant. I would go there, do interviews, and didn't prepare because we didn't know who would be coming in. One day Bobby Darren walked in...and Jimmy Hoffa. I got used to interviewing famous people and not-so-famous people.

I loved it, I loved asking questions—I still do—and that was 51 years ago. I had no idea that I'd be on worldwide television. I was on the radio for two years and then got a television show, so I always did both TV and Radio.

Radio and TV at the same time?

Yes. I did one radio show and one television show. I left radio in 1995. Although my television show is simulcast now, I had no idea there would be a network, satellites, or anything like that. My dream was to be a broadcaster and that part of the dream has totally come true.

Who inspired you when you were younger?

I was affected a lot by Arthur Godfrey who was a great radio broadcaster. Later, I got to know him very well. Fred Barber who was the announcer for the Dodgers was a mentor; I worked with him later on. I was a great admirer of Mike Wallace who became one of my best friends.

I have a lot of heroes, but I was taught early on by Arthur Godfrey who told me something that has remained with me a long time. He said, "The only secret in this business is that there's no secret," ...which is just to be yourself. People are going to like you or not like you. Just don't be afraid to be yourself. A lot of people are; they think that when that light goes on they have to be somebody different, they have to sound different or look different. I've never thought that in my life, so that's a bit of advice I've always carried with me.

While I had mentors and people I admired a great deal, I have imitated no one. I'm just me.

You always seem so cool and your program runs so smoothly. What do you attribute that to?

That's easy to answer. It's an old joke that it's not brain surgery. I have never looked at this as earthshaking or world affecting. I may have had an effect on politics or world events by simply asking questions and eliciting answers—that may have affected people in how they voted or how they thought—but I never thought about it.

I go on the air to ask good questions, keep them short, and let it transform from me to the viewer or the listener. I'm a conduit, but it isn't that big a deal. It's hard to say it, but it's only television. I'm no different before the show than when the show is on.

How do you know when you have hit one out of the ballpark, so to speak, one that you are really excited about, because you felt you asked questions that enabled people to tell their story well?

That's intuitive. Whether it's Ross Perot saying, "If you put me on the ballot, I'll run in every state," Malcolm X describing what it's like to be a young black boy growing up in Massachusetts, or Martin Luther King Jr. talking about his life, it's an intuitive thing. You know when you've really scored one, but it's only as good as that day's show. You've got another show to do the next day.

I have always had a sense of pace, this is natural to me. I know how to keep a show moving, I know how to interrupt when you have to interrupt. I'm not much better now than I was when I started; I'm still the same person. I've got more experience under my belt, but I'm basically the same guy.

How do you handle it when two of your guests are fighting with one another on issues?

That's the easiest, you just provoke it. You make sure that each gets the same amount of time to be heard, that one person doesn't get an edge over another. You interrupt if one person is controlling the conversation too much. You can keep the fireworks going, and you do that by interjecting at just the right time.

215

Sometimes you just sit back and let them go. You don't have to be present all the time, it's just a feeling, but those are the easiest shows to do when two people are in conflict.

When you're bringing two or more people together, is it your intent to get people with different views?

The producers book the show. I've never had an agenda in my life. I've never gone on the air saying, "Boy, I'm going to get a fight tonight, or I'm going to learn this tonight." If people disagree with something, I'm going to go with it. Do I know what to expect? No. Do I want to know what their answer is going to be? No. Do I want them pre-interviewed? No, I want to be surprised.

Obviously, if one person is for McCain and one person is for Obama, you know they're going to have difficulty, but they may have types of personalities that are not conflicting. In other words, they're reasoned, they don't interrupt each other, they have solid opinions on both sides and respect the other side. Or you could have two volatile people.

I don't know how it's going to go; I take it where it goes.

Do you feel that the last presidential campaign went too long?

Yes, but it is what it is. There's never been a campaign or an election like that one (referring to Hillary Clinton and President Barack Obama), and we've never had a black challenge a woman. It seemed to go on endlessly.

Larry, you've interviewed many world leaders and other people who we would consider visionaries. Have you found some common threads that run through their lives?

Yes. All visionaries, just by the nature of the word, see tomorrow pretty well. And if they're wrong, they don't let that hurt them or set them back. That's a common trait. One can be more outspoken than another, one can be shy, one can be outlandish, but they all have an ingredient, which is they look *forward*. They tend not to look back. They tend not to have regrets. They're visionary in that they see better than other people do and see tomorrow pretty well.

My friend Edward Bennett Williams is one of the smartest men I ever knew. I asked him if he was optimistic or pessimistic, and he said, "Of course I'm pessimistic, I'm smart." Pessimism can be a good thing; you can take a negative and make it a positive.

What I've learned is that persistence pays off. You know Woody Allen says 90% of success is showing up, and in part that's true—just to be there, to be in the hunt. One thing I love about what I do is I get up and go there every day. I like the hunt and visionaries like the hunt.

Kurt Krikorian is a good friend of mine. He's 91 years old, he is worth I think $20 billion, and he's out buying stock tomorrow. He's out thinking about Ford, General Motors, all these hotels in Vegas and where that's going. When I have lunch with him, I'm dazzled by his mind. He never thinks, "I'm 91 years old, why am I doing this?" He's doing it because that's him.

Is that a game some men and probably some women play?

Ted Turner told me once it could be toothpicks. Do I have more toothpicks than you? It happens to be dollars for businesses, but it could be the game of toothpicks. It's striving to win. Yes, it is a game. Life is so short and it's partially all a game. I want to do better than you.

Mel Brooks once said, "If you fall down a manhole, it's hysterically funny. If I cut my finger, it's a tragedy."

You said you thought you wanted to be a comedian.

Originally, because I'm funny. When I do speeches, and I do a lot of speeches, I always do funny stuff. I try to make people laugh, and a lot of people have told me I should have been a comedian. In fact, the biggest kick I get is when I go in front of a room and make them laugh, because that's an "I love you" from a crowd. There's nothing like that, and you can't fake it.

I recently heard you tell a story about going to Ted Turner's Montana ranch. Would you share that?

I went to his ranch, and we were driving around one night in a Range Rover. We stopped, it was very dark and there were about 800 buffalo surrounding us. We're sitting there in the car. and he says the two words that you never want to hear, which are, 'I'm lost.'

"You're lost, wonderful."

He says, "There are three ways we can handle this: We could sleep in this car all night with the buffalo around us; we could drive around aimlessly, or we could follow the stars." Since he was the captain of the ship, we followed the stars and got home.

It wasn't funny at the time, now in telling it, it's funny. This great world figure who has captained ships and won races is telling me we're lost...at midnight with buffalo looking at us around the car.

Buffalo** **are** **huge creatures.

They are huge, and their eyes at night are blue. They're staring, and I'm wondering if I'm their next meal, because I don't know about buffalo. There's no buffalo walking down the street in Brooklyn. But that's one of the things I admire about Ted, he wasn't going to look at that as a negative. He was going to figure it out.

He figured out options before he told you he was lost.

He's the greatest person I've ever worked for. Being around him, he's an intuitive. CNN started when he got into a little Toyota, in Atlanta. He turned on the radio and the announcer said, "You're listening to WGST—all news, all the time."

He said, why can't that work on television? He didn't take any trial agendas, he didn't do any pre-things; he just started it. That's what makes Ted who he is. You always get an answer from him; he never says, "I'll get back to you." If you went to him with a question, he'd answer it. He never lied, and his handshake was worth it.

Isn't that great in the long run, being really honest, being sincere?

It's the hardest thing to be. The hardest thing to say in the human language, for me, is to say no. But Ted can say no and make you feel good. You can say to Ted, "How do I look?"

"Not so good."

Don't ask him if it's borderline.

219

If you're a little worried, don't ask him, because he will give you a direct answer. He's a beautiful man. He was the best man at my wedding, and Al Pacino did the reading of the Cumming's poem. Yes, that was some day.

It sounds like an unforgettable day. On a different note, do you have a cardiac foundation?

Yes, the Larry King Cardiac Foundation. I had heart surgery back in 1987. After it, someone asked me how much it cost, and I had no idea, because I was insured. I got to thinking about the people that aren't insured, so we started this foundation.

My son runs it, my wife is Chairman, and we help people who can't afford it. We've done hundreds and hundreds of procedures, from heart surgery to bypass to quadruple. We give prescriptions to children, and we work with hospitals all across America.

It's the proudest thing I do, when I call somebody up and tell them we're going to do their surgery and then call them back afterwards and compliment them on how well they've done. There's no bigger kick than saving a life.

Are there some visionaries you'd like to interview that you haven't had a chance to yet?

I'd like to interview Castro; he's a visionary of a different kind. Osama bin Laden, I wouldn't call him a visionary, but I'd call him a man who affected the whole world. I don't know any journalist who wouldn't want to interview Osama bin Laden.

Then I'd like to do people on the forefront of health. We need to do more about the surgeons with new concepts in surgery, more philosophers, and more people who by their writings have changed things. If I had to pick one person, though, it would be Castro, because no one has led a country longer. He retired after 50 some odd years.

Why do you have this passion for baseball?

Baseball is my favorite thing in life. It's my passion and it has been since I was a child. I'll go again tomorrow night, I take the whole family. The kids love it, my boys play Little League. I'm a Dodgers fan, and I get no bigger kick.

Baseball is an intriguing game. Every time I go to a game, I see something I hadn't seen before. I learn something I didn't know before. It's a wondrous game to me. If you start with it in childhood, you can get two guys talking baseball and they can go for hours.

I was in Cuba and I passed this corner, a big lot with hundreds of people in it. I asked my guide, "What is that?" He said, "That's our baseball lot." He said that people come there every day just to talk baseball. There's nothing like it, it's a thinking man's game.

It's been a great delight to talk with you. Thanks for your time, Larry.

Although Larry left *Larry King Live*, after a period of time, he went on to do another show, *Larry King Now*, on RT TV, weekdays at 9PM and 11PM. He was featured interviewing Bonnie Raitt at the Del Mar Paddock and Turf Club on September 28, 2013.

- Visionary Spotlight -

RICHARD PARSONS

Chairman of Citigroup, former Chairman and CEO of Time Warner, Inc.

Dick Parsons is somebody that I have always admired for his foresight in being able to look to the future and see the broader picture. We met at the Trumpet Awards in Atlanta where he was being honored and had a brief conversation about "being relevant" in the work we do and the way we involve ourselves in the world at large. Here is what Dick had to say about being relevant:

"Being relevant is important. It means that you are doing something that positively affects your community and the country in which you live. Maybe you have skills as an auto mechanic or have good computer skills or are a sales person. But if you are not doing something that is a part of the larger picture, then to what end? Being relevant means going further than just self-gratification."

BOB SAFIAN
Editor of *Fast Company Magazine,* as well as Fast Company online

Bob Safian is editor and managing director of the award-winning monthly business magazine *Fast Company.* He oversees all editorial operations, in print and online, and plays a key role in guiding the magazine's advertising, marketing, and circulation efforts. Bob came to *Fast Company* in 2007 from *Fortune,* where he served as executive editor. Prior to that, he was an executive editor at *Time* and headed *Money* as its managing editor for six years.

Doris Lee: With your cutting-edge magazine, Bob, how do you pick the people you feature in your articles?

Bob Safian: What we're trying to do is to encapsulate the spirit of change that is part of a progressive business and where it is moving in the future. We try to identify individuals whose actions have the ability to inspire other people's activities to move forward.

We talk about fast companies and what we mean by fast companies. The irony is that when I talk to groups of people, I ask them "Is your company a fast company?" Almost every group says, "No." Almost everyone thinks their own companies are not fast moving, including the CEOs of companies that you might think of as innovative.

Can you give us a few examples?

Companies like a Nike, IBM, Intel or Cisco may not necessarily describe their company as fast, because they're conscious of the things within their own enterprise that don't work as well as they would like them to.

What we try to do is to encourage people to make *their* part of the company the fast part. What that means is being willing to take risks and to question the existing way that a business operates. It often happens when you start a new job, you immediately can see the things that don't make sense. You step in and try to point out what they should change, saying, "Maybe we should think about this differently." After you've been some place for a while, it can be very hard to see those same things; you get so close to it.

What we're trying to do is to encourage people to think differently about how they do things. We use the expression "thinking outside the box" and most of the time people are just thinking in a bigger box. When we choose people to write about in the magazine, we're thinking about people who may be inspiring. I'm going to give you an unexpected example.

In a recent issue, we wrote a story about the actor Ashton Kutcher. He has built an extremely robust following on Twitter, Facebook, and other social media that he is using to help market other large brands; Nestle, Kellogg, and so on. The subtext of the story is that if this guy can figure out how to work with new technology and social media, then so can you. If he can figure out how to spend time in Silicon Valley and get to know the right people and understand how it works, then you can do it too.

What he's really trying to do is remake the model of what people think of as an entertainment and an advertising company. He's coming from the perspective that the way Hollywood works now is under threat. The kinds of products that they have produced have made a lot of money, but they may not be able to make money in the same way because of changing distribution.

Ashton isn't beholden to the old model. He hasn't spent 30 years embedded in it. Why is it that Nestle can't go and spend two years on its own figuring out social media but Ashton Kutcher can? It has something to do with his age, who he is, and what he can then bring to them as a different perspective.

I already have people who are using their lists to get the word out, which is another form of what Ashton's doing. Beyond making money, it's a new form of making a contribution to the world, of sharing visionary perspectives through social media streams.

In the USA, our bottom line has been our Gross National Product. I just came back from the country of Bhutan, high in the Himalayas, where their bottom line is Gross National Happiness, and I see the two cultures somewhat conflicting at times.

I think our lives are more complicated here, and sometimes that leads to different things. I think there are people who are happy and contented here, but you don't always necessarily find them in the halls of power in business.

I'll offer you another character, a different kind of leader that we wrote about a few months ago, a kid named Chris Hughes. Chris Hughes was one of the founders of Facebook, and he went on to help build the online arm for Barack Obama's presidential campaign. He's a young guy in his twenties. You'd look at him and think that he's a teenager, and yet he has had a critical impact on two very successful new institutions, new brands. Although he works with technology in building these sites, he's not really a technologist. His particular talent and vision is about understanding how people connect with each other—understanding the passion points and the critical things that make people really want to communicate with each other.

What a great example!

Is he in it for the money? Not really. In fact, he was asked to join the Administration when Obama won the election, and he chose not to. He is working on new projects, trying to find the next way that he can advance this cause of meaningful communications between people.

So for him, it's not necessarily about the dollars; it's more about creating a successful community. Although it's a different kind of community than you might find in Bhutan.

Yes, that's a great example, because creating and sustaining meaningful relationships is an area that we could improve in our country.

How do you typically find the people that you feature in your magazine? Do they often contact you and put their ideas in front of you?

Sometimes the people contact us, but most of the time it's one of our own reporters, who reads or hears about someone interesting, that makes us reach out to get them in the pages of our magazine.

What would you consider a visionary?

To me, the definition of a visionary is someone who sees where the world is going in the future, but not so far in the future that it becomes fantasy. I think that is often the challenge that we have when we're looking at who we're going to write about. Is this a person in a business, or is this a topic that you're going to be hearing more about three years from now, five years from now, ten years from now? Or is it someone who's got a great idea, but that idea will not likely end up escalating to being something of scale?

Or they're too far ahead and can't bring the world with them.

That's absolutely right. You can be too late, and you can be too early. We sometimes use the term "innovators" to describe visionaries, and you can be an inventor and invent something before its time. An innovator is someone who can take that invention and, at the right time, bring it to fruition, bring it scale, bring it to a great many people…popularize it at the same time.

What do you see in the future? Are you feeling positive about America? Are we going to come out of this economic downturn?

I'd say that most media spend a lot of time finding problems and trying to ferret out wrongdoing and things that need to be fixed, and that's a terrific service that I think the press offers. But, for us, we like to look for possibilities and try to keep people's spirits up, because without believing that tomorrow can be better than today, you just don't take the chances, you just don't try. We really do believe that there are a lot of possibilities out there and a lot of great inventions still to come.

Visionary Reflection on...

Your Untold Story

What is your untold story? What gifts and abilities do you possess that have made a difference in the lives of others? And how would you like to share these gifts in the future?

CHAPTER 11

CLOCKWISE L to R: Surgeon Kenneth Kamler, M.D.,
Oceanographer Don Walsh, Ph.D., Josh Bernstein,
and Angela Fisher with Carol Beckwith

*"The human future depends on our ability to combine the
knowledge of science with the wisdom of wildness."*

- Charles A. Lindbergh,
the first man to fly non-stop, solo from New York to Paris

CHAPTER 11

The Spirit of Exploration
When Courage Meets Curiosity

• • • • • • • • • • • • • • • • • •

KENNETH KAMLER, M.D.
Microscopic Surgeon, Author, *Surviving the Extremes*,
Explorers Club Board Member, sometimes wears a wetsuit to
work underwater with NASA

Dr. Kenneth Kamler has done some amazing things in his lifetime. He is a very active member of the Explorers Club and is on the Board of Directors, where we first met. He has written a book called *Surviving the Extremes*. You may have heard him on one of Larry King's programs, where he has contributed as a medical expert. He was once given permission by the King of Bhutan to evaluate how to improve the health conditions of Eastern Bhutan. He had also planned on going to the summit of Mt. Everest but only made it to the second level beyond base camp on that trip because four of the trekkers needed medical assistance for frostbite. He performed surgery right there on blow-up mattresses on the side of the mountain.

Doris Lee: You are not only a traditional doctor with your little black bag, but you also take care of people in peril in very remote places. How does one get started at doing some of those unusual things you've done?

Dr. Kenneth Kamler: It actually happened because when I grew up in the Bronx, in New York. I was living in a housing project surrounded by other buildings and not much open space. And I found a book in the house that my father had received called *Annapurna. Annapurna* was the story of what was at the time, in 1950, the highest mountain ever climbed.

I read that book. It was a revelation for me to see that the world was filled with these wide-open spaces and big mountains and empty places, and the idea just captivated me. I was a poor kid then, probably about eight years old. Where I lived in New York City, no one ever talked about mountain climbing. If you mentioned it people looked at you funny, so I never acted on my desire to see what that was all about.

As, I got older and became a doctor, but I never lost the idea that I wanted to explore those big open places. I became a micro-surgeon because I found out that it would be easier to explore through a microscope when you live in the Bronx, and I did my exploration that way. I was very happy with that, and I still do microsurgery—that's my field.

Ken, you and a colleague were invited by the King of Bhutan to go to one of the very remote places in his country and do a health survey. You were the very first outsiders to be invited there, so what was that like?

That's actually a very interesting story. A friend of mine did some charity work in Bhutan and became friends with one of the princesses and fell in love with the country. He asked me to go with him to Bhutan on his next trip, so I did.

Bhutan is a remote mountainous area, a very isolated kingdom in the northeast corner of India, like on the shoulder of India. It's squeezed between Tibet and India. It has very few natural resources, so the world has left it behind, and it remains the last Himalayan kingdom.

They have a true king. There are four queens that he's married to with a host of princes and princesses. Nevertheless, the king is a progressive man. He speaks English. He is Western educated, as are most of the ministers and the princes and princesses.

The country is progressive in one way, but the king is very careful about guarding his culture, and he doesn't want his country overrun by Westerners. He wants to keep the Bhutanese culture intact.

Five of my friends and I just returned from a trip to Bhutan and were charmed by both the people and their culture. So I understand the importance of maintaining the culture. We experienced the elegant but still practical customs of their citizens through dress, festivals, and culture.

That's so true. It remains a beautiful country with a lot of ceremony. The king wants to retain that, because that's fragile. He doesn't want it overrun by television and technology. He has allowed people to visit the western part of Bhutan, which is slightly more advanced in that sense, but he's kept the eastern part of the country completely off limits to foreigners. You are only allowed so far, maybe halfway through the country, then that's it.

Even the western part is not very developed. The capital city of Thimphu doesn't even have a traffic light. They put one in but nobody liked it, so they got rid of it. You can walk around the city of Thimphu in about 20 minutes. The cities are open to a limited amount of foreigners.

My friend and I actually wanted to go to the eastern part. He spoke to the princess, and she said that she could get us authorization to go to the eastern part of the country. We went to Bhutan with that idea, but when we got there the king said, "No. I don't care what the princess says, I'm not letting you into eastern Bhutan."

My friend is Mike Hall, a professor of computers at MIT. So what we did was we went to the Minister of Education. Mike said, "You're an educator, and I'm an educator. We're both professors, so why don't you let me go?" And the Minister of Education said no. Then we went to the Minister of Communications, and Mike said, "I'm a computer guy, and you're a computer guy. Why don't you let me go?" And the Minister of Communications said no.

We were figuring that this wasn't going to happen, but then Mike had a thought: Even though I wasn't traveling to Bhutan as a doctor on purpose, and was just coming as his companion, he said, "Why don't we try the Minister of Health?" So we went to the Minister of Health.

We found out that the Minister of Health had never been to the eastern part of his own country, because there are no roads there and it's mountainous. I proposed to the minister what amounted to a Lewis-and-Clark-type expedition. I said, "Why don't you send the two of us to eastern Bhutan? We'll come back and tell you what's there—what the health problems might be and what the general state of health is for the people." He thought that was a great idea. He petitioned the king, and the king saw it in a new light and granted us permission. He wrote us a little proclamation, granting us permission to go to eastern Bhutan, but it wasn't easy.

Bhutan is a very isolated country; it's the size of Switzerland, but they speak seventeen different languages. Every time you cross a mountain pass the language changes. It's that isolated. The people in the eastern part each speak their own language. They're not just simply slight dialectical differences; they're completely different languages. So, just because you can speak one doesn't mean you can speak the next one.

So we went to eastern Bhutan, taking with us a guide who himself had never been to eastern Bhutan...and didn't speak any of those languages.

Major problem?

The local language is Dzongkha, and he spoke Dzongkha. But he didn't speak the languages over the next mountain. As we were moving more and more to remote areas, we ran out of road, which ends in a dead end. At the last village, we found a college student—which is rare in Bhutan since they only have one college—who spoke English and Dzongkha. We recruited him to go with us to further remote areas in eastern Bhutan where there are no roads, but he didn't know how to get there. He said he'd been there once when he was seven years old, but that wouldn't be enough to guide us there. He said his father used to go there very frequently as a trader, so we recruited his father. But his father didn't speak English. His father only spoke Dzongkha.

So you had to be guided by both of them together.

Yes, but even that wasn't enough, because the next village over the mountain spoke another language called Sharchopkha. As it turned out though, the father spoke Dzongkha *and* Sharchopkha. We had the son who we could communicate to in English, who could communicate to the father in Dzongkha, and the father could go from Dzongkha to Sharchopkha. So we needed all these people to make this connection.

Did you go on horses?

No, on foot. They have horses there, but they don't often ride the horses. They ride them sometimes, but it is very rugged terrain. Most people use the horses to carry supplies. The horses are led with the packs on and you walk, for the most part.

We stayed overnight in the village at the father and son's house, and that night the local monk from the monastery came down to visit us. He didn't speak English either, but our guide spoke to him in Dzongkha. He was very interested in what we were doing. He said to us that he would go with us to the eastern part of Bhutan, because he hadn't been there in some time—but he knew the way very well. We were very honored by that, and the next morning, we set out with the son, the father, the monk, the two of us. And Mike's assistant from Boston also came on the trip with us.

Now there were six of us setting off into the wilds of eastern Bhutan. All of us were wearing our L.L. Bean gear, our hiking boots, all this kind of stuff, and the monk shows up in flowing robes. It was incredible.

What a contrast.

He was gorgeous. He had a magenta robe with an orange sash and absolutely looked spectacular. He looked like a monk, but on his feet he was wearing Italian loafers and nylon socks, and we all had hiking boots on. We set off on the trail with the father and the monk. The monk was moving too fast for us to keep up with him. He was flying

234

ahead in his Italian loafers. It was a very arduous kind of trail. The trail went up and down and over and around.

We wanted to get to a specific town. The local people estimated that it would take us about four hours to get there, but they had no idea that we were Westerners and not nearly as able as they were in the mountains. We were incredibly slow by their standards, and there was no way we could do it in four hours.

We were moving along at a very slow pace. Eight hours into the hike, and we still weren't there. We had envisioned a much shorter trip, so we were running low and then completely out of water. The monk was in the lead. It was interesting, because every once in a while he would stop, and when he did, he would turn to a tree and actually talk to it.

Talk to a tree?

Yes. We didn't understand what he was saying, because he was talking in Dzongkha, but it wasn't like a prayer. It didn't have that sing-song, lyrical sound. He was talking almost casually to the tree. Then he would stop, pick some leaves off the tree, and sprinkle them on the ground. Then he would move on a little further, and he would talk to a rock in a conversational tone, taking some pebbles and sprinkling them on the ground.

Then he moved on, and he would talk to a stream. And there again, in a very conversational tone, he would talk to the stream and sprinkle water on the ground. He was doing this periodically, and we were grateful for this, because it gave us a chance to catch up with him when he did that.

Oddly enough, in his backpack the monk had a liter bottle of Coca-Cola. We saw it sticking out of his backpack. My

235

friend Mike and his assistant Charlotte were saying, "We've got to keep up with the monk, because sooner or later he's going to stop and open that bottle of Coca-Cola." We wanted to make sure we were near enough that he had to offer it to us, because we were dying of thirst. It was hot and the trail was much longer than we ever expected it to be.

We got up to a 14,000 foot pass and there were prayer flags at the top. We said, "This is where he's going to stop, so let's catch up to him. Sure enough, he stopped at the very top. There was a little altar there, and he stopped and put out a blanket...and opened the bottle of Coca-Cola. We said, "This is it, we're in position now!" But he took the whole bottle of Coca-Cola and poured it on the altar. The entire thing! He didn't even get a sip for himself. The whole bottle gets spilled out into the air, because he wants to appease the gods!

I said to Mike, "Wait a minute, stop him! We need the Coca-Cola more than the gods do." But to no avail. He poured the whole thing on top and then he moved on.

We came down the pass on the other side, and we were actually getting somewhat close to the village. We passed the area where they speak Sharchopkha. The most remote eastern part of Bhutan is inhabited by a group of nomadic people who are yak herders. They have no permanent home; they just wander back and forth across the border from Tibet and Bhutan herding their yaks. They stick to themselves, and they speak a different language called Bumthangkha, which no one else speaks.

So you're running into a language problem.

Yes. We've got English. We've got Dzongkha. We've got Sharchopkha. But we don't have Bumthangkha. What happened was we were probably out on the trail ten hours by now, and Charlotte was absolutely at the end of her rope. She just couldn't take it anymore. She said she couldn't take another step and collapsed on the trail. She sat down, started crying, and said, "I just can't do this." We were not that far from the village by this point, but she wouldn't move. She was really in a state of mental and physical collapse. At about that time, we started seeing the Bumthangkha people on their yak trail, and they started coming past us.

From a Western point of view, they were very unusual. They live off the yaks the same way the American Indians lived off the buffalo. Everything depends on the yaks; they herd the yaks, use the yak's skin to make clothing, eat yak meat, drink yak milk, and use the yak to pack in their supplies as they move from place to place, setting up new huts as they go. They're entirely dependent on the yaks.

They have a red dye that they use. They dress in yak skin clothes—yak skin dresses, pants, tops, and apron-like pieces that are all dyed red. They also weave the yak fur into a very tightly knit felt hat, because it rains a lot in Bhutan. The hat has braids of yak hair coming down the front and the back of the hat. The idea is that the rain hits the top of the hat and gets caught in the braid and comes down past their faces. In other words, it stops the water from hitting their faces.

Wearing their completely red outfits, from our point of view, they looked like they were from another planet.

They only speak Bumthangkha and, again, nobody in our group spoke Bumthangkha. They all pass by us, and then

237

what looks like a husband and wife with a few yaks come by. The wife looks at Charlotte laying on the ground sobbing and signals to her husband to go on ahead with the yaks, and he does. The woman stops next to Charlotte, sits down with her, and puts her arm around her. There's no hope that these two people can ever speak to each other. The woman only speaks Bumthangkha and has spent her life in the mountains. Charlotte is a graduate student at MIT in Boston. Two people couldn't be further apart on the planet, and yet the woman puts her arm around Charlotte, consoles her, gives her something to drink, and pats her on the back. The woman holds Charlotte's hand, helps her to stand up, then walks with her into the village. This woman did what none of us could do. She was able to get Charlotte up and motivated to go to the village. The two of them had no hope of ever speaking to each other. Their cultures were diametrically opposite, yet they had this common woman bond.

The Bumthangkha woman was able to transmit this kind of sympathy and empathy for Charlotte, which motivated her and gave her the energy to get up and get going. It showed a kind of universal trait between human beings that crosses cultures, nationalities, and language barriers. And it was just much more powerful than the two of us men who tried to reason with her. That eastern Bhutanese woman was able to reach across all those barriers and get Charlotte to get up just based on one human being contacting one another.

Showing her caring through that?

Yes, her caring is what it took. She got Charlotte into the village and sat her down in a hut there, and we all came around. In the village there was somebody who spoke Bumthangkha as well as Sharchopkha, so we were now able to set up a line of communication.

238

The woman wanted to talk to Charlotte, so it went like this:
She spoke in Bumthangkha.
Someone translated Bumthangkha into Sharchopkha.
Someone else translated Sharchopkha into Dzongkha.
And then Dzongkha was translated into English.

We needed four people to get this done. The first thing the woman said to Charlotte was, "Where are you from?" She had never seen people like us before. Charlotte said, "I'm from America." The woman said, "What's that?" She had never heard of America. We said it's a country on the other side of the world, and she barely understood what a country was, because they had no concept of that. They were nomadic people who just wandered across to Tibet and Bhutan. Wherever the yaks needed to go, they went.

We stayed in that village a couple of days, assessing healthcare. The monk was with us, and that first night he came to join us. He was staying in somebody's house, and we were staying in somebody else's house. He came down and again, through the translation, I told the monk how honored we were that he would accompany us to this village.

Through translation, he said, "When I came to visit you before you set off on your trip that evening, I looked at the three of you, and I said, 'You're going to need all the help you can get.' I thought I ought to accompany you, because I was afraid to let you go on your own. I knew the route. And more importantly, I would help you with all the deities along the way, because you don't know where they are."

He stopped at the rock, at the tree, and at the stream, because those were where the deities lived. What he was doing was talking to the deities asking them to grant us safe passage.

The monk was praying.

In fact, it was effective. We had safe passage, and we were able to stay in the village several days. We were honored guests, because we had a proclamation from the king.

The national sport in Bhutan is archery, and even though it wasn't the season for archery, they set up an archery tournament in our honor. They gave us bows and arrows, and we participated in the contest. At the same time, I was able to assess the healthcare, talk to the people through the translators, and see what their health needs might be.

We left after three days having made great friends there and went back the way we had come. We came through the capital, Thimphu, and then I actually wrote a 17-page report for the Minister of Health on what I had seen and observed in the people, what I thought their health needs were, where I thought they needed a lot of help. He actually took that report, read it before the parliament, and used that as somewhat of a basis to direct their future healthcare.

It was very effective, and I've been invited back to do this again in other remote regions of Bhutan.

We're grateful to you, Ken, for leading us along so many interesting trails...and for the monk that guided you.

- *Visionary Spotlight* -

SIR EDMUND HILLARY

First man, along with Tenzing Norgay, to reach the summit of Mount Everest, knighted by Queen Elizabeth, New Zealand's Ambassador to Nepal and India

I had the pleasure of knowing Sir Edmund Hillary over 25 years, and when asked about the most memorable interviews I've had in my 3,500+ interviews, I always mention Ed. For all the things that he accomplished over his lifetime, he was always humble. I regard him as one of the finest men of the last 100 years. Although he often spoke of the risky things he had done, he was never boastful. He also talked about experiences in which he did not think he would ever survive. But survive he did...

The Sherpa people had worked as cooks, porters, and guides on his many expeditions in the Himalayas. After his record-breaking climb, Sir Edmund asked the Sherpas how he could help them. They said they needed schools and a hospital. This turned out to be a life-long commitment to the Sherpas. He was able to build 27 schools, two hospitals, and numerous runways for altitude sickness climbers who needed to get down from the high altitude in a hurry or perish.

A former beekeeper from New Zealand, Sir Edmund said, "Together we shall build a school." And they did. The first school, Khumjung, opened in 1961 with 58 children in grades one through five. Today the school has 355 students. In total, 2,600 students, in all grades, are attending the twenty-seven schools in Nepal. One of the first students of the Khumjung School is in charge of the Himalayan Trust that Sir Edmund set up—a trust that supports an additional 36 schools. To learn more, visit www.himalayantrust.co.uk.

As for the two hospitals, one is located in Phaphlu and another in Hunde. There are also a dozen smaller health clinics in remote villages throughout the area. The staff originally was supported by doctors from Canada and New Zealand, but today most of physicians are Sherpas.

In the 1970s, Sir Edmund built the airstrip in Lukla, an area for climbers. However, the many visitors to the area took a toll on the landscape. In need of firewood, people stripped the hillsides of trees, which ultimately resulted in erosion. Conservationist Mingma Norbu of the World Wildlife Foundation noted at that time, a climber and his support group used ten times as much wood as the average Sherpa family.

Together, Mingma Norbu and Sir Edmund founded Sagamartha National Park. Ed also provided for five Sherpas to study Natural Resources Management in New Zealand. In a 2003 interview with *The Explorers Club Journal,* he said, "I came for the mountain and stayed for its people." He went on to say, "If that one day on Everest has allowed me to do what I do, so be it. Today we are wielding hammers, not ice axes. Working with our Sherpa friends, we are fashioning the rocks we used to climb into school house walls."

Jamling Norgay, Tenzing's son, honored Ed by saying, "Sir Ed Hillary was like a father to the Sherpa people and will be remembered in our community, not only for his achievement on the mountain with my late father, but also as a great humanitarian for his efforts to improve the lives of the Sherpa people."

Through his son, Peter Hillary, Sir Ed Edmund Hillary's work will be remembered always. (In 1990, Peter and Sir Ed were the first father/son duo to summit Mt. Everest.)

- *Visionary Spotlight* -

LORIE KARNATH
Explorers Club President 2009-2012

Lorie Karnath was the late President of the Explorers Club, and I am pleased to include her visionary perspective on women explorers and where she sees the exciting field of exploration going in the future:

The annals of women explorers are as lengthy as history, although the accompanying recognition is distinctively shorter. Amongst their number were visionaries, scientists, artists, as well as those that sought out distant places for the pure adventure that such travel would bring. In doing this, these women oftentimes were faced with tremendous dangers: natural disasters, hostile native reception, encounters with treacherous animal, insect and plant species, shipwrecks, and a wide range of other calamities. They had to surmount numerous hardships, including exhaustion, hunger, loneliness, and a yearning for home. There was also a stigma that accompanied the efforts of women explorers, which for some, precluded them from ever being able to return to the homes they longed for. Yet they persisted, inspired by the wealth of untapped knowledge that lay beyond their borders. Their contributions, often unheralded or obscured, served to greatly increase our understanding of the world.

Over the centuries, the nature of exploration and discovery has changed. Today's explorer can, in most situations, select from a portion of the map already identified. However the format by which the explorer views these named places has changed. An expedition no longer sets a goal solely to reach a location. Today's expeditionary quest is to help to articulate knowledge of the world within a specific context, to gain an understanding of a specific place from a multitude of scientific and cultural perspectives: from its environmental resources to its human history.

For sure, the role of the explorer remains an important one as there remains still a lot to uncover. Exploration is increasingly scientific in nature; nonetheless this scientifically oriented discovery—whether it takes place in the field or in the laboratory—requires the same instinct of the earliest adventurers: to seek out and explore so that we all can learn.

The explorers of today and tomorrow, both women and men, will continue to embody the qualities of vision, courage, and determination required to enable discovery and further new findings. The discovery process will remain at the forefront as we struggle to find ways to balance and manage our natural world while providing for its peoples. More field research will aid in monitoring and maintaining environmental equilibriums and providing analytical evidence to help pinpoint where natural buffers and balances effecting ecological landscapes have broken down. Exploration may still embody a personal quest, but today's discoverers are tackling concerns relating to planetary survival relevant to all.

Just as was envisioned in its early mandate, the Explorers Club remains a place of congregation for explorers and field scientists from around the world, with the notable addition that women today strongly factor in this gathering.

DON WALSH, Ph.D.
Oceanographer, Honorary President of Explorers Club, world's deepest diver with Jacques Piccard—record-holder for 50 years

Don Walsh is an American oceanographer, explorer, and marine policy specialist. He and Jacques Piccard were aboard the bathyscaphe *Trieste* when it made a record maximum descent into the Mariana Trench on January, 23 1960, to the deepest point of the world's ocean.

Doris Lee: Don, you had the chance, with Jacques Piccard, to do some things that nobody else had ever done. What was the most exciting part for you about that experience?

Don Walsh: I wouldn't say exciting. Maybe pleasurable, in the sense that we had promised we were going to do this. Nobody believed us. In the Navy there were, and still are, penalties to be paid if you say you're going to do something and you don't. You might not ever get promoted, or something like that, but we had a hard-working team of 14 people, both military and civilian, that worked with us. We were at a Navy base for about six or seven months at Guam in the Western Pacific, because Guam is close to the deepest place in the ocean. It was seven days a week, 10-12 hours a day of training.

What we were doing were progressively deeper dives. We started out in the harbor, a few hundred feet. And then by November of '59, we had made a dive to 18,000 feet. In early January of '60, we made a dive to 24,000 feet. And then a little bit later, we made the deep dive to 35,800 feet.

Thirty-five thousand feet, and you were the first persons to do that?

Yes.

It must have been interesting to be able to work with Piccard on this project. This was a major underwater dive that most of us, and even the Navy, didn't think you could do.

Yes, I was a junior Navy lieutenant at the time. I promised the admirals we could do it, and they didn't believe me. I am sure they thought, *what did he know*?

You knew in your heart that it could be done.

Yes, I knew and was confident with all the technology involved, as well as the operational procedures.

You have said that there is a significant portion of our oceans, the trenches, that have not been explored and where you believe many medicinal possibilities can be found?

Not so much that. It's more about understanding fundamental geophysical processes on our planet. You just can't exempt that much area from being explored and say we're not going to study it. The deep trenches, of course, are where the seafloor is being subducted into the interior of the earth where it is "recycled." Today, there are no manned submersibles which can visit these places to do the fundamental research.

The seafloor is created in the rift zones; that is the mid-ocean mountain ranges, like the mid-Atlantic ridge and so on. New seafloor is being built there, and then like being on a conveyor belt, it moves slowly across the seafloor. Finally, at an age of about 200 million years it is recycled at the subduction zones (trenches), and it is returned back into the interior of the earth. We haven't done that many studies in that area, so I think that's an important new frontier for us to look into, but it's very expensive.

The submarines that go that deep are quite costly. For example, the two Russian subs, the Mir submersibles, which can only go to 6,000 meters or 20,000 feet, cost over $50 million in 1989. So today they would be much more expensive. And to build a manned vehicle for 35,000 feet would be quite expensive. However, I don't think we need fleets of these things. An alternative would be unmanned submersibles which would be less costly. In fact since 1995, two unmanned submersibles, one Japanese and one U.S. built, have made a total of three dives to the deepest place. In my opinion it is also important to take humans with their trained eyes and brains to those depths. I think one or two of the deepest diving manned systems could satisfy deepest ocean research needs.

We need only one or two?

Yes, but it is not just the submersibles alone. These operations require a seagoing system with a proper mothership being most important. I envision a system that would be an international asset available to scientists from all countries.

I think a good model for that is the Deep Sea Drilling Project. The program is run by the United States Government through the National Science Foundation. They make ship time available to legitimate scientists all over the world. They have to pay their way, but they only pay for a small portion of time. They don't have to carry the whole ship on their budgets.

That sounds like a great idea.

I see that model working with the deep manned submersibles too.

Is there one final thought that you would like to share?

Think deep! There is much to be found down there and, at present, we are not putting enough effort into the exploration of this vast area of our home planet, Earth.

JOSH BERNSTEIN
Explorer, Educator & Environmental Advocate

Doris Lee: With so many places already researched and explored, are there other remote locations worth exploring?

Josh Bernstein: It's true that much of planet Earth has been explored over the past 150 years, but the majority of those expeditions have focused on land—the mountains, the jungles, the poles. For whatever reason, there hasn't been an equal focus on our oceans, which is odd given that our planet is mostly water. Since 1960's successful trip to Challenger Deep by explorers Don Walsh and Jacques Piccard, few others have ventured into the watery realm with the same sense of intrepid purpose—although I must acknowledge the fantastic work of my friend Dr. Sylvia Earle. The inner-ocean—that area 1000 feet below the surface down to 1000 feet above the sea floor—remains largely unexplored. Perhaps Sir Richard Branson's newly announced Virgin Oceanic initiatives will usher in a new realm of exploration...only time will tell.

Beyond the oceans, there are also those locations outside of Earth itself—specifically Mars, Jupiter, and the planets and celestial bodies beyond, although these expeditions are, understandably, much more expensive and need to be funded by government agencies.

In addition to the physical realms, though, I believe we still have tremendous opportunities to acknowledge and explore metaphysical and mystical realms in much greater depth. Western culture was born from the Greek schools of reason and logic that depended heavily (if not completely) on the physical world and the human senses that process it. Many other cultures teach that the physical world is just one layer of many. Dreamtime, altered states, and shamanism all feed into the mystical realm that Western culture often views as superstition or taboo. I won't say this realm is unexplored. But that knowledge has often been subjugated in the name of "Science," and I feel that further exploration into these mystical realms could create a paradigm shift into our understanding of nature, disease and our planet's well-being.

Our humanity is much greater than just what our five senses can detect. This, to me, is the greatest area of exploration left open to those who seek to venture into the unknown...explorations into consciousness.

How do you best handle dangerous locations?

First, I think it's important to understand that what's "dangerous" is subjective. There are people who no doubt think crossing a busy street during rush hour in Manhattan is dangerous, yet others wouldn't give it a second thought. And there is a difference between *perceived* risk and *actual* risk. Some locations are perceived as dangerous simply because of how they're portrayed in the media.

For example, the Middle East is often depicted as a war zone, yet many cities there are totally livable. When I lived in Jerusalem during the First *Intifada*, my friends and family in the U.S. were distraught that I was going to get blown up while buying groceries or walking around town. While I did see a number of "suspicious packages" and had to be careful where I went and how I visited places, it wasn't as dangerous as the media portrayed it. Like most things on television, what's depicted on the news is often an exaggerated, compressed version of reality. Having said that, I have had to be more cautious than usual while traveling through Yemen, Zimbabwe, and other less stable countries. And there was a slightly tense moment in Papua New Guinea when we thought a local tribe might attack our group.

But, by and large, I've always done my best to approach people with a friendly smile, an open mind, and a sincere sense of respect. I think that helps tremendously.

Regarding dangerous expeditions involving, say, long rappels or deep dives, I rely on proper training and good risk management procedures. I maintain my gear, double-check my ropes and analyze my gases. It's often the simplest errors that lead to the costliest mistakes, so I do what I can to mitigate all risks. If there are legitimate areas of risk that can't be reduced completely, I proceed with an appropriate amount of caution.

Do you keep a log of your encounters and, if so, how has it been helpful?

I do. I keep a schedule that records where I am and what I do every day—every country, every flight, every hotel, every site, etc. It's been tremendously helpful as I've had to look back over the past 500,000 miles and figure out where I've been, where I've stayed, and what I've done. For my book on the making of the *Digging for the Truth* TV series, that was invaluable, as were the photos I shot every day while traveling. Between my calendar and close to 80,000 photographs, I can recreate what I did every day since 2004. And, of course, I log every dive.

What traits are helpful to new adventurers starting out?

There's a saying that "adventure is what happens when things go wrong." Most of the explorers I know prefer to avoid having "adventures," as expeditions have enough challenges staying on course. That's not to say explorers aren't adventurous—we certainly are. But when it comes to expending financial and human capital to achieve a scientific objective, it's best if things are done with purpose, and "adventuring" isn't usually a part of that higher goal.

As for traits, whether young or old, an explorer should possess the ability to move between diverse points on the emotional spectrum: be passionate yet removed, organized yet flexible, serious yet humorous, and determined yet open-minded. It takes a certain quality to plan and lead an expedition, to create an environment in which others feel confident to follow your lead and also comfortable to hang out. Oh, and of course, almost all explorers I know have an insatiable curiosity to travel, to learn, and to experiment— basically to celebrate the wonders of life here on earth.

How has The Explorers Club been of help to you?

Here's a good example. In a few weeks, I'm going to Iceland to lead a trip for a client. While I've been to Iceland before and have a good sense of what kind of experience I want to create and where I want to go, I needed to find local people for logistical support—vehicles, horses, rafts, etc. I sent an e-mail to The Explorers Club members that live in Iceland and, within just a few days, everything was set. It's a fantastic resource and the Club's greatest asset is, without a doubt, its membership. There are some truly inspiring people in the Club.

Thank you, Josh. I appreciate your exploration of the inner and outer realms!

RISK

John Geiger, author of *The Third Man Factor: Surviving the Impossible*, Senior fellow at Massey College, fellow of

Explorers Club. For more information, visit www.thirdmanfactor.com

As Kenneth Kamler wrote in *Surviving the Extremes*, "No animal in its right mind ever intentionally puts itself in danger by going somewhere it doesn't belong." Yet, as Kamler notes, human beings do go where they don't belong."

In a recent article in *Neuron*, British researchers also identified a neurological basis for people going where they don't belong. Human beings in their right mind do put themselves in danger intentionally. **Our brains, it turns out, reward risk.**

In an experiment carried out at the Wellcome Trust Centre for Neuroimaging at University College London, scientists measured blood flow in the brain. The researchers found that the ventral striatum, which is involved in processing rewards through the release of neurotransmitters like dopamine, is more active when subjects shunned the safer options to experience the unusual. This is called the "novelty bonus". Risk it seems, is part of what it is to be human.

During the Edwardian era, Britain was more prosperous that at any other time in its history, and it gave rise to discovery, including the first South Pole explorations of Robert Flacon Scott and Sir Ernest Shackleton.

The 1950s was one of the most prosperous eras in American history. In the United States, unprecedented numbers of families reached middle class status. It is also the decade that gave birth to space exploration, and saw the British conquest of Mt. Everest.

In developed countries, the subsequent six decades have been highly prosperous, the societies stable. Home has been a good place to be and, one would think, to stay. These same populations have produced a large and growing number of people who have placed themselves at great individual risk, engaging in exploration, extreme sports, and adventure travel. Voluntary risk has never been more pervasive.

Two billionaires, tied at #261 on Forbes's 2009 list of the world's wealthiest people, with fortunes of $2.5 billion each, embody this point. Virgin Companies founder Richard Branson and Cirque du Soleil founder Guy Laliberté can afford lives of great luxury and comfort, yet Branson has repeatedly risk his life and come close to dying in attempts to set distance records in hot air balloons. Laliberté, meanwhile, is scheduled to blast off on September 30 aboard a *Soyouz* spacecraft, becoming the seventh civilian to fly alongside astronauts and cosmonauts on the Russian spaceships.

Risk-taking it seems, is both part of our neurological makeup and an integral part of contemporary society. As W. Grey Walter, author of *The Human Brain in Space Time,* argued, "The urge to explore is part of our nervous equipment…The human species is unstable in stable environments."

Exploration is a way for people to gain insight not just into the world, but to better understand themselves. Without risk there is no gain in scientific knowledge or in understanding one's self.

One of the most intriguing manifestations of risk is a subject I have been studying for years. People at the very edge of death, often adventurers or explorers, reported experiencing a sense of incorporeal being who is beside them and who encourages them o make one final effort to survive. This phenomenon is known as the "Third Man" factor, and it has been experienced by scores of people, from Shackleton and aviator Charles Lindbergh to polar explorer Ann Bancroft, climber Peter Hillary, diver Steffi Schwabe, and many more.

Risk is innate to human beings, and so much a part of us that our brains dispense "novelty bonuses" to encourage us to take the more adventurous path. Risk is also powerfully influenced by the great wealth and comfort enjoyed by those of us lucky enough to live in the West. We seek extreme and unusual environments to gain insight into the nature of our planet, but also as a testing ground of the human spirit.

- *Visionary Spotlight* -

Angela Fisher & Carol Beckwith
Photojournalists capturing African culture

For over 30 years, Angela Fisher and Carol Beckwith have traveled to remote African tribes to photograph and document their cultures. Tribal leaders have befriended these two adventuresome women, ensuring the care and protection that would give them the freedom of movement and cooperation necessary to do their important work—to document the lives of these extraordinary people and capture the tribal customs that may be lost as the countries move further into the twenty-first century.

I had an opportunity to ask Angela and Carol about the contrasts they find between African and Western cultures. One of the aspects that stands out the most for them is how the Africans relate to the elders of their communities. They shared how the older generation does not live in isolation, nor do they die in isolation. Instead, they are surrounded by the love of their families as they pass on.

Carol said, "We've seen, in some parts of Africa, the modern life sweep away the values of traditional Africans. And these people are in very difficult states, especially in the cities. It's our hope that, as African people move out of their societies and into cities and urban life, they will carry their values with them."

Angela and Carol's latest book, *Dinka*, is monumental in size and scope. The photographs, taken over a four-week period, are truly mesmerizing...even profound. Also capturing the beauty and integrity of African cultures, their other books include, *African Ceremonies, Africa Adorned, Nomads of Niger*, and *Maasai*.

To learn more, visit: www.africanceremonies.com

Visionary Reflection on...

Curiosity

Albert Einstein once said, "The important thing is not to stop questioning. Curiosity has its own reason for existing. One cannot help but be in awe when he contemplates the mysteries of eternity, of life, of the marvelous structure of reality." A thirst to explore is perhaps one of our greatest gifts as human beings...leading to awe-inspiring discoveries. Today, adopt an attitude of curiosity as your primary state of mind...and see what happens!

CHAPTER 12

Top to bottom: Justice Sandra O'Connor (ret.);
John Templeton, M.D.

CHAPTER 12

True Democracy
An Exploration of Freedom & Responsibility

• • • • • • • • • • • • • • • • • •

JUSTICE SANDRA O'CONNOR (ret.)
United States Supreme Court

In September 1981, President Ronald Reagan nominated Justice O'Connor as Associate Justice of the United States Supreme Court. This was the first time in the 191 years of the Supreme Court's history that a woman was nominated. Her participation in the court over the years has often given her the well-deserved title of one of the most powerful women in America.

After 25 years of service she moved to a retired position with many honors. Now she is very active going throughout the country and the world, speaking out on important issues of the courts. With a career in public service, totaling more than 50 years, Justice O'Connor has certainly contributed greatly to our country here in the United States.

What most people don't know is that Justice O'Connor is an enthusiastic golfer, and she also was known in her childhood as a cowgirl. She was recently inducted in the National Hall of Fame of the Cowgirl's Association. She has written a book with her brother, *Lazy B - Growing up on a Cattle Ranch in the American Southwest*, about those early years growing up on a 267-acre ranch in a very remote area of eastern Arizona.

I think that growing up in an environment where she worked with so many cowboys on a pioneering ranch made it possible for

257

her to work with all the other Supreme Court Justices in a special way. She helped to encourage a workable environment in the court.

Today, Justice O'Connor speaks out about three main topics: Civics and its importance in our schools, the significance of the courts, and the American position as we work toward a more collaborative world. I am honored to have the Justice in my last three books.

Doris Lee: Let's start out with the subject of Civics; I know that's an important topic for you. You and I grew up with Civics classes in school but it's no longer being taught in all schools?

Justice Sandra Day O'Connor: When I went to school back in the last century, we had courses in American History, courses in Civics, and we learned the structure of our nation's government and various state governments. Civics was considered important knowledge to be conveyed in our school system. Certainly, in high schools, this was a required course.

If you look statistically today at what's done in high schools across the country, about half of our states no longer make it a requirement for high school students to take Civics, Government, or American History. I think this is a great danger to our country. The system of government that we have is a rather complicated one, and you have to learn how it works and how citizens have a role to play within that system.

Is this happening because of budget cuts?

I'm sure that's part of it, but there's something else that I'm about to discuss that I think has played a role.

We agreed as a nation that we would have some of our high school students tested and compare the scores with those from high school equivalent levels in other countries. When we did that, it turned out that the United States young people's test scores on math and science were below those of most other nations. This was a wake up call.

Congress and the President both agreed that it called for corrective action. They decided they would make federal money available to schools that managed to have students with good test scores in math, science and reading. That was put into the No Child Left Behind legislation.

It did provide financial benefits for schools that managed to teach their children enough to do better on test scores in those subjects. What happened, however, as an unintended consequence, was that there was no federal money available to teach American History and Civics. Then there was no testing for those subjects by the schools and they just dropped them by the wayside. That is what happened as a practical matter. It's unfortunate; I don't think that was the intent of the members of Congress and the President, but it was an unintended result of the system.

How can a country have real democracy without knowing the advantages of the system?

It's not just the advantages, you have to know how the system works. Today, according to polls taken by the Annenberg Center, no more than one-third of Americans can even name the three branches of government. Imagine that! They can't even name them, much less say what they do.

We have fallen into a situation in this country where our citizens are woefully uninformed about our system of government. As a result, they are not going to be effective as citizens participating in it.

When I think of the sacrifice that our country's founders made so that we can have democracy, I am amazed. It is the reason why so many people from other countries still wish to make their home in the U.S.

We've been a nation through the years that has welcomed immigrants, and we've always had many people applying for entry into the country because they thought that this country offered some opportunities not available where they were.

In relation to this topic, what do you see as significant with our courts today?

The significance is what it has always been in the past; we are a nation that has set up a pretty decent judicial system both at the state level and the national level to resolve disputes. The courts spend a lot of time handling criminal cases. Every nation has to have a system for handling criminal charges brought against people and we do as well. We have a system of resolving disputes between citizens, whether it's business or private, and these disputes are handled in courts rather than just fighting it out on the streets. Every nation has some kind of a court system.

People around the world have generally admired our federal court system because we tend to get well qualified people to serve as judges on our courts. Some of our states, on the other hand, have partisan election of state court judges, at least since the days of President Andrew Jackson.

Originally, when we became a nation and the colonies became states, every state selected their judges much like we do at the federal level. The appointment was made by the governor. When Andrew Jackson came along, he was more of a populist leader and he encouraged states to move to a system of election of judges in partisan elections. Eighteen of our 50 states still follow that system and elect their judges.

No other nation in the world has partisan election of judges or any kind of election of judges. It is not regarded in any other nation as being a desirable way to pick judges and I agree with that. The electorate is usually not able to be well-informed about the long list of candidates for judge and it just doesn't work well in a partisan context.

What we want for judges are people who will be well qualified, fair and impartial. We don't want people on the bench who hold allegiance to some other entity or person, and we don't want judges who have received a great deal of campaign money from some lawyer and then have that lawyer appear before them in court. That's pretty risky and yet that's what you run into in states that allow partisan election of judges.

Should we switch to the merit selection?

I think that's a better system of selecting judges, yes. A bipartisan commission can be set up of citizens to consider applications from people who want to serve as judges. The commission then investigates their capacity and ability, provides a list of qualified candidates to the appointing authority, which might be a governor, and lets the appointments be made in that fashion.

I think retention elections are alright, so that after a period of time the judge that has been serving appears on the ballot for voters to decide whether to retain the judges or not. If the voters think a judge has been doing a bad job they can vote against the judge.

It sounds like a much more practical way of doing it because judges have already proven that they were worthy of that position.

Yes, it works better.

Why did you go into law, Sandra? You grew up in a very remote section of Arizona.

I grew up on a cattle ranch, and we didn't have any lawyers. We didn't know any lawyers or judges.

I applied to Stanford and went there as an undergraduate student and then to law school. During my undergraduate years at Stanford, I took a general course offered to undergraduates on law from one of the law professors. The professor was a man named Harry Rathbun. He was very inspiring, incredible, and the best professor I ever had. It was because of him that I decided to apply to law school.

What is happening with women in the court system now?

Through the years we've actually seen a gradual increase in the number of female judges both in state courts and in the federal courts. I applaud that, because women make very fine attorneys, and they make very good judges too. I expect that general trend of an increase in the number of women will continue.

When I went to law school, only one percent of the law students nationwide were female and now 50% or more in law schools are women. We have had a real revolution in this country in opportunities for women.

As an observer, I would say that you were partially responsible for that 50% jump.

I came along at a time when I think opportunities for women were just beginning to emerge. In World War II, most of the men between the ages of 18 and 40 went to war. They were drafted into the military service and they had to leave their jobs. In those years women then took up most of those jobs and went to work.

After the war, when the soldiers came home, men were entitled by law to get their jobs back. However, women had learned that they could do the work and they could do it well. Therefore many women wanted to stay in the workplace and they did.

Looking now at the world's situation and America's role in it, it is clear that we're facing troublesome times. How do you see us putting our best foot forward in a constructive way?

Our country has to be part of those prosperous countries that try to help others feed and clothe themselves and do a decent job of helping the people who live in those countries.

We have not done a great deal in terms of foreign aid; I think we can do better. We work through our diplomatic service and with Peace Corp volunteers to try to help others around the world in ways where we can be helpful.

We don't own the world and we can't do it all, but we can be helpful. I hope we will continue to try even harder to help those in need in other countries.

In many parts of the world, there are countries trying to move more toward democracy.

Many are. We have more democracies today than we've ever had in the past, and I think the majority of countries have some sort of democratic government. It doesn't work everywhere, but the countries are learning by trying it.

What would you say to the Baby Boomers that will have to face some health situations such as Alzheimer's? Do you have a word on care-giving?

In the first place, we are living longer than we did in the past, and with longer lifespan comes, unfortunately, a longer period in which to develop some very debilitating medical problems—and Alzheimer's is one of those.

The doctors say that one in two people over 80 will develop Alzheimer's and that's a very debilitating disease. It is very sad to see what happens. There is no cure for it. Therefore, I think people will try to live a healthier lifestyle in their younger years in order to prevent them from getting Alzheimer's and other diseases.

Perhaps some day there will be a cure, but there isn't at present. It is very costly for drug companies to develop and test new medications. It takes a lot of time and a lot of luck to find something that's helpful.

What brings you the most joy in your life these days?

Now, as in the past, it is doing work that's worth doing.

Great statement. What do you suggest for people like Bill and Melinda Gates who have a huge foundation to direct their research to? What specific topics, in addition to Civics, do you see as very important?

There are so many. I think everyone should just try to find some kind of work that's worth doing, as I have tried to do. There is plenty of need, so there's a lot available to be done. For example, people can go into many areas of science and contribute enormously, or they can go into medicine and help millions of people.

I applaud your efforts. I think the word "retirement" should certainly not be associated with your name because it seems like you've gone on to do a lot of other things.

Yes, I am busier than I've ever been, so I'm not sure that retirement from one's paid job necessarily means retirement from efforts to help the world.

JOHN TEMPLETON, M.D.
CEO of John Templeton Foundation

Doris Lee: Dr. Templeton, today we're talking about four major topics that the Templeton Foundation has researched: forgiveness, anger, frugality, and moral values. The foundation has always done such a wonderful job of taking on major questions instead of skirting them, so I'm grateful to you for your work. A major magazine just came out saying that we have lost our values.

John Templeton: Forgiveness is never a simple thing. Of course, it depends on how great the offense is. Our post-modern culture causes such harm to human nature, though human nature is good.

Little anger can become big anger, and then resentment, and nothing gets resolved. You need something as powerful, or *more* powerful, to cause people to think differently.

I cannot think of a more transforming impact in a person's life than if they conscientiously turn into a grateful person. Begin to focus on small things. Even mechanically write down three things you're grateful for every morning when you get up. And continue with the discipline.

Good exercise– three points each morning that would help you appreciate something.

You have to start small. You can't start dramatically, so you have to build up a habit of gratitude. If you start each morning by writing down three things that you're grateful for, you may find some come back two or four days later. That doesn't matter. Write whatever is in your heart getting up in the morning.

By the end of a month, you'll feel that just being able to breathe is something to be grateful for. You can be grateful for very rudimentary things, but it's the attitude that counts.

My father used to talk about an "attitude of gratitude." If one has a sense of gratitude, then it opens one's heart to deal with the tougher issues that remain unresolved in one's life.

Let's say Pol Pot kills your entire family. That's a hard thing to forgive. Maybe in the end it's not that you're forgiving Pol Pot, but you're forgiving the circumstances or someone who did what Pol Pot told them to do because he was scared.

Scared…a powerful word. Are you studying this on an international level? For example, what about the larger needs of countries like the Congo?

When so-called UN troops rape women and steal from people, that's a failure of leadership at the sergeant, captain, colonel, and United Nation's level. One of the biggest culprits is the United Nations.

How can that be addressed to make a change?

I've been in the military, but only as a doctor. I have a sense of what it means, at least in the American military, to teach people codes of conduct. But I think the United Nations is just glad to get ten nations that will send troops, and they don't have any UN standards or codes of conduct.

It has to come from the top down with accountability. They should all know the code of conduct, and they will have to answer for violating it. These standards have to be maintained.

Now, looking to the topic of frugality, how have you addressed that?

Frugality was one of Benjamin Franklin's favorite words. In the focus group testing we have done, people think frugality means being a cheapskate. That's not the message that my father or the John Templeton Foundation want to get across. In fact, for those 19 character values that my father held up as spiritual realities, he has *thrift*, but he doesn't call it frugality. So I'd like to call it thrift.

At its core, thrift means a sense of stewardship. Stewardship acknowledges the blessing of being able to earn what we have, that we have the capacity to earn it. We should be grateful for the capacity to use our mind, intellect, and innovativeness. We should also be grateful for the way that our ability to take risks enhances some of the assets that we have. It's like the Parable of the Talents: Two men put their talents to work. One man, a

267

cheapskate, put the talents in a hole. He did not understand stewardship.

When his master came home, he was thinking he would be happy, and he wasn't because the talents didn't go anywhere.

One has a lifetime responsibility to prosper what one has, including prospering the nation that you are blessed to be a citizen of. Stewardship is not just a matter for the individual. It's a matter for the entire nation.

We have lost 200 years of a passionate conviction for thrift. Up until the 1920s, when times were generally good for most citizens, Americans saved 20% of every dollar they earned. There were tens of thousands of thrift clubs. Weekly, farmers' wives would get together to look at their budgets, their food purchases, and how to get the best food value.

I learned from my father and mother not to turn thriftiness into a burden. Savings should be an adventure. In the Depression, when he and my mother were newly married, they moved to New York. He began his investment career, and my mother was doing advertising. They both worked and saved 50 cents on every dollar.

Why was that? It was not that they were opposed to spending. But you could make up a budget for what you next hoped to have. They never bought a house on debt. They had always saved the money ahead of time.

In their six floor walk-up, because the rent was lower on the sixth floor than it was on the first floor, they needed a comfortable chair to sit in. They went to Goodwill. They didn't pay attention to the color or design. They just touched it and made sure it was a good quality, strong, and comfortable chair. That's all they needed, and they bargained for a $5 purchase.

When they made up food budgets and when they went to the food store, they had dinner first so they didn't make decisions while hungry. They had a purchase list of the food for the week, and it was already thought through so they weren't tempted to buy more.

The final element of thrift of a spiritual sense is that you're a steward of your assets, which in the end, don't belong to you. You have a sacred responsibility to make them prosper, and that includes your own children. You must prosper in them a sense of resiliency, capability, and the capacity to be independent. Your greatest joy is to release them the way a bird releases their little fledgling that can now fly. As humans, we don't completely break ties, but you would never want to raise a child with traits of dependency, which we see a lot.

The final aspect of thrift and stewardship is the Judeo-Christian tradition of tithing. You know about tithing, yes?

You give away ten percent of all you make.

As you make up your budget for the year, you put the tithe first. You probably have an income of $50,000 if you're middle-class. So you set aside $5,000 at the top of your budget. If the top of your budget is for giving to a church or benefiting others, that creates a concept of priorities.

Another high priority is having clothing and a safe place to live. When you get to the bottom of your budget, you realize you don't need many of those things. We have enough left for a few birthday presents and so on, but we don't need all those personal indulgences. I think there are many people who have become enthusiastic testimonial givers about tithing. They often say they wish they'd started sooner.

269

Americans had a vast love affair with thrift in the 1920s, as they had for 200 years. In the 1920s, on average, people saved 20 cents on every dollar. In 2007, when most people thought that the economy was good, what was the average savings rate? Minus three percent!

The average family owes $10,000 in debt in the U.S., correct?

The average college student's freshman packet includes five credit card applications. They fill them out and get $17,000 of credit card debt, separate from tuition debt and boarding debt.

If alcohol was one's weakness, to the extent that it made you non-functional, you would say one is addicted to alcohol. Our culture is addicted to debt. Who would you say is the most addicted to debt in our society? The government.

The government is massively addicted to debt and in four month's time has come close to tripling the national debt compared to what it was a year ago. That's an addiction. It's other people's money. Those people elected to office aren't stewards. You don't hear elected people say anymore what you and I used to hear, which is, "I am a public servant." This means, first of all, "I am a steward of your taxpayer money."

There is another aspect about culture that relates directly to thrift.

Do you think as an American citizen that you have an unalienable right to have a private house? Do you think Thomas Jefferson, James Madison, Abraham Lincoln, or even F.D.R. felt that every American has this right?

Like the government would have to give you a house?

You put your finger on it. If one thinks that every citizen has the right to have a house, then somehow the means to acquire one, one has to be given to them.

It's the entitlement situation that we're struggling with?

Over the past 30 years, Congress passed harsher, stronger laws in two directions: 1) To impose heavy fines on banks. 2) More importantly, intimidation by federal regulators who said to these banks, "We will block any future growth of expansion you have if you don't give a certain percentage of all of your assets to loans to people who don't even have one dollar."

That whole culture then went eventually to Fannie and Freddie, which dramatically lowered standards. By 2001, you literally did not have to put up any collateral or down payment for a house.

That's not a culture given to thrift.

One other bill that's currently pending in Congress collects $100 billion or $200 billion in taxes. Does every American have an unalienable right to a television? This bill will assure that the government will pay for the conversion from analogue to digital television.

So then that just gets worse and worse. It's like that entitlement just seems to grow and grow. How do moral values fit in?

What percent of people do you think feel that there are absolute rights and wrongs?

The younger ones think they are entitled to all kinds of things.

That's entitlement, but I'm addressing a bigger issue. In all circumstances, there is an absolute wrong and an absolute right. But let's talk about the concept of *moral relativism,* which means there are no absolutes.

So here's a cultural statement: You can pick an area of the country where there are a number of churches. You can take high school juniors and seniors and ask them, "Who thinks Jesus Christ is the One?" 70% might raise their hand. You then ask, "Are there any absolute rights, wrongs, or truths?" 70% will say, "No; everybody knows there are no absolutes." They just said Jesus is the absolute truth, and then later they said everybody knows there are no absolutes. They don't even make the connection. They just know that they have been taught, either through teachers or more profoundly through the media, that everything is moral relativism.

What difference might have been made if Bernie Madoff was taught the Ten Commandments every day? He's a product of a culture of moral relativism. Why shouldn't he cheat people? There's no reason not to. His only remorse is he happened to get caught, not that what he did was wrong.

An alternative theology that really upholds that there are standards of rights or wrongs in the end will defeat a society of moral relativism. Moral relativism is a guaranteed prescription of extermination. There are people of profound convictions who hate the West and the culture in the West. Their intention is to destroy the West because it's morally bankrupt and they can win. If moral relativism is not seen as one of the most profound harmful world views, then hope is at risk.

You and I have very strong feelings about this country and are trying to move forward with positive things. How do you see us turning that around, Dr. Templeton?

Let's go back to thrift. There's a renewed interest in thrift, but it's weak because it's based on need or practicality. If you've lost your job, your pay has been cut, or your bank account is down, you just have to spend less.

What's truly key is to embrace thrift as a passionate conviction. It's a blessing to be thrifty and have an adventure, like how my father saved 50% of what he earned. He just said *plan for what you spend, don't be an impulse buyer.* If it could be done during the Depression, why can't it be done today?

In 1920, the State of Kentucky passed a law mandating the teaching of thrift, industry, and hard work for a minimum number of minutes every week to their students. If you have a good teacher who thinks something is important enough that they take time to teach it and use positive reinforcing examples to persuade you that she or he is right, you begin to have an impact.

The most dominant cultural voice for America's teachers is the teacher's unions. If the unions do not take on a national agenda to teach thrift as a passionate conviction, most teachers aren't going to do it, but they could.

If the unions made this a five-year national agenda, what might you see? You could develop a very well put together six-week course on financial literacy, which includes concepts of prudence, budgeting, and learning what bubbles are.

Madoff was a bubble. The housing mortgage situation was a vast bubble. Nobody has ever taught them what the bubble is. Do you know of the tulip mania in Holland in the 1600s?

No, I don't know that.

Holland had a specialty of not only growing tulips, but bringing in new varieties. There were new colors and petal patterns. People loved them and began to buy them, so the prices went up. People in Holland were convinced that this was an unlimited, increasingly prosperous thing to do. It would cost you five times more to buy four new tulip bulbs than what you paid in buying the older tulip bulbs. The whole bubble collapsed, and people who put all their resources in lost everything. It is a massively illogical concept that something is ever permanently prosperous.

That's a wonderful lesson to teach to kids. As a part of a curriculum on financial literacy, you can pick out 20 core maxims or what my father called "laws of life." One of them said to give no credit to "a great promiser."

Suppose Bernie Madoff met you at a cocktail party and was saying he found a system that would guarantee a 10% return in every up market and down market. You would never lose money, but he doesn't let everybody participate. He'll let you know in a week whether he would accept you in his fund. Everybody psychologically wants to belong to it.

In the back of your mind, you hear your grandmother teaching you maxims, like "give no credit to a great promiser." Then you call back and say, "No thank you Mr. Madoff."

So, those are some thoughts on those core areas.

I have one other suggestion. Most people never ask themselves what their *assumptions* are or even question them. We are prisoners of our assumptions. They very much affect small and large decisions that we make.

Let's say you had a poll that asked, "Is freedom guaranteed and permanent?" What percent of Americans today at every strata, educational level, income level, and ethnic level would say "yes"?

I think most of them think it is permanent.

Yes. I'd say 90%. Why do they think it's permanent? They don't know how tough it was to win freedom, to preserve it against dedicated enemies.

Think of a building at the water's edge that's held up by 15 pillars, so it's above the danger of the waves. If those pillars are, in effect, the pillars of freedom, some of which might be as basic as free speech, protection of personal property and so on, and they are being eroded away or even broken, there comes a point when you can no longer support the house, or sustain freedom.

One of the most dangerous assumptions in America today is that freedom is permanent. Freedom is never permanent.

I gave a talk recently about the culture that gave rise to the financial chaos that we're in. A memo that my father, Sir John Templeton, wrote in June 2005 titled "Financial Chaos" predicted it with uncanny accuracy. He knew the reason why it was coming.

Another cultural question is: Is my physical security permanent?

Before barbarian invaders from the German tribes finally swept over Northern Italy, broke through the walls of Rome and captured it, what do you think the assumptions were of the vast majority of Romans 40 years earlier?

That they were safe. That no one could possible do that.

They just went around them.

John, how can we change people's attitude? You talked in my book America's New Future *about how you could never get your dad to wear a seatbelt until one day you said the right thing. You said, "You might go through the windshield and I could sew you up." Your father hadn't realized that an accident could affect his brain and his thinking. That got him to start using a seatbelt. Is there some way we can do that in this country?*

You'd have to figure it on a socioeconomic level. For example, Americans who are planning to leave something for their children should ask: What is more important, leaving them with a house and money, or leaving them with a culture that enables them to have the freedom to earn that house themselves, start a business, and be able to prosper?

People should ask themselves, "What did Thomas Jefferson mean at the end of the Declaration of Independence where it says in effect, *"...with trust in divine providence we pledge our lives, our fortunes, and our sacred honor?"*

There were signers of the Declaration of Independence who died so that they might have liberty, or they died penniless, but not one of them lost their sacred honor. Those people understood what sacrifice was.

That is outstanding. When I finished America's New Future, *I went back to Philadelphia and Boston to see The Freedom Trail and to reread the sacrifices of our forefathers.*

There's a sense about the importance of giving, and you'll hear people talk about social justice or charitable giving. Somebody is hungry and you need to give them food and so on. I have come to the conclusion that it's all a one-way street. Those who have it are required to give to those who don't. What does that mean in either spiritual or human psychological terms? It means you are talking about people who are permanent givers and permanent receivers. The latter no longer have what spiritual people would say is the "Image of God." Even though God honors and respects the poor, he doesn't want them to *be* poor. He wants them to have that sense of human dignity. They themselves, in time, can become givers.

Society is going to fail if it doesn't try to get across the concept of a social contract. It is a two-way street. People have an opportunity to be able to be a contributor, but the focus should be so that everybody becomes a contributor.

Everybody has the capacity to be much more on target with things, but they have to believe that they're called to be a contributor—a real active contributor, a steward.

And then it's not about *owning* it. It's about *prospering it* by what you do with it.

Your father would be so proud of you. I'm sure he was all along. I feel like he's still around even though he's in Heaven doing his own thing. I bless you for all that. Thank you so much.

Visionary Reflection on...

Responsibility

Writer Robert Heinlein said, "I am free because I know that I alone am morally responsible for everything I do." Rather than opposites, freedom and responsibility are intimately linked. When we are willing to *respond* to the world—to love it, to be a part of it—we are free to live our most extraordinary life. What can you take greater responsibility for today?

CLOCKWISE L to R: Dr. Robert Schuller and Les Paul with
Doris Lee

*"Music speaks what cannot be expressed, soothes the mind, and gives it
rest, heals the heart, makes it whole, flows from the heavens to the soul."*
- Anonymous

CHAPTER 13

The Joy of Living
Music, Laughter & Optimism

● ● ● ● ● ● ● ● ● ● ● ● ● ● ● ● ●

- Visionary Spotlight -

BARRON HILTON
Former CEO Hilton Hotels, CEO, Conrad N. Hilton Foundation

Barron Hilton shares his "special formula for success"…

My father, Conrad H. Hilton, had his special formula for success, as set forth in the last chapter of his autobiography, Be My Guest. *I have followed his formula since early manhood, and it worked well for me.*

1. Find your own particular talent.
2. Be big; Think big; Act big; Dream big.
3. Be honest.
4. Live with enthusiasm.
5. Don't let your possessions possess you.
6. Don't worry about your problems.
7. Don't cling to the past.
8. Look up to people when you can; look down to no one.
9. Assume your full share of responsibility for the world in which you live.
10. Pray consistently and confidently.

ERNESTINE DILLARD
Beloved American gospel singer

Ernestine Dillard is a gospel singer, vocal coach, and mentor to singers, who may be best remembered as the singer who helped heal a nation during the memorial service for the victims and families of the Oklahoma City bombing tragedy, as she performed "God Bless America."

Hearing Ernestine sing, as I have many times at the annual Trumpet Awards Celebration, has always been one of the high points of that event. Her vocal range and her passion for her message permeate the entire audience. All are silent in order to hear every word. Ernestine and I talked recently about her passion for music.

Doris Lee: Ernestine, what are your favorite songs or CDs?

Ernestine Dillard: From my own collection, what I liked most is called *Songs to Heal.* My reason is that a portion of it was recorded live, and I got reports back that people had had special healing experiences happen during that concert.

The song that I like most is "God Bless America Medley." It's a medley of "God Bless America" and "America the Beautiful." That's probably the one that is most popular. Some people say that this song is very healing. I'm singing it a lot with veterans and seniors, and that seems to be very inspirational to them.

You sing from the soul. Is this something that you discovered early in life?

I did discover it early in life, but I think it's just a part of my family, the community that I grew up in. And it's just part of my heritage to be able to sing what the feelings are.

If you know the American spirituals, you know that they were sung to do many things, actually, to help people overcome very difficult circumstances. So I think it's just the way the African-American community communicates through music, and it comes from a very deep place in your heart.

You write lyrics and music. How do you usually do that?

I'm what you would call a song stylist. Occasionally, I will get songs where words come that have not been heard before. But mostly, I style music that other composers have written and composed. It seems to work best for me that way—interpret the music the way I feel it and put it into my own personal space.

As a psychologist, I know that music often holds a healing quality that takes place in a person's soul, in their body and in their minds, long before they may be able to verbalize that. Sometimes people don't feel comfortable coming to a psychologist; whereas, they can listen to music and it helps stir feelings and ideas inside of them, as you're suggesting happens with your CD Songs to Heal.

Right. You know I'm deeply spiritual and my faith base is very strong. What I've studied in the Bible talks of other times and other characters that have used music as a healing tool, and I think God intended it to be so.

Those of us who have been given the gift—and it's a precious gift that I hold dearly and try to be a good steward of—we have that ability. And if we use it properly, I think it has that ability.

There is this saying, "music is a universal language." The live portion of "Songs to Heal" was recorded live in Paris.

Obviously, we don't all speak the same language, but when you hear music, it somehow reaches that special place.

It sounds like you do some traveling, too. I think our world is filled with so much hurt and pain. When I hear of some of the atrocities going on in Africa, people in Iran trying to fight for democracy, what's happened in Myanmar...there's a lot of hurt out there, Ernestine, that needs healing.

Absolutely. My purpose, I know, is to bring about unity and healing, as much as possible. There may always be this kind of difficulty, but I think it is too widespread now, and it can be better.

At first, music might not seem as significant in this vast chaotic "thing" that's going on, but I think it is. I think it's going to be part of healing. Of course, there are some practical solutions that have to be happening as well, but I think music is one of those.

I know your deep-felt connection with church. Do you see this as something that reaches beyond the church?

Yes, absolutely. As a matter of fact, just recently I was in New Hampshire with a group of veterans from our Armed Forces who happened to all be female. Not only did I have a chance to share the music with them, but I also became aware of the plight of the veterans and their families and their deep problems and concerns that we should all be aware of. I'm having a lot interaction with VFWs and that kind of thing.

I'm also presently negotiating to be spokesperson for, isn't it interesting, the Humania Insurance Company, which provides healthcare for seniors. The beginning of my life I spent as a nurse. I'm amazed at the connection—here I am negotiating to be a Goodwill Ambassador for the Humania Company, which is a healthcare provider.

As a psychologist, you know that the needs of our men and women in combat when they return home are great, psychologically and emotionally. The way that the military and healthcare pieces are tying in with music, it's just amazing to me.

Yes. God has an amazing way of making the necessary connections. On the West Coast we would say that's awesome.

Yes, I'd say it's awesome.

Do you see yourself just going on singing until there's no more breath left inside of you?

Absolutely. I promised my children I would do that. On my last note I will just go away to whatever God has prepared for me after this life.

In the meantime, I would like to provide a home for struggling young women. That drop in the bucket would help to provide a home for them, to re-group and recuperate, to get them grounded and stabilized through education and knowledge. I see that as one of my visions– a large home for them to live in until they are more grounded.

What's happening with this vision right now?

I'm working on starting a home outside of mine, but in the past ten years, I've had about seven to ten women live in my own home. Anywhere from four months to sixteen months, they live here to re-group financially and to learn some coping skills to handle the problems they have in society.

I've had as many as two living here at one time, and they vary in ages from 20 to 40 years old. That's what I've been doing on a limited basis, but I would like to create a more structured type of situation for them.

Have you thought of doing a fundraiser for this, where people come and hear you sing and have the proceeds go for the new facility?
Absolutely. That's my goal. As we speak, we're planning something of that nature. I have people working on that.

What final word would you give to our readers?

I think that my goal and focus is to bring unity and peace between people—and I mean all cultures. Music is a very important part of that, but I think understanding and actually getting to know each other is more important. Music is an avenue, but there are many other ways that we can work together to learn to know each other, so that we can get along better.

Ernestine, I appreciate your time and I'm looking forward to getting your CDs.

Thank you so much for having me.

- *Visionary Spotlight* -

LES PAUL
Father of the Electric Guitar; Played at the Iridium Club to age 93

At an age when most people have long since retired, Les Paul was still playing with great enthusiasm every Monday night at the Iridium Club in New York City. He played to sold-out audiences who came early and stood in line even in the cold and rain to hear this master who was often referred to as "An American Legend." He often invited other musicians, young and old, to come and share the stage with him. They were just pleased to be able to play along with the Grand Master.

At one show, I had requested to talk with Les and was fortunate to get an invitation into his green room. As many people know, the "green room" is often not green but rather gray. However, the gray tones of the room were brought to life by the colorful people milling about.

After the concert, while standing in a long line of people waiting to get his autograph, Les asked me to sit down next to him and keep him company during the signing. What a delight! He told me, "Music is a very special way of transferring feelings—that can't be done any other way. It's great therapy for the listener and the player."

Les had a particularly special way of transferring his own feelings when he played, often making interesting sounds while his face let you know that he still had the thrill and joy of being able to communicate with his audience through music.

- Visionary Spotlight -

AUDREY GEISEL
President and CEO of Dr. Seuss Enterprises, Philanthropist,
often called Mrs. Dr. Seuss

Dr. Seuss (aka, Theodor Seuss Geisel) was a very highly evolved Visionary. He made his words and characters come alive, and he stretched our imaginations to wondrous frontiers of creativity. Uplifted by writing that was almost musical in its rhythmic cadence, he helped us to think about how we too can put interesting words together. The hours of quality time between parents and children around the world would be impossible to calculate.

Ask anybody at University of California, San Diego about Dr. Seuss and they all have a special connection. "The Geisel Library is where I go to study," says Kelly. "Every year on his birthday the whole university is invited to eat cake in celebration of his life!" In the gardens surrounding the library is a sculpture called "Dr. Seuss and the Cat in the Hat," after one of his best-loved books.

Audrey and I live in the same town, La Jolla, which is in the San Diego area. Every year, there is a special 4th of July parade on Beaumont Avenue in La Jolla. The theme of this legendary parade one year was "Oh, the places you'll go down Beaumont Street," taking off on another one of his books. Families and neighbors came together to make colorful floats, and there was a wonderful variety of Dr. Seuss characters represented in the parade. Two of the stand-out costumes were the green-faced Grinch and twin babies as Thing 1 and Thing 2. Of course, there were also many Cats in the Hats.

The San Diego Art Museum did a retrospective of Dr. Seuss some years ago featuring a huge *Cat in the Hat* figure peeking over the top of the tall museum building. I personally cherish a picture of Ted signing a copy of *One Fish Two Fish Red Fish Blue Fish* as a keepsake for my family to enjoy.

The inspiring woman who keeps these creative and far-reaching stories alive is Ted's wife, Audrey Geisel. "She is the only one I would trust choosing colors for my figures or commenting on my stories," Ted said to me some years ago.

Audrey has taken on the creative side of Dr. Seuss Enterprises, which enables many of us to continue enjoying the Dr. Seuss characters that have so enriched our lives.

Visionary Reflection on...

Passion

No matter our age, finding our passion may be as important as food, air, and water. Enjoying our days, finding what makes us sing, and allowing ourselves to laugh heartily and often shouldn't be left for "someday." Allow yourself to tap into optimism and joy today. What would be possible in your life if you fanned the flame of your passion?

CHAPTER 14

Top to bottom: Her Majesty the Queen Mother Ashi Dorji Wangmo Wangchuck of Bhutan with Doris Lee, His Majesty King Jigme Khesar Namgyel Wangchuck and Jetsun Pema, the Queen of Bhutan

CHAPTER 14

Another Kind of Visionary
What Can We Learn from Bhutan?

• • • • • • • • • • • • • • • • •

In traveling to Bhutan and staying with a local family, I was greatly impacted by the sense of well-being and happiness I discovered amongst people everywhere. This led me to write a book called, *The Magic of Gross National Happiness*. In preparing and writing the book about visionaries, the leaders and citizens of Bhutan were at the top of my list. Whether talking about a country, a city, an organization, or a family, what could be more visionary than prioritizing balance, well-being, and happiness?

The term "gross national happiness" was coined in 1972 by Bhutan's fourth king, **King Jigme Singye Wangchuck**. As a true visionary, he used the phrase to underscore his commitment to building an economy that would serve Bhutan's unique culture based on Buddhist spiritual values. What started as a somewhat casual remark became a concept that has come to define this profound nation. The concept was taken seriously, and the Centre for Bhutan Studies developed a sophisticated survey instrument to measure the population's general level of well-being. Over time, Gross National Happiness has become a unifying vision for the people of Bhutan, as well as other countries that are now adopting the concept to create their own version of the survey and index.

The fifth and current king of Bhutan is **King Jigme Khesar Namgyel Wangchuck**. Being a young man (who was officially crowned in 2008), His Majesty is bringing a voice of encouragement to the youth of Bhutan to work hard and continue striving for a high standard of living.

The interviews that follow will shed much inspiring light on what Gross National Happiness really means in the lives of the Bhutanese, and it just may give rise to new ideas for spreading happiness within your own community.

Visionary Spotlight– the next generation

PRINCE JIGYEL UGYEN WANGCHUCK
Son of the Fourth King of Bhutan

The opportunity to meet with Prince Jigyel Ugyen Wangchuck arose and it was a pleasure to see him once more. When I first met Jigyel, he was representing his country at the Smithsonian Annual Festival. He was asked to speak and as he approached the podium. The audience seemed to appreciate his colorful outfit from the 14th century. But most importantly, they admired his colorful hand-painted boots. His friendly, outgoing personality was instantly communicated.

After the Prince spoke, Governor Rick Perry of Texas strode to the platform with his very large lizard-skin cowboy boots. As he came to the podium, his first words were, "This is the first time that anyone has out-booted me." The audience responded with a great deal of laughter.

The fifth king, Jigme Khesar Namgyel Wangchuck, honored Jigyel by making him Chairman of the Bhutanese Olympic Committee.

Jigyel also serves on the Tarayana Foundation Executive Board of Directors, an organization aimed at reducing poverty by helping isolated villagers sell their products. He is doing a wonderful job of continuing the legacy of happiness in Bhutan.

HER MAJESTY THE QUEEN MOTHER, DORJI ASHI WANGMO WANGCHUCK
Queen of Bhutan

Doris Lee: I think it's phenomenal that you and Jigme, your Secretary General of Tarayana, have walked to many of your small villages.

Queen Ashi: Yes, we have walked all over the country.

Of the things that you brought with you, what was most helpful to the people in the villages?

On our journeys to the remote parts of our country, which happened in 2001, we found some amazing things in the indigenous population. Let me begin first with one community that's in southern Bhutan. To get into those villages, I had to cross the river many times, sometimes in swift currents. We knew that we would have to cross the river, so we were prepared. We had to make sure that we didn't have to take our shoes off each time we crossed a river, so we decided to wear plastic slippers [flip flops]. I bought plastic slippers for the entire team. After crossing the river 24 times, I noticed that my feet were totally cut and blistered because of the new plastic slippers. We stopped so I could bandage my cuts.

Then we had to brave leeches. I'm petrified of leeches. There was this torrential rain after that hail storm, and we were totally drenched. We walked into this village we had never been to before. It was very remote. The place where

291

we were supposed to camp was the school football ground. By the time we reached there it was late and our tents were totally soaked, so we had to take shelter in the school. The next day, we couldn't leave because the weather was so bad. So we met all the villagers in town. I gave them a variety of vegetable seeds so that they could improve their nutrition.

We sat down and had a meeting. It was so wonderful. They didn't know who I was, because I didn't tell them. We had a question-and-answer session. I asked them about their crops and their hopes and aspirations. I said I had come to them because of His Majesty, from whom I derive my total inspiration. In the early years, he had envisioned a way of life for his people called "gross national happiness." I could have ridden to the villages, but I wanted to walk; to experience the hardship, if even for a short while. I walked into the villages to explain the king's mission, and I also wanted to realize His Majesty's concept of Gross National Happiness. I wanted to be with the people in their own homes and to experience their difficulties, to learn about their dreams for the future, and in some way make them come true. So we sat and ate with them and visited their places of worship.

In the meetings, there were many questions asked. For instance, they were very interested in the vegetables they had never planted, like broccoli. They wanted to know about the different kinds of vegetables and how to grow them, and that's why Jigme, the Secretary General of Tarayana, had been working for the Ministry of Agriculture. She has the expertise; she went to Cornell in the U.S. and got her Master's degree. She was a wonderful person to travel with.

At one meeting, after we had spoken about nutrition, health, the school system, the earth, and everything that they wanted to talk about, one person asked us, "Who are you?" I thought that was the most refreshing, wonderful gift, because I wanted to go among them and let them feel comfortable without any inhibitions. That was one of my first trips in southern Bhutan.

We walked into that very village, an indigenous community and also quite poor. They didn't have proper housing; they were like huts on stilts. There was a school that was put up by the government, but the children didn't have uniforms. The parents didn't have the means to buy the uniforms, and they had to go to school without shoes and couldn't buy the books. Some of them wouldn't go to school at all because of the lack of these basic needs.

I thought about this a lot, and I said, "What can we do for them?" The first thing was basic shelter. If you have a proper home then your health improves because your basic security is there. Another thing I should put in before anything else is the education of the children, because with education you improve everything; and then nutrition and income is generated, etc.

There was so much to do, and suddenly I said, "Okay, it has to be a total package, a total holistic program." There was a cluster of three villages close by, so we decided to work in these three villages. It was really one large village by the name of Little Kochu and broken up into A, B, and C. So I suggested three names that came to mind: Jigme, Singye, Wangchuck.

How wonderful.

This is the first time this has ever happened, Doris. I said, "Okay, let me question villagers A, B and C in Little

Kochu. Let me call them Little Kochu Jigme, Little Kochu Singye and Little Kochu Wangchuck. This is the first time that a cluster of villages has ever been named after His Majesty." His Majesty doesn't like anything being named after him, but I didn't seek his permission. I was just spontaneous and did it. I said, "The reason why I'm naming the three villages after His Majesty is that I will take a very solemn vow, because I honor my duties first and any wish that I say to him I will do it 100% to make it right."

They were very happy to have His Majesty's name for their villages. We celebrated that night with a ceremony; we sat and danced with them in a circle, ate and prayed together. It was a wonderful beginning.

This is the story about their hopes.

After that, I spent three nights there. I visited every home and then adopted a very beautiful lady—an older lady—Angonee's grandmother, Sarah. She looked just like you, a complexion just like yours, very clear and translucent, lovely hair. We adopted her. One of the first things I did in my earlier travels was to adopt ladies who had spent a lot of their time and energies being mothers, and I wanted to honor the mothers of the community. It's because of them that we are who we are. I had done this in other places, but in this village, the lady Anga-Sarah, is a very serene lady. I adopted her, and by giving her a sense of dignity and respect, we made her feel special, and she now contributes again to her family. We adopted a little boy, and that's how we started.

Over time, we supplied uniforms to all the children of the village so they could go to school with confidence. Then we built permanent homes for all residents who didn't have them. Most importantly, we showed them how to build the homes because they didn't have the skills. We took a pre-built home and taught them masonry, so they now all have permanent homes. Also, in that village, we set up a community center.

We also set up a factory in that community where they make stationery paper, envelopes, and many other things. We trained the local men in the art of craftsmanship and how to market the products, so there's no middleman cost for them, and they get exactly what they should be getting.

Also in that same village, we lifted their spirits. There was not a single person who had gone to college, so we got a sponsor. The first college graduate—we call him "The Doctor"—was educated on the condition that he would come back to the community. Now we're trying to get from that community the first engineering degree student. They didn't have one at that time. The most highly-educated person in that village had graduated from 10th grade. We've come a long way in that community, and there's a sense of pride. We have kept our promise to them, and they are doing so much better now. That's one of our success stories.

We've operationalized His Majesty's concept of GNH. We've taken this concept to other villages in Bhutan. In this village, it's definitely taking hold. In other villages, like those in the Mongar district, we have created necessities for them so they can make bamboo baskets and other products. This is something wonderful for this region. In two years, the community regenerated itself with the profits from their bamboo baskets, which gave them a sense of accomplishment. We market all the products from the communities that create them. The villagers weave the baskets, and now we are in 36 villages and five districts.

Our desire is that we can do this in just about every village in Bhutan.

What does Tarayana mean?

Tara is the name of the goddess of wisdom and compassion. Yana means vehicle. When we put them together, it becomes a vehicle for wisdom, making it possible for the development of rural areas.

How much time do you spend in board meetings for the Tarayana Foundation?

Actually the board meetings don't take too much time. We schedule to meet twice a year, but I'm almost involved on a day-to-day basis with Tarayana activities, and I'm very passionate about it.

With all the people that I've had the privilege to interview over the years—the ones who were the most satisfied and successful—the number one trait they have shared is having a great passion for what they were doing.

I'm not sure I've even scratched the surface of what I really want to do. The possibilities are enormous. The challenges are: 1) you need the funds, and 2) you need the infrastructure. Right now, we have 21 people working with Tarayana.

It is possible to attain the goal of having a poverty-less country. Can we have a free Bhutan?

Oh yes, most definitely. Nothing is impossible if you have your heart in the right place; if you have the funds, energy, and a whole network of committed volunteers. If everyone joins hands, nothing is impossible.

Your king still continues to give five acres away to anybody who has no land at all, is that correct?

Yes, I'm not sure about the acreage now, but His Majesty gives land away.

One of the domains of GNH is time-use. Would you say a little bit about that? We all have just so much time. How do you see that best being divided?

Time management is very important. You devote time to your work, to your family, to keeping yourself in good shape—physically as well as spiritually. If one gives the right time in proportion to the needs, then the quality of life goes up.

Is there anything else you would like to share with our readers?

Today is a very happy day for me since I met you, Doris. I think we need more people like you to bring a whole network of social workers and philanthropists together. It makes it possible for social workers like us to do our job; to bring together people who care deeply about the world can make a real difference in uplifting life.

You have brought all of these people together with one goal, and that is to make the world a better place for all of us. I salute you for that, Doris. You're one lady who has put a beat in my heart.

Visionary Reflection on...

Happiness

Today, make a list (long or short) of everything that brings you happiness. Without censoring yourself, simply notice what shows up on your list. As an awareness exercise, notice what people, activities, possessions, experiences, and circumstances bring you happiness.

CLOCKWISE L to R: Nicholas Kristof, Bob Buford, President Bill Clinton, James Cameron, and Senator John Glenn

CHAPTER 15

Forging a New Future
Making Commitments & Taking Action

●●●●●●●●●●●●●●●●●●

BOB BUFORD
Social Entrepreneur and author of *Finishing Well, Halftime, Game Plan,* and others

Bob Buford is a cable-TV pioneer, social entrepreneur, author, and venture philanthropist. He co-founded Leadership Network in 1984, became founding chairman in 1988 of what was initially called The Peter F. Drucker Foundation for Nonprofit Management, and popularized the concept of "Halftime" through several books he authored, demonstrating that life after 60 can be productive, exciting, and fun.

Doris Lee: Could you tell us about halftime?

Bob Buford: Carl Jung, the Swiss psychiatrist, wrote about the first season for males being a warrior season, where you're proving yourself and making your mark. That's what I call *Life One.* You're raising a family and seeing if you can stay with the same woman more than six months without getting a divorce. I'm now in my 47th year of that trial and find it better than ever.

Life Two happened for me in my mid '40s, where I changed from success to significance.

The *Third Season,* according to Jung, is that of being a sage or a person who has special knowledge as a result of his or her experiences. In that season, I've written four books. My next book, which is titled *My Next Book*, is available for free on the web; a chapter every two weeks. I'm writing a book on the part of the journey that I'm now living.

There's no other age or place I'd rather be than where I am right now. I think when you get to what I call halftime, you basically say, "I've been there, done that, and whatever it is that I've been doing to project my veneer to the world, I'm satisfied on that part—or dissatisfied, as the case may be—but now it's time to go on to something else."

In my case, it was a transition from success to significance. I went from being the chairman of the board of a television broadcast company that morphed into a cable television company. I think when you do that, there are three things that are critical to know about that most people don't know. One is to know what your strengths are. Most people think they know their strengths, but what they know usually is their role as a mom, nurse, entrepreneur, financier, or something like that. You start with what you're good at, and in a more theological sense, the way God made you. I think God made every one of us for a purpose. I think the second half of your life is when you have the opportunity to discover what that is.

There it is—the life that has been waiting for you. Now you have the opportunity to take control of your life and do what Peter Drucker calls "managing yourself" at last.

How do you see that working in people's lives as they get older?

God has redeemed us, but for a purpose. Jung called it "your life task," and most people don't know what that is. *It is the thing that reawakens your original passion.* It's something that's been in your life a long time, and you begin to get a sense that it's time to get around to it at last.

301

Halftime is when you step aside and say, "It's time to figure it out."

In my case, I had an experience where my assistant, who was older than I was and wiser as well, walked into my office when I was managing a television station and said, "You're really a frightening person. You frighten people who work for you."

I said, "Say more."

She said, "You are so intense about getting wealthy and making cash flow in your business targets that you're kind of scary." That caused a moment of pause. I went outside and sat under a tree with my Day-Timer in my lap and asked myself three questions:

1. Is she right? (I answered that: "Yes, she is.")
2. What am I going to lose in all this target-lock focus that she's describing?
3. What's truly important to me in my life? If my life worked out, what would be the elements in that? Stephen Covey calls this "beginning with the end in mind."

One of the things I saw was for my son to have high self-esteem. It was the next family priority, and he did, up until the moment he died at 24.

Was it hard to accept your assistant's personal comments?

No, not a bit. I said, "It sounds right to me. I'd better go dissect this a bit." Better to have a train wreck in a conference room than out on a train track. Do it in your mind rather than in real life. That altered my life, and I began to think about what my mission was.

Fortunately, at that time I'd developed a relationship with Peter Drucker who was, from my point of view, the most practically intelligent person alive on earth at that point. I think that was providential, because he began to turn midway in his career of thinking about how organizations are managed and thinking about how society works from business to what he called the social sector. He and I began to think about what contribution management could make to the social sector.

We worked first on the application of management to the scalability of churches, so we created Leadership Network, where we sought to find the people who had the best ideas—not management leaders but church leaders. A whole industry developed, and I've had the good fortune of being surrounded for 30-40 years by people trying to do virtuous things for other people. I may live to 200 if I can stick around those people. I expect you're one of those.

One of the reasons I'm compiling this visionaries book is because I'm excited to tell people about individuals who have discovered their task in life. Bob, you don't wait for someone to add your ideas to the system, you just start the system.

Do you feel for that you were supposed to meet Peter Drucker? You both seemed to have inspired one another.

Absolutely. I came along about the time Peter had written all his major works on business. In 1974, he combined those in a book called *Management: Tasks, Responsibilities and Practices.* He always called himself a social ecologist, and he came to the belief that the social sector probably had more to do with preservation of what we call the American way of life. Remember, he came from Europe at about the time Hitler was starting a war that cost fifty-five million people their lives. I think Peter resolved that it shouldn't happen in the United States and the main thing that would keep it from happening is the proper management of organizations: government, business and, finally, the social sector. That's what I was interested in, and that's what he was interested in about the time I came along. He coached me for 25 years in how to do it, and it worked.

Peter was almost exactly 30 years older than me, and we began to talk about the opportunity that people have in the second half of their life to live the life they were designed to live in the first place. Most of us don't have that in the first half. We set it aside for other things; money, fame, and power are the three main culprits. We wake up one day and wonder, "What shall I do with that? It's a big puzzle, and most people never figure it out.

How do people go about identifying what will make the second half of life fulfilling and meaningful for them?

On the "how" side, I'd say there are three major components:

1. Identify your strengths.
2. Discover what ignites (or reignites) your passion; what causes you to whistle while you work.
3. Know what drives your economic engine.

The thing that kills a lot of people is retirement, where they simply lose their purpose in life, and they lose their life pretty shortly thereafter. You do need enough money and resources to survive; that's an important practical question.

There was a Polish poet named Czesław Miłosz, who was about Peter's age, and all his poetry toward the end of his life was wondering whether he had completed his calling on earth. I don't live with regret, nor did Miłosz.

How do you handle it when something doesn't work out the way you want it to?

I quit doing it.

How can people get in touch with you, Bob?

The best way is to look up what's called <u>ActiveEnergy.net</u> or <u>BobBuford.com</u>, either of those two.

Every two weeks, I write a different chapter. It's usually about what's going on right now, so it's very current.

Is there anything else you would like to say to our readers?

The hope I have for people is that they find that life work that was prepared beforehand for them to do and they get busy doing it! They'll live happier, more productive, more purposeful lives, and they'll also have more treasure in Heaven.

- Visionary Spotlight -

NICHOLAS KRISTOF
Author, Pulitzer Prize winner, award-winning journalist for the *New York Times*

Nicholas Kristof is a world-renowned *New York Times* journalist who grew up on a sheep and cherry farm in Oregon. He graduated Phi Beta Kappa from Harvard College, then went on to study law at Oxford University on a Rhodes Scholarship with first-class honors. As a student, he backpacked through Africa and Asia, writing articles to cover his expenses. While traveling, he encountered everything from malaria, to mobs, to an airplane crash in Africa.

Traveling the world has gotten into his blood. For the *New York Times*, Nicholas has served as a correspondent in Los Angeles, Hong Kong, Beijing, and Tokyo. He later became Associate Managing Editor of the Sunday editions of the *Times*.

In 1990, Nicholas and his wife Sheryl WuDunn, who was also a journalist for the *Times*, won the Pulitzer Prize for their coverage of China's Tiananmen Square democracy movement. Subsequently, Nicholas visited the Darfur region of Sudan more than ten times, writing columns that have often focused on global health, poverty, and human trafficking. He won a second Pulitzer in 2006 for his commentary, which the judges called "his graphic, deeply-reported columns that, at personal risk, focused attention on genocide in Darfur and that gave voice to the voiceless in other parts of the world."

I met Nicholas at the Clinton Global Initiative in New York City in 2011. While there, he interviewed Mahmoud Ahmadinejad, the President of Iran, procuring the only print interview the President gave on his visit to the UN General Assembly. Despite his many commitments, Nicholas was kind enough to share a few thoughts aimed at young people and how to have a positive outlook:

> *For all of recorded history, it has been routine for each generation to lament the shortcomings of young people. In the same way, it's common to hear adults today groan about today's youth.*
>
> *But I'm very optimistic about young people. Sure, there are some dregs, but I also run into so many*

high school and university students who are working passionately on behalf of the less fortunate at home or around the world. Some of it is calculated to make them look better in college or fellowship applications, but much of it is absolutely sincere and deeply-rooted in a value system that I greatly admire.

They're not only empowering others but also empowering themselves. One of the things I've learned is that although our efforts to help others have a somewhat mixed record, these efforts have an almost perfect record of helping ourselves.

- Nicholas D. Kristof

Nicholas and his wife are authors of *Half the Sky: Turning Oppression Into Opportunity for Women Worldwide.* He has a Facebook fan page and a channel on YouTube.

- Visionary Spotlight -

PRESIDENT BILL CLINTON, CLINTON GLOBAL INITIATIVE, and CLINTON GLOBAL INITIATIVE UNIVERSITY

It seems fitting to include in this book about visionaries President Bill Clinton and his paradigm-changing work through the Clinton Global Initiative (CGI) and Clinton Global Initiative University (CGIU). If I were to summarize former President Bill Clinton's tremendous work and ongoing contribution in one word, it would have to be **commitment**. Through the Clinton Global Initiative (bringing over 130 world leaders together to take action on global challenges) to CGI University (launched in 2007 to engage the next generation of leaders on college campuses around the world), President Clinton has been inspiring people around the globe to *commit to take action*. The results have been nothing short of remarkable.

Secretary of State Hillary Clinton, Chelsea and President Bill Clinton

CLINTON GLOBAL INITIATIVE UNIVERSITY

A recent meeting of CGIU took place in my home town, at the University of California, San Diego, in April 1-3. Nearly 1,200 attendees came together to make a difference in CGI U's five focus areas: Education, Environment & Climate Change, Peace & Human Rights, Poverty Alleviation, and Public Health.

Here are some of their outstanding commitments to date:

- *Made more than $1.3 million in infrastructure*
- *Improvements to schools and libraries in countries including the U.S., Rwanda, Nigeria, and Laos.*
- *Raised nearly $2.8 million for college scholarships, nearly $400,000 for humanitarian relief and more than $800,000 for global health programs and hospitals.*
- *Provided more than 150,000 people with better access to health care and social services.*
- *Collected more than $100,000 in books, laptops and other educational supplies.*
- *Built 44 schools and libraries.*
- *Engaged 2,700 people in workshops on conflict resolution, diplomacy, and peace.*

- *Established and maintained over 90,000 square feet of community gardens.*
- *Introduced more than 3,000 bicycles on college campuses within the U.S. as well as in communities in Ghana, Uganda, Kenya, Cameroon, and China.*

CLINTON GLOBAL INITIATIVE ANNUAL MEETING

In his closing speech given at the Annual Meeting of CGI in New York City in 2010, President Clinton shared some real numbers that tell an important story about what's possible when people act on behalf of humanity. He talked about how CGI had, as of 2010, already generated 1,900 commitments worth $63 million, which positively affected 3 million lives in 170 countries. At that point in time, he said that 900,000 people had interacted with CGI on Facebook, and there were more than 200 tweets an hour. He concluded by saying:

"People are catching on and tuning in to what CGI members are doing. We operate through a minimum amount of talking in relationship to doing.

Why are we doing this? Why are people so committed to disaster relief and economic empowerment? Many are worried that in this recession, we would lose our confidence in our shared future. People should remember meaningful accomplishments and what we're attempting to do. Even with limited resources, people still care about their neighbors. Interdependence is the number one issue of the 21st century. We have a responsibility to the next generation to ensure positives outweigh negatives."

Making commitments is not only about pledging to do something; making commitments is intimately linked to engaging ourselves, to *taking action*. The Clinton Global Initiative and CGI U are two of the finest organizations in the world today for putting our desires to make a difference in the world, into motion.

For much more information, go to www.clintonglobalinitiative.org. The CGI community also includes MyCommitment.org, which engages a select group of young CGI members for leadership development and collective commitment-making.

CLINTON GLOBAL INTIATIVE September 2011
Sheraton Hotel, New York City

What is the Clinton Global Initiative?

More than 1,200 members attended the 7th Annual Meeting of CGI to brainstorm creative solutions to address the three topics presented at the meeting: Jobs, Jobs, Jobs; Generating Employment for the 21st Century; Sustainable Consumption; Ensuring Long-term Prosperity on a Finite Planet; and Girls and Women; Scaling What Works.

CGI members have made more than 2,000 commitments and have improved the lives of more than 300 million people in more than 180 countries since CGI began seven years ago in 2005. Established by President Bill Clinton, this annual conference has brought together 150 current/former heads of state, 18 Nobel Prize laureates, hundreds of leading CEOs, major philanthropists, heads of foundations, leaders of nongovernmental organizations, and the media to devise and implement innovative solutions to some of the world's most pressing challenges.

Here are some of the many topics that were presented at this conference:

ENDING CHILD MARRIAGES

Archbishop Desmond Tutu, chairman of the Elders, and **Mary Robinson**, the first female Irish President joined the Ford Foundation and NoVo Foundation to announce an initiative to end child marriage. The Elders are an independent group of global leaders who work together for peace and human rights.

On the Topic: "Conversations on Courage" at CGI 2011
Archbishop Desmond Tutu interviewed **Aung San Suu Kyi**, the General Secretary of the Nation League for Democracy, who had personally decided to stay in her house in Myanmar (Burma) to openly protest the lack of democracy in her country. She was interviewed over Skype. Aung San Suu Kyi is the daughter of Aung San, considered to be the father of modern-day Burma. Aung San Suu Kyi was awarded the Nobel Peace Prize in 1991 for her efforts in fighting for democracy in Burma.

TECHNOLOGIES FOR BUILDING SOCIAL AND ECONOMIC VALUE

Other CEOs and Presidents spoke out on International Issues

Tarja K. Halonen, President of the Republic of Finland
Andrew N. Liveris, Chariman & CEO, The Dow Chemical Company
Bob McDonald, Chairman, President, & CEO, Proctor & Gamble
Judith Rodin, President, The Rockefeller Foundation
Wale Tinubu, CEO & Managing Director, Oando PLC Group

Madeleine Albright (Master of Ceremonies, Chair of Albright Stonebridge Group) and Former US Secretary of State led a panel on **ORGANIZING CHANGE.**

311

MICROSOFT committed to bringing technology access to one million low-income youth. They launched a three-year program to give one million students from low-income families in the U.S. the benefits of software, hardware and broadband Internet service so they can have the training they need to compete in the global market. This project also aims to increase employment opportunities and contribute to their community's economic recovery.

Sports as a Tool for Social Good–Robin Roberts, as you all know, has been on anchor of ABC's "Good Morning America." When not traveling around the country or the world covering breaking news events, she is at "GMA's" studio in Times Square conducting interviews with a diverse group of newsmakers.

Here are other main topics addressed at the CGI:
Clean Water, Combating Ocean Trash, Global Smoke-Free Work Sites, The Burden of Cancer, Increasing Food Production, Stop Sex Trafficking, Breeding Cattle in Haiti, Intertribal Council on Utility Policy (COUP), Green Jobs Initiative, and more.

Now there are over 200 creative ideas brought to the CGI events. **Three Projects I found most innovative that can be used particularly in the Developing World were:**

1. The sOccket – One that attracted a great deal of attention came from four Harvard students: Jessica Lin, Julie Silverman, Hemali Thakkar, and Jessica O. Matthews. They were challenged by their Harvard professor to build something that would help African villages.

They invented the sOccket which was a soccer ball that captures energy when playing soccer to charge batteries and LEDS inside the ball. Jessica, herself, came from a small village in Africa where 90% of the population has no electricity and lives off the grid. The group of four figured out how to make this special soccer ball that could be used by local young people, with a special mechanism inside. After playing soccer for a short period of time, it is able to gather the energy to power up electricity for later, such as for reading lamps, cell phones, etc. More specifically, fifteen minutes of play can light three hours of LED light. Amazingly enough, Jessica believes that the sOccket soccer ball now costing $70.00, but she is trying to get it down to $10.00. To find out more about this, go to: www.soccket.com.

2. Rolling Water Tank - Women have traditionally had to carry jugs on their heads to get water for 4-8 hours. However, a new invention manufactured by *Kopernick* can change that. The new 13-gallon donut-shaped plastic container can be used by a family of five for one week. It can be easily moved by pulling a rope to and from a well and is now being used by men as well as women to transport water more easily. This can be a huge cultural shift, as carrying water is now not just limited to women anymore, but can also be considered a "masculine task."

3. The ZamBike - Bamboo bikes co-founded by Vaughn Spethmann, 24 in Zambia. This project is extremely eco-

313

friendly, using the fastest growing woody plant-bamboo and low-tech production to make bike frames that are light weight and easy to carry; can also be sold in America.

It was delightful to hear the many commitments to projects and the action that will or has already been taken on them. For more information, visit www.clintonglobalinitiative.org under "Our Meetings" – "Annual Meeting 2011."

The Next Clinton Global Initiative was called
"DESIGNING FOR IMPACT"
NYC September, 2012

It is always interesting to see some people we have read about in the news, for example, involved with CGI. The following were 2012 featured panelist:
• **Michael T. Duke**, president and CEO, Wal-Mart Stores, Inc.
• **Her Majesty Queen Rania Al Abdullah**, of the Hashemite Kingdom of Jordan
• **Ban Ki-Moon**, secretary-general, United Nations
• **Jim Yong Kim**, president, World Bank Group

One of the announcements was the Panzi Hospital, of Democratic Republic of Congo. They were receiving $150,000 over two years for sustainable and renewable energy, from Suntech Power Holdings Co., Dr. **Zhengrong Shi,** Chairman, is a member of CGI and is also in *VISIONARIES.*

P&G, **Proctor and Gamble,** along with Musician **Smokey Robinson**, are joining efforts for clean drinking water. Smokey emailed his friends and asked them to join the effort.

Another person who is highly respected and follows in his mother's footsteps is **Dr. Timothy Shriver**, who has worked with Special Olympics, along with his family for many years.

Special Olympics provides year-round sports training and athletic competition in a variety of Olympic-type sports for children and adults with intellectual disabilities, giving them continuing opportunities to develop physical fitness, demonstrate courage and experience joy.

I once went on a plane with some of the Special Olympics to Ireland. Halfway through the flight we were detained in England for 4 ½ hours. Many guests complained but not the Special Olympic athletes. They shouted and yelled when we finally arrived at our destination.

HONOREES WERE GIVEN RECOGNITION FOR THEIR CONTRIBUTIONS

Denis O'Brien, chairman and founder of Digicel Group. Digicel has extended its operations to 31 markets, with over 12.8 million subscribers in the Caribbean, Central America, and Pacific regions. O'Brien is one of Ireland's leading entrepreneurs, with extensive investments across several sectors, including international telecoms, radio, media, property, aircraft leasing, golf, and other leisure interests. One of his greatest contributions was that he made it possible for people to donate even small amounts of money like $5 or $10 with their cell phones to help rebuild Haiti.

For more information concerning the Clinton Global Initiative
Established in 2005 by US President Bill Clinton, the Clinton Global Initiative (CGI) convenes global leaders to create and implement innovative solutions to the world's most pressing challenges. As of 2012, CGI Annual Meetings have brought together more than 150 heads of state, 20 Nobel Prize laureates, and hundreds of leading CEOs, heads of foundations and NGOs, major philanthropists, and members of the media. To date CGI members have made more than 2,100 commitments,

which are already improving the lives of nearly 400 million people in more than 180 countries. When fully funded and implemented, these commitments will be valued at $69.2 billion (From the Clinton Global Initiative Office).

One of my joys in attending the Clinton Global Initiative was that I was able to hear Chelsea Clinton moderating an outstanding panel. She was poised, well in control of the session and I was very pleased to see how she has beautifully developed her ability to speak confidently while staying very professional.

When she left, I ran to the next session of Clinton's Press Conference. When I arrived I was told that I was thirty seconds too late. I was very disappointed and thought about leaving; but somehow a special voice inside me said, "Stay, stay, stay." Five minutes later the door opened and President Clinton was right in front of me. I just happened to be holding my new book, *REMARKABLE LEADER*. I quickly told the President how pleased I was that he was featured in the book and how great it would be if he could do a testimony for it. He looked at it and said, "It looks interesting, send it to my office." You can believe that the very next day I did just that.

Doris Lee talks with President Clinton

I just returned from PRESIDENT CLINTON'S HEALTH MATTERS INITIATIVE CONFERENCE held on January 16, 2013, in La Quinta, CA. The event was mainly sponsored by the health insurance group, HUMANA, and retail corporation, WALMART.

316

If your company is not doing well, this is a winning model you will want to seriously consider. They started out the Health Day and in the following days, combined it with the PGA golf event with top golfers.

The HEALTH DAY started with an exercise and work out which was followed by regular tea and coffee but also the best blue berry smoothie I have ever had. It was so good that I went back for seconds. True to Clinton's style, the program was filled with strong supporters of a healthy lifestyle.

Did you know that Coachella Valley also has an active non-profit called, HIDDEN HARVEST, that goes into the fields and picks up vegetables and fruits left behind and gives them to the needy? The founder and Executive Director is Christy Porter.

Confident and very capable, Chelsea Clinton moderated a panel at the event. I told her that I was pleased to include her in my book soon to be launched book *REMARKABLE LEADERS: Risk Takers Who Dare Us*. She gave me a big smile and hug.

Lunch followed this and started with fennel and salad (something not usually in my diet but very tasty). Next we had Black Sea Bass and a healthy desert.

Barbara Streisand was there with her husband to announce her commitment of $2 MILLION for a WOMEN'S HEART program. Did you know that more women die of heart failure than all other health problems like Cancer, diabetes, etc.? I didn't!

The 16th SURGEON GENERAL OF THE UNITED STATES, Dr. David Satcher, head of the Satcher Health Leadership Institute at Morehouse School of Medicine was there. We talked briefly about Dr. Benjamin Mayes, one of my dear friends who

317

led the first class of non-violence at that institution where he invited young, Martin (Luther King Jr.) to be a student in a class with the top professionals. He also spoke on Mental Health and Addictions.

When Clinton dives into a project he chooses a big, no, a gigantic one. He always brings along some of his many friends. His pattern is to encourage them to make a commitment (service or donation) with following through to taking action on their stated project and a year later he asks for their progress.

To get Coachella Valley healthier is a major challenge. The 3rd Health Matters Conference in 2014 we will see how well that goal is carried out. With his past record, I am sure that we will see great positive change.

Chelsea Clinton gives Doris Lee a big hug

PUSHING FOR AN EXCITING FUTURE

Steve Forbes, Editor-in Chief Forbes Magazine

"I think that the united States is entering an era that will change the way in which we live and in which we work in as profound a way as did the industrial revolution in the last century. The new ways that we are moving into are symbolized by the microchip, which is extending the reach of the human brain in a way machines extended the reach of the human muscle. It's going to affect even

the most mundane businesses, such as retailing, and will create
many new businesses and industries that we can't even imagine
now. We are going into that era, symbolized also by technology,
fiber optics, and digital technology in screens. This will obliterate
the traditional differences between telephones, TV screens, and
computers."

Steve, as well as his father before him, said, "KEEP YOUR
CURIOSITY. IF YOU LOSE THAT, YOU'RE BRAIN DEAD."

- *Visionary Spotlight* -

SENATOR JOHN GLENN
The First Astronaut to Orbit the Planet, Senator of Ohio, and Honorary Chairman of Explorers Club

As you may remember, John Glenn blasted into orbit at 17,500 mph, 160 miles above earth February 20, 1962.

If you have a yearning for adventure and exploration, one place to find it is in the Explorers Club. It is an international organization filled with people who want to climb new mountains, dive in the deepest waters, pass over Earth's poles, and break new records. To our amazement, John Glenn said the same thing as James Cameron about curiosity being the most important trait individuals can have. And why? It's because it pushes them to further achievement. They ask themselves why they cannot do better than the last person that was working on the project.

When President John F. Kennedy challenged the country to be the first in outer space, an elite group, the Mercury Seven, were chosen to fulfill the challenge. They were considered to be the country's best and the brightest. John Glenn, a retired US Marine Corps pilot and a future US Senator was one of those seven. He became the first American to orbit the Earth in 1962. Those of us who witnessed this triumph remember announcer Walter

Cronkite's on-air excitement over the successful orbit. Later, after Glenn left NASA, he was elected to the Ohio Senate as a Democrat, serving for four terms. At age 77, he again flew on the shuttle Discovery, and still holds the record for being the oldest man in space.

Although Glenn is now age 91, he is in great shape and strongly involved with the John and Annie Glenn School of Public Affairs at Ohio State University. Both John and Annie were born and raised in New Concord, Ohio.

The club's 109th annual dinner was held on March 16 at the Waldorf Astoria in New York City to honor John Glenn and Scott Carpenter (the two surviving astronauts from the Mercury Seven team), and producer/director James Cameron.

Glenn and Carpenter each received the "Legendary Explorers Medal" at the party, Cameron received the "Explorers Medal."

I had an opportunity to personally talk to Senator John Glenn and Anne before John was honored. We had both gone to the same undergraduate college so it was nice to touch base with former schoolmates.

My main question to John: "What was the most important trait that we as individuals have?":

> *Every bit of progress made in human history has come because someone was curious about how we can do it better, but too often we fail to act. Shakespeare put it very well: 'Our doubts are traitors, and make us lose the good we oft might win, by fearing to attempt.'*

Since then, John Glenn has been asked and accepted the Honorary Chairman of the Explorers Club (International).

- *Visionary Spotlight* -

JAMES CAMERON
Academy Award-winning film director of *Titanic* and *Avatar*, recipient of the Scripps School of Oceanography Nierenberg Prize, and Deep-ocean Pioneer

Academy Award-winning film director and deep-ocean pioneer James Cameron descended to the Mariana Trench, the deepest place on Earth, on March 26, 2012. He went down below some seven miles in a single, piloted vehicle, which was co-designed with members of La Jolla's Scripps Institution of Oceanography. Capitan Don Walsh was also part of assisting James. In addition Captain Walsh who along with Jacques Piccard had held the world championship for the deepest dive for 50 years. Interestingly enough, Jacques Piccard is the father of Bertrand Piccard, who recently flew around the United States without any fuel, only solar disks.

Cameron is also known for his feature-film, "Titanic", for which he won 11 Oscars. His 2009 film, "Avatar", which earned $2.8 billion worldwide, is the only film to surpass it financially. Cameron is the founder of the Avatar Alliance Foundation, a non-profit with a focus on studying climate change and the loss of indigenous lands and cultures.

I was interested in hearing what James Cameron said about what the most important trait a human can possess is. To my surprise, he said, just as John Glenn did, that curiosity is the most powerful thing you own. Imagination is a force that can actually manifest a reality; it drives people to new achievements. In his *Ted Talk*, James said,

> *"No fame, no glory, no money. What are you doing? You're doing it for the task itself, for the challenge...for the thrill of discovery. ...*
> *Don't put limitations on yourself. Other people will do that for you — don't do it to yourself, don't bet against yourself, and take risks."*

- Visionary Spotlight -

BERTRAND PICCARD and ANDRE BORSCHBERG
Pilot of the *Solar Impulse* Project, Flew around the US with No
Fuel, but with 10,851 Solar Disks

Bertrand Piccard, son of Jacques Piccard who was a deep diver, along with Brian Jones, has been noted to make a record to become the first to circle the earth in a hot-air balloon nonstop for a duration of nearly 20 days in 1999.

On May 3rd, Bertrand Piccard and the *Solar Impulse* departed from NASA's Moffett Airfield at the Ames Research Center in northern California. They were sent off by members of the Explorers Club, whose contribution helped fuel the plane. They landed 19 hours later at Phoenix's Sky Harbor International Airport, on the first leg of "Across America" tour. The tour went on for four more legs for which Andre Borschberg took the craft from Phoenix to Dallas for the second leg, Piccard took the craft from Dallas to St. Louis for the third leg, both took the *Solar Impulse* from St. Louis to Washington D.C. for the fourth leg, and for the fifth and final leg, left Washington D.C. and landed in New York in early July.

The only major difficulty they had came before the Washington D.C. to New York at the John F. Kennedy Airport. The difficulty resulted from an 8 ft tear in the left wing, but they managed to land safely. A helicopter which flew over the plane determined that the plane would be able to continue to fly without any need for assistance.

The two pilots kept us informed during their flight and in one email they said:

> *You have just joined a community of pioneers working together to challenge conventional thinking. We want to*

322

inspire innovation, hope, and action among citizens and policymakers by pushing boundaries and proposing solutions to real global challenges.

The *Solar Impulse* Project is a concept plane, **a plane able to take flight without the aid of fossil fuels**. Instead, attached to the wings are solar disks that store energy overnight and powers the plane through the day. The *Solar Impulse* has a wingspan of 63.4 meters and its wings are covered with 10,851 solar disks. People kept telling them that the goal of their project was going to be impossible to achieve. But they did it. Their plane flew around the country without the aid of any fossil fuels, and landed safely in New York. The demonstration flights from the *Solar Impulse* will help the team with the construction of the *Solar Impulse HB-SIB*, whose ultimate goal would be to circle the globe in 2015.

I asked Bertrand when he was the speaker at the Explorers Club, why he spent so much time letting children and adults look more closely at the plane, he said, "I like to inspire people and to show them how difficult things are possible as long as you hold onto your strong desire of completing the project. It took us some time to figure out how to do this difficult thing to store energy overnight as opposed to using regular fuel and spewing that into the environment. So, we have put 1,200 solar disks on the wide wings of our airplane which only 3 feet shorter than a commercial 747. They told us it was impossible, but we did it."

Why is curiosity so important to other people?

Years ago, Malcolm Forbes told me "Don't ever lose your curiosity, or you will be brain dead." And now Steve Forbes, the Editor in Chief at *Forbes Magazine* is saying the same thing.

When Melinda Gates was asked by CBS Charlie Rose about what attracted her to Bill, she said, "His curiosity and optimism about life."

Chuck Yeager was asked how he broke through that famous flight that nobody had ever done before. He said, "The plane was rattling and shaking but he went on and, for the first time, broke through the sound barrier.

Lili Zanuck, writer and producer of the film *Driving Ms. Daisy*, was asked what Lili did when the producer told her that her movie was not good enough to be produced. Even her husband told her to stop pestering other producers. She, however, was extremely pleased when she and her husband walked down the aisle, for winning an Academy Award.

Katharine Graham, Chairman of the Board of *The Washington Post*, she replied by saying "quality requires infinite patience and demands a willingness to take risks, and compels acceptance of failure. It takes courage to take risks and be willing to fail and try again.

Fifty years after President Kennedy was assassinated, his words still resound in the minds and hearts of many individuals. He left a strong dedication for us all when he said,

"My fellow Americans, ask not what your country can do for you, ask what you can do for your country."

DORIS LEE MCCOY– THE AUTHOR SPEAKS OUT

In the United States, each November on Thanksgiving Day, we pay tribute to the 102 Europeans who traveled on a tiny ship across the Atlantic in search of religious freedom. They had the courage to leave their homeland for a new, unexplored place called America. This ship didn't carry scholars or statesmen but ordinary people that came to be called Pilgrims.

They landed in Massachusetts, but before they left the ship they wrote out an agreement known as the Mayflower Compact, distilling the political and philosophical thinking of over 330 years. They agreed that they would elect men to rule over them and they would respect their rule. Thus began American democracy— government of the people, by the people, and for the people.

Foreshadowed in that little document were the Declaration of Independence, the Bill of Rights, and the Constitution. They were rather smart people, the Pilgrims, and they were tough. It took incredible fortitude and strength to take the risks they took and to make the progress they made.

What progress are we making? Is life getting better for us and our families? Our leaders suggest ways of sharing our time, ideas, expertise, and surplus resources with others. But they also leave us with some questions. As we move to a more connected global world, are we able to accept and even embrace our differences? How will the people who are enraged enough to turn into terrorists come to believe that life—all life—matters? Can we have a world that lives in peace?

These and other remarkable leaders in this book show how a few dedicated and focused people can make a difference. What will you do today and tomorrow to help make this a more humane and prosperous world—a world that we will hand over to the next generation?

Here are just a few words of advice, ideas that I like to aspire to...

- **Time—use it wisely**
- **Live simply—go back to the basics**
- **Remain curious**
- **Speak kindly to one another**
- **Take pride in your country**
- **What you take from the land, you must give back**
- **Respect, honor, and cherish senior citizens**

In short: Love generously, care deeply, and leave the rest to God.

The richest person is not necessarily the one who has the most material possessions but the one who has lived out his or her true journey in life and has contributed to the lives of others.

May you fully live all the days of your life, for it is an exciting journey. I wish you well with every single day of this blessed gift!

Visionary Reflection on...

Commitment

Your Visionary Commitment: I commit to _____

_____

—

in order to ensure a more positive future for this world and my fellow

human beings.

Signed _____ Date_____

Other Non-Profits Making a Difference– A Resource Directory

Organization	Address	Email/Website	Phone Number
Airline Ambassadors International	418 California Avenue, PO Box 459 Moss Beach, CA 94038	airlineamb.org	Toll Free: (866) ANGEL-86 Ph: 650-728-7844
Alliance for African Assistance	5952 El Cajon Blvd. San Diego, CA 92115	alliance-for-africa.org	Ph: 619-286-9052 Fax: 619-286-9053
The American Ireland Fund		irlfunds.org/aif	
American Lung Association of California	2750 Fourth Ave. San Diego, CA 92103	californialung.org	Ph: 619-297-3901 Fax: 619-297-8402
American Youth Foundation	147 Canaan Road Center Tuftonboro, New Hampshire 03816	ayf.com	Ph: 231-861-2262
Autism Speaks	2 Park Avenue 11th Floor New York, NY 10016	contactus@autismspeaks.org autismspeaks.org	Ph: 212-252-8584 Fax: 212-252-8676
	Los Angeles 5455 Wilshire Boulevard Suite 2250 Los Angeles, CA 90036		Ph: 323-549-0500 Fax: 323-549-0547
Clinton Foundation	55 West 125th Street New York, N.Y. 10027	clintonfoundation.org/contact/	
Fine Art Society around the World	734 W. Beech St Suite 100 San Diego, CA 92101	www.sdfas.com	Ph: 858-205-4354
Floresta	4903 Morena Blvd. Suite 1215 San Diego, CA 92117	info@floresta.org www.floresta.org	Ph: 800-633-5319
The George G. Glenner Alzheimer's Family Centers, Inc.	3702 Fourth Avenue San Diego, CA 92103	information@glenner.org halzheimerhelp.org Note: One of the best in the nation whose system could be followed by other centers.	Ph: 619-543-4700
Heifer Project International	1 World Avenue, Little Rock, AR 72202	heifer.org/gift (To buy a heifer is $500, a share is $50; or buy a pig , water buffalo, chicks, etc)	Ph: 800-422-0474

327

Organization	Address	Contact / Web	Phone
Intervarsity	9525 Via Pereza San Diego, CA 92129	Scott Phillips filamfam@sbcglobal.net	Ph: 858-538-767
La Jolla Presbyterian Church	7715 Draper Ave La Jolla, CA 92037-4380	ljpres.org	+1 858-454-0713 +1 858-454-2677 +1 858-729-5500
Charles A. and Anne Morrow Lindbergh	Lindbergh Foundation 2150 Third Avenue North, Suite 310 Anoka, MN 55303-2200	lindberghfoundation.org info@lindberghfoundation.org	Ph: 763-576-159
New York Women's Foundation	434 West 33rd Street, 8th floor New York, NY 10001	info@nywf.org	Ph: 212-261-458 Fax: 212-564-73
Nile Sisters Development Initiative	6035 University Ave, Ste. 22 San Diego, CA 92115	sistersinitiative@sbcglobal.net nilesisters.org	Ph: 619-265-295 Fax: 619-265-29
Nu Skin – Vitameal	One Nu Skin Plaza, 75 West Center, Provo, UT 84601 USA	nuskin.com	Ph: 801-345-100 Toll Free: 800-48 1000
The Paragon	P.O. BOX 4068 Lawrenceburg, IN 47025-4068	theparagon.com	
Patrons of the Prado	P.O. Box 928530 San Diego, CA 92192	patronsprado@aol.com	
Project Concern International	5151 Murphy Canyon Road, Suite 320 San Diego, CA 92123	Washington D.C. Office: 1140 Connecticut Ave. Suite 500 Washington, D.C. 20036	Ph: 858-279-969 Fax: 858-694-02 Ph: 202-223-008 Fax: 202-296-28
Samaritan's Purse	International Headquarters Samaritan's Purse P.O. Box 3000 Boone, NC 28607-3000	samaritanspurse.org	Ph: 800-282-198
Sierra Club	85 Second Street Second Floor San Francisco, CA 94105-3441	sierraclub.org	Ph: 415-977-550 Fax: 415-977-57
Spirit of Casa, Inc.	P.O. Box 469 La Jolla, CA 92038	westcoastclaire@aol.com	858-456-9226
The Stanford Challenge		giving.to.stanford@stanford.edu	Toll-free: (866) 5 0243 (USA) International: (650) 724-0627
Synergos	51 Madison Avenue, 21st Floor New York, NY 10010 USA	synergos@synergos.org synergos.org	Ph: 212-447-811 Fax: 212-447-81
Sundt Memorial Foundation	9404 Genesee Ave., Ste. 210 La Jolla, CA 92037	sundtmemorial.org	Ph: 858-551-700 Fax: 858-551-185

World Vision	P.O. Box 9716	worldvision.org	Ph: 888-511-6548
	Federal, WA 98063-9716		
World Vision Gift Catalog	P.O. Box 70359	worldvisiongifts.org	Ph: 888-511-6511
	Tacoma, WA 984481-0359		
Y-Malawi	PO Box 2170	y-malawi.org	Ph: 951-492-3025
	Hemet, CA 92546-2170		

In Appreciation of Churches and Synagogues

We acknowledge the many churches, synagogues, and other religious organizations that tirelessly raise funds for non-profits organizations.

Travel Companies

Many travel companies contribute to the countries that they visit, such as MTSOBEK, Go Ahead Travel, and others.

World Vision Gifts

This is a very unusual gift catalog that will stretch your imagination. Through this organization, you can buy mosquito nets, fast-growing seeds, a goat, chickens, ducks, rabbits, an oxen, pigs, cows, even a donkey or a clean water well. You can buy life-saving medicines and food for children, school supplies, and fruit trees. You can also help sexually exploited girls or send a girl to school. Alex Trebek, host of Jeopardy, is a supporter and urges for you to join him in helping change lives. **Visit: www.worldvision.org**

Testimonies

"I don't know how she does it, but Dr. McCoy always gets interviews with the most interesting people. Her questions draw out answers that are sometimes unexpected. If you like to think, and like books that are a quick and easy read, this book is worth it. Watch out Barbara Walters."
--Jess Todtfeld, *SpeakingChannel TV Formerly with Fox & Friends*

ABOUT THE AUTHOR

Doris Lee McCoy, Ph.D. is an Author, Interviewer, Psychologist, International Keynote Speaker, TV Moderator and Producer. She has interviewed over 3,000 successful entrepreneurs, politicians, celebrities, artists and athletes. Her first book*, MEGATRAITS: 12 Traits Of Successful People* includes interviews with: Malcolm Forbes, Supreme Court Justice Sandra O'Connor, Ronald Reagan, Gerald Ford, Mary Kay, Charlton Heston, Gregory Peck, Norman Lear, and others. She was featured on 100+ television and radio shows to speak about the book. **Nightingale Conant and Discovery Tapes released** a six-cassette audio album in conjunction with *MEGATRAITS.*

Dr. McCoy moderated and produced 20+ television specials and three television series, including *"THE CHANGING WOMAN"* television series. It discussed the art of balancing highly successful careers with family, friends and future goals with interviewees including First Ladies Betty Ford, Mrs. L.B. Johnson, and Walter Cronkite. They were shown on Cox Cable stations.

In Kenya, Beijing and Mexico City, Dr. McCoy covered the International UN Conferences on Women. Her television special, "WOMEN OF THE WORLD" was aired throughout the U.S. and featured her interviews with UN delegates from Asia, Europe, Africa and the U.S. American Airlines aired her interviews for the "This I Believe" audio-cassette series.

An NBC TV Commentator said about Dr. McCoy: "Her many years in television, teaching, speaking and consulting qualify her as a communications specialist. High-energy professionalism and personal warmth characterize her on and off the screen. Whether shooting on location in the rainforest or interviewing top American executives, her crisp, energetic, 'from-the-heart' flair comes through."

To have Dr. McCoy speak to your group, call (858) 459-4971.

To order any of Dr. McCoy's eight books or her CDs/DVDs, go to www.dorisleemccoy.com. In addition, Dr. McCoy provides private counseling on "HOW TO GET TO HARD TO GET TO PEOPLE."

American Spirit Foundation

Doris Lee McCoy, Ph.D. Founder/President

The American Spirit Foundation is an organization whose mission is to help young and mature people discover their talents. The foundation strives to assist these people by helping them understand their God-given gifts.

The assumption is that every person can contribute positively to their lives and others if they only discover how. The foundation strives to make a change in the attitudes of young Americans who are discouraged, and to show them that the future is not dismal and desperate. We do this through interviewing successful people, and writing about them in books, and giving speeches.

We hold sacred the values that make this country great: integrity, honesty, patriotism, personal faith, self-discipline, diligence, hard work, compassion, self-esteem, teamwork, and service to others.

It is the foundation's hope that sponsors will come forth to support a TV special or series interviewing some of the leaders in this book. These then could be shown on TV with copies later used in schools, after school programs, and service clubs. Please contact the foundation if you would like at:

Ph./Fax: (858) 459-4971
Email: dorisleem@gmail.com
Web: http://www.americanspiritfoundation.com/